And You Thought It Was All Over!

And You Thought It Was All Over!

MOTHERS AND THEIR ADULT CHILDREN

by Zenith Henkin Gross

ST. MARTIN'S / MAREK
New York

Design by Mina Greenstein

Library of Congress Cataloging in Publication Data

Gross, Zenith Henkin.
    And you thought it was all over!

    1. Adult children—United States—Family
relationships.   2. Mother and child—United States.
3. Middle aged women—United States—Family
relationships.   4. Parenting—United States. I. Title.
HQ799.97.U5G76   1985   306.8'74   85-12504
ISBN 0-312-03636-1

First Edition
10 9 8 7 6 5 4 3 2 1

TO

My parents, Rose and Harry Henkin

My husband, Sid

Our children,
Katherine, Kenneth, and Lawrence

. . . and our extended family,
Barbara, Justin, and Peter

Contents

Acknowledgments

No book of this kind can be completed without the active assistance, encouragement, and support of many people.

My first thanks must go to the hundreds of women who gave so much time and energy to answering my questions in written and spoken form, to participating in group discussions, and to sitting patiently for endless hours of telephone and in-person interviews. Their warmth and generosity in allowing me into the intimate spaces of their family lives will always be deeply appreciated. Any misinterpretations of their stories or inaccuracies in reporting their experiences are, of course, solely my responsibility.

Next, my thanks must go to two outstandingly professional, competent, and savvy women. One is my editor, Joyce Engelson, whose lucid guidance gave the book shape and ease, and whose belief that women over 40 need not be invisible accounts for the existence of this report at all. The second is my hard-working agent, Linda Nelson of the Charlotte Sheedy Literary Agency, who believed, persevered, and mothered when things were at their most difficult; that she remains a valued friend as well is one of the unexpected delights of years spent at hard labor.

A strong thanks is due to Kathleen Goforth, a former colleague in corporation land, who was to have been my collaborator on the book. Kathleen helped formulate the initial concept (see the preface) and aided in designing the questionnaire. She also did some of the early interviewing and writing. Kathleen was especially helpful in sharing the work on Chapter 5 before she left to pursue other career opportunities.

My special friend and former colleague Mary Greene did much of the enormous job of handling the hundreds of questionnaires and helping tabulate the results. Her witty good humor and steadfast belief that our struggles to make sense of mountains of data would eventually result in good things for women were a constant bulwark and stay against discouragement.

A warm thanks is also owed to Jane Garmey, herself a talented food writer and gifted educator, who was the book's "godmother," bringing me together with the literary agency that was so well equipped to handle a women's project.

No woman completes a task outside her home without somehow replacing herself on the domestic front. For the first part of my work on this book, our long-time "assistant mother," Rebecca Cohen, held the fort at home. When she retired, Ada Higgs took over the job. Without these two women, the task would have been even more formidable.

Important in my feminine network were my daughter, Katherine, and my daughter-in-law, Barbara, who showed me in a hundred comradely ways that they knew how hard it was to keep ordinary life going while trying to write a book. Their understanding eased the path at several points and I'm grateful.

By the nature of this book, most of my debts are owed to women, but several men were crucial, also. My husband, Sid, read endless drafts with sweet-tempered helpfulness that was a balm to exhaustion and doubt. My sons, Larry and Ken, gave practical advice that picked up drooping spirits when the road was rocky and revved up enthusiasm when things were going well.

My debts to these and many others who helped and encouraged along the way are very great indeed, and I can never fully repay those debts. I can only say that my gratitude is real and my appreciation boundless.

Z.H.G.

Preface

This book is about a new stage of motherhood—the one that begins when the children leave home.

It's about how women are living in changing ways with those special people, their grown-up children, as told by the mothers themselves. We will hear women describe how they daily weave the fabric of a new relationship with adults who, as children, were so central to their lives. They tell how that fabric is made of joy and sorrow, strain and conflict, reward and satisfaction, tears and laughter, in the second half of women's lives.

I call this new stage, which never existed before in earlier generations, for all kinds of historical and sociological reasons, the "orbital" stage of mothering because it follows the children's launching into the world outside the shelter of home.

The book is about how women are feeling and thinking their way through this new phase of family life with their grown children, and it is written only from their point of view. For two reasons this is not a book about mothers and fathers parenting together.

One is that mid-life women whose children are today grown up were raised to believe that mothers are the psychological center of the family, bear the major responsibility for child care, and thus take full blame (but little credit) for how the young adults turn out.

In short, they see themselves as accountable for the lives of their adult children in ways that fathers usually do not, and in this book, women describe how they are living with that accountability.

The second reason we will hear of these experiences only from mothers is that their lives with their children from birth to this moment are so different from the experience of fatherhood that mid-life men report, that it would take a separate book to adequately detail the differences and similarities that befall the two sexes in modern-day America in the parenting enterprise. (However, in Chapter 7, there is a brief report from mothers on how the fathers influenced their own maternal behavior and how they see the fathers relating now to the grown children.)

Most American women have been told repeatedly that it is the first stage of mothering—from pregnancy through birth, until the child grows up and leaves home—that is absolutely critical for the child's well-being.

But after that, runs conventional wisdom, the process is pretty well completed. The job is done for good or ill. There is no life after the first stage, women are told; it's all over (if you are "healthy" and don't meddle in your children's lives). In other words, when they are grown, they are gone and that's that. Finis.

As a reporter, writer, and mother who has talked to hundreds of other mothers, I have discovered belatedly that far from the job being over, it has simply *changed.*

Now it turns out that relationships with the grown children are more subtle, complex, persistent than most busy contemporary women ever expected. The reality is that the mothering task goes on in some form forever, *and not always because the mother seeks a tight hold on the child's life,* but rather because generational *inter*dependence is a need on both ends of the equation.

In the last quarter of the twentieth century, women remain important in their children's lives, financially and emotionally, beyond anything anyone ever expected for this stage of parenthood, and the adult children remain important to their mothers, no matter what age each generation may achieve.

And this relationship, I have found, is more than just metaphorically significant; it calls forth active mothering on many fronts—refereeing adult sibling rivalry, slackening and tightening economic ties, working through maturation processes for both generations, serving as eternal mediator and translator between the adult children and their father and other siblings —a whole host of mothering tasks in a different time frame and at a different level of intensity than when the children were at home.

Even though today's young people are having fewer babies than did their parents, and thus offer fewer occasions for grandparenthood, still grandmothering *is* being done and is another step in the long service performed by mothers. No one seems to have noted that mothers are almost never given an honorable discharge from duty, or battle decorations made up of crossed checkbooks with curled telephone wires.

Because the contemporary image of a "good" mother is that she stays out of her children's lives, makes few demands, fades into the wallpaper, waves cheerily as their lives roar past her, and becomes visible only when needed on ceremonial occasions, many women are puzzled, confused, not a little guilty, as well as mightily surprised, to find that second-stage mothering is so involving and takes so much more time, money, energy, and attention than they ever expected.

They are also amazed at how often the continuing relationship *is sought on some level by the young person* and is not at the mother's initiation.

The surprise packages in second-stage mothering are endless, women report. The conflicts, strains, and tensions of the past— inherent in all of family life—certainly do not disappear magically when the first duffle bag is packed for college or the first job is successfully landed. And conversely, the joys and rewards of seeing their young adults moving strongly and competently from the home launch pad into a good orbit of work, love, and play offer to mothers a happiness and satisfaction they find sweet beyond what many dared hope.

This new relationship between mothers and their grown children will last for a very long time, given the new eighty-years-plus life expectancy for contemporary American women. This is such a startlingly new aspect of human affairs that we don't even have an up-to-date label for it; "postparental" is the one most often used, but that doesn't tell the tale at all in most cases. For middle-aged women, I found, are not "post" much of anything with their adult kids—they're right in there, helping with weddings and home purchases and babysitting the grandkids and lending the car for moves to new jobs, not to mention help with crises and emergencies. "Postlaunch" is perhaps closer to describing the real scene, but that, too, has some limitations, as we'll discuss in Chapters 1 and 2.

As often happens when new life stages are investigated, my decision to look into what seemed to be a big gulf between the myth of the finished job and the reality of a new relationship that isn't even supposed to exist (most people define mothering as caring for very small children or adolescents at the latest) arose from my own life events.

"Doesn't It Ever End?"

An idea that there *might* be a new relationship taking form with my own three adult children was crystallized by one of those seemingly small, but echoing, incidents that often mark the arrival of insight.

My own life as a mother was, perhaps, an unrepresentative one, because I had unusual career opportunities during World War II. As an aspiring young reporter, I found job openings not often available to women of my generation, because of men's wartime absence.

As a result, though my boss told me clearly that a newspaper office was "no place for a girl," the dearth of males meant I got a chance to work on newspapers (dailies in two Ohio cities) and for a major wire service (the Associated Press), and to get a crack at journalistic coverage of nationally significant developments in education, medicine, the law, and half a dozen other fields while on the information staff of a large midwestern university.

Marrying, moving to New York, and having three children kept me at home for more than fifteen years, but I was able to do free-lance public-affairs writing at home while my children were smearing peanut butter on the curtains and dismantling their toy boxes. Because those peanut-butter-and-jelly years provided very real and serious life experience, and because my journalism background was unusually solid for my era, I was atypically well positioned to return to paid employment. Thus, in 1967, I found myself working as a writer-researcher corporate executive in a Fortune 500 company when my youngest child was eight years old and the two older ones were nearing or in junior high school.

One of the pleasures of being youthfully middle-aged in my corporate job was that I could be a mentor for younger women. I found it a good way to have some of the pleasures of parenting without any of the real responsibility.

The little grain of sand that makes the pearl arrived one day when I was already ensconced in a management-level corporate office on the fifty-first floor of a New York skyscraper—the very model of a modern Mom. Gone were those unmourned days of eating the sandwich crusts the kids had left at lunch; now I lunched with other grown-ups in grown-up places.

Like so many other mid-life women of my generation, I had proved to myself and my husband and children that there was really life after Spock, when the kids are away at school or working, no longer under the family roof.

On this particular day, I was scheduled to have lunch with one of my younger colleagues, the single mother of an adolescent son. We were to talk over both the upcoming company annual report, in which we both were involved, and her perplexing days and nights as the mother of a young teenager about to curdle. Since both my sons were now in their twenties, the assumption was that I'd have some words of comfort, if not wisdom, for the storms of adolescence.

In midmorning, the telephone rang. It was the youngest, our daughter, far away in college on the West Coast, asking a small favor. "Mom," came the breathless request, "listen, I've got to run so I'll make this fast. Exam week starts tomorrow and I just realized that Millie's big twenty-first birthday is about three days away. [Millie was a treasured friend from kindergarten days.] And you know, Mom, there's really nothing I'd like to send her from this little town. Could you, would you, mind dashing across the street to that fancy Fifth Avenue store and pick out something just smashing, just real New York-y, you know, you have just such wonderful taste. I'm sure whatever you choose will be great and if you did it today and had it sent out, it would get there in time. Would you mind, please, Mom? I'll pay for it, of course, and it would be *such* a help. Gotta run, thanks a million, million. . . ." I said, "Sure, honey, and I'll call you later and let you know what I sent."

When I called my colleague to postpone our meeting for an hour and prepared to "dash across the street" to tend to the chore, I found my coworker pleasant about changed plans, but curious about my assignment.

As we were ending our telephone call, she said, "Of course I understand; it's okay, but I'm just wondering—how old is your daughter now?"

"Twenty," I answered. (Her son was 14 at the time.)

"Twenty!" she echoed. "My God, doesn't it ever end? Will I be still running around for Chuck when he's twenty or even thirty? Does it really go on forever?"

"Doesn't it ever end?" drummed in my mind as I slowly replaced the receiver. What jelled in my head at that moment was not the minor little favor my daughter had asked—that was really nothing—but my colleague's questions evoked much stronger feelings that had been subliminally woven through these new "freedom years" my husband and I were truly enjoying. Suddenly, those feelings became clearer: our sorrow for our son's pain when he was divorced; our anxiety about our other son's future in the entertainment business, which appeared to us a most chancy way to earn a livelihood; and our worry over the new money grant our daughter would need if she did eventually decide on graduate school.

Did it, indeed, never end?

Or were we the problem—parents too involved, parents too indulgent, a mother believing she could go on protecting and helping forever, a father deeply concerned over his children's financial and emotional well-being forever?

Were other parents feeling like this and how were all of us going to get along with our children as they moved into adult lives of their own once they left home? Would we still be connected, and if so, how? If we as parents did not become involved in our children's lives and if we diligently pursued our own activities and interests with little regard for theirs, did that mean that eventually all that would be left between us would be empty duty and sterile obligation? To be "good," noninterfering parents, did we have to forgo warmth, love, laughter and sorrows, sharing and caring, in order to allow each of the generations plenty of independence and living space? Where was the magic middle line to walk between caring and connectedness and overinvolvement?

There was only one way to find out: Ask other mothers. I chose to ask mothers for the reasons I listed above—they are still widely seen as the fulcrum on which the family rises and falls— and also because I knew from myself, friends, and relatives that women take primary responsibility for how their adult children's lives turn out.

I had to ask these questions of other women because Spock had abandoned me long since. Like a faithless lover, he had taken me from pregnancy through toilet training, braces on the teeth, and homework, and then dropped me flat when the uproar of the first driver's license had ended. I hurried to other books; very few had anything to say about this new stage of motherhood, except a team of splendidly literate and humane British workers in the field of family studies who wrote, with what seemed to me marked understatement, ". . . the lights of active parenting do not go out in a flash."[1]

I determined to explore what other mothers would answer to the question "Doesn't it ever end?" I would also explore with them what the "endlessness" consisted of, if, indeed, they were experiencing continuing mothering involvement in their lives beyond the empty nest.

Questions and Answers

My reportorial training would come in handy, but at first the problem of reaching a large number of other mothers and determining what questions to ask was a knotty one. Eventually, I drafted a fifteen-page questionnaire, which asked for no less than ninety-nine separate pieces of information, ranging from simple factual data like ages and sexes of the grown children to more complex questions like "Do your children expect things from you now that surprise you?" I was too inexperienced a questionnaire-designer to realize that the document was too long and would take nearly two hours to complete; the experienced professional social scientists to whom I showed it warned me that it would have to be shortened, should include fewer essay questions, and would be too hard to tabulate. (See Appendix for the questionnaire.)

Nevertheless, I sent it out to what professionals call "a sample of convenience"—that meant every woman I could reach by any means: friends and relatives in four states, my dentist's receptionist, the teacher of an adult class I was taking, all my coworkers at the office—in short, the outermost circle of friends and acquaintances that I and my work colleagues (who were eager to help) could possibly reach.

The only selection process I used was that women had to have lived through a genuine (not vacations or brief periods) separation from at least one child for at least a year, or long enough for the mother to get some idea of how the young person would still figure in her life, on what changed basis they might begin the new relationship that would take them to the end of the mother's life. This real separation was the sole criterion for receiving the questionnaire; there were no limitations of age, race, economic background, or any other factor that would keep some women from being asked to participate, and obviously, no attempt to make the first group a representative sampling of American women.

I was able to start with a nucleus of fifty names. Because of the length of the questionnaire and because many women had never thought about some of the questions since their children had grown up, I was prepared for a return rate of about ten out of fifty. Instead, I got forty-six back!

But the most surprising thing was that the women were breathlessly eager to pour out their stories; they wrote in margins and on the backs of pages, they appended additional letters and comments. They were clearly anxious about this unexpected new part of their mothering lives and wanted to share experiences and information, as well as pride and satisfaction if they saw the job as going well.

The next astounding development was that almost every one of the initial forty-six who sent back their answers asked me for five, ten, or even twenty more copies of the questionnaire for friends, relatives, and colleagues at work. These were accompanied by notes saying things like: "I thought no one ever noticed how hard this part of mothering is" or "It's really a lifetime job, isn't it?" or "You bet it never ends! It goes on forever, worrying and enjoying, both. . . ."

Soon, as word spread of what I was attempting to investigate, a large number of women volunteered to help. Friends who worked within community organizations offered to distribute fifty questionnaires at a clip at club meetings and political rallies; relatives who taught adult classes took twenty and thirty questionnaires at a time for students who were interested. My husband even got his business associates to ask their wives to fill out the questionnaire and our by-this-time far-flung children on both coasts asked the middle-aged mothers of their friends to answer my questions.

In this way and almost outside my supervision, the questionnaire rolled across the country and into four foreign countries, to be returned to me by women whom I did not know and most likely will never have the opportunity to meet.

In the end, more than 500 questionnaires were mailed out; a total of 407 were returned, another almost unbelievably high return rate.

From this very large group, I and some volunteer helpers culled 175 of the questionnaires in which a wide variety of women had been the most sharing, most forthcoming, and most complete in their answers. These were the questionnaires that told the most about this later-life mothering and they formed the nucleus of the sample, the core of the respondent group.

But the larger group of over 400 women (with an average of 3.2 children apiece, they were relating to a total of considerably more than 1,200 young people) also provided much valuable data on specific questions, if not on all of them.

And the whole group indicated clearly that they were bursting to discuss many subjects I had not even included on the questionnaire. This pointed to the place where my journalism experience would be helpful. I could do face-to-face interviews with several dozen women in my geographical area, do telephone interviews with others, and arrange group discussions for the mothers to share experiences. I did nearly fifty personal interviews, two dozen group discussions, and fourteen telephone interviews. From these, I chose the notes taken from interviews ranging from two hours to three days and put together a group, again, of the "best" ones, a total of thirty-three lengthy conversations.

Therefore, the women who responded can be thought of as one large group (a total of 407) and a smaller, core group of 175 written responses plus 33 person-to-person talks, making a base of 208 mothers of young adults who participated fully.

Describing the Core Group

There are a number of points to be stressed about the sample group of women whose voices the reader will hear repeatedly throughout this book.

The two most important points are these: This is a self-selected sample of women who were willing, nay, eager, to talk with a stranger about their second-stage lives with their grown children. This automatically excludes the woman whose relationships with her children are so troubled that the pain is too great for sharing, the mother too distressed to talk with either me or other mothers about her situation, or the woman whose family is a nonfunctioning one. I encountered such mothers, of course, along the way but they quickly removed themselves from participation, sometimes after initially showing some interest in receiving a questionnaire or being interviewed.

It cannot be stressed too frequently that even though some of the mothers and a goodly number of the young adult children have had various kinds of psychotherapy at various times, according to their own accounts, the mothers in this group saw the family as essentially a functioning unit with most of the members in reasonable communication with one another. In no way does this negate the tensions, strains, and conflicts inherent in family life (or just in life), but it did rule out families in which trouble had escalated to the point where conflict, anger, and even hate were the ruling themes of the family's life. The mothers of such families eventually removed themselves from my attempt at investigation and their stories are not reflected in this collection of maternal accounts of second-stage mothering.

The second important point about the smaller group—and indeed the larger sample—is that it is not totally representative;

it is not a perfect cross-section of the racial, religious, ethnic, socioeconomic pattern of the United States population.

Let's look more closely at the 208 women in the core group whose case histories we'll examine in the following pages.

The Women in the Core Group: Who Are They?

As the questionnaire moved across the country, handed from one woman to another without my intervention, and as women cooperatively agreed to sit for long hours or brief chats to talk with me in person or on the phone, the profile of this group emerged:

• Respondent women lived in twenty-three states, and their children in thirty-nine states and four foreign countries, over the five-year period the questionnaire was circulating.

• The women were concentrated in the Northeast, but all regions are represented, with fairly substantial numbers from California, Arizona, Nebraska, Wyoming, Florida, Kentucky, Ohio, and Alabama.

• Respondents are mostly white, mostly middle- and working-class women, with about a quarter divided evenly between wealthier women and working poor. Black, Hispanic, and Asian women made up about 7 percent of the total. There are, sadly, no Native American women because I did not have knowledgeable and sensitive access to that group.

• Educationally, I estimate that from 80 to 90 percent of the core group completed high school or its equivalent; more than half had some education beyond high school, or a college degree, and three percent had advanced degrees. Nearly 60 percent were working; about a third held managerial or administrative jobs. The rest were in lower-paying traditional female occupations such as secretary, sales assistant, or service jobs such as cashier, beautician, or receptionist. Fewer than 5 percent were in law, medicine, social work, teaching, or other professional fields.

• The question on religious affiliation was not specific. I asked whether religion played a part in the family's life, leaving it to the women to specify their religious affiliation if they wished. Among those who volunteered to list a formal religious affiliation or specify a religion as part of their own backgrounds, all the major faiths of the United States were included. The group included a higher percentage of Jewish women than is typical of the United States population; 17 percent of the sample identified themselves as Jewish, while Jews with formal affiliations comprise between two and three percent of the population. The remainder were Protestant and Catholic mothers, plus a large minority who denied a role to *formal* religion in their families' lives, regardless of the religion of their own parents. I spoke briefly with two or three Moslem women, but they did not wish to fill out the questionnaire or be interviewed.

• The pattern of religious nonaffiliation so strongly sketched by my core group is in line with trends reported recently that Americans as a whole seem to be turning away from organized, highly structured religious activities, while continuing to seek individual, personal spiritual values and meaning for their lives.[2]

• A number of women discussed strong ethnic ties, which they differentiated from religious ones, and said that culturally they felt that their family lives were more influenced by the country of origin of their parents and grandparents than by a current formal religious affiliation. It should certainly be noted that, as is well known, racial, ethnic, religious, and educational factors play strong formative roles in shaping women's notions of motherhood, but I was unable to weight the responses to account for all those factors as completely as would perhaps be ideal. While it would have been interesting to view the mothers I talked with from the perspectives of *all* the social sciences, my major concern was rather the universal aspects of second-stage mothering.

• I wanted to look at the mothering goals that seemed to cut across barriers of race and class when women confronted the new task of building relationships with their grown-up children.

These were feelings and attitudes that women held in common, despite marked differences in socioeconomic and cultural backgrounds. Such feelings included the hope for a fulfilling life for their children, concern over deviations from the life course if children chose inappropriate mates or failed at school or work, and a touching and wistful hope for grandchildren. Not all women reacted in identical ways to these goals, of course, but they represented the hopes of the large majority of women with highly varied histories.

• The women in the entire group ranged in age from the mid-forties to the early seventies. Their median age was 54; the average age of their young adult children was 26.

• Unfortunately, I was not able to include queries to women who are in extreme situations of economic, sexual, and racial oppression—women whose mothering tasks have been cruelly complicated by poverty, discrimination, ill health, lack of education, and frequently unresponsive social and political institutions. We all know at first hand that many mothers, caught in such difficult lives, have nonetheless performed truly heroic feats of care and nurturance in all stages of mothering, often with awesome stamina and poignant joy and hope. Others have been casualties, defeated in every attempt to help themselves and their children. These lives are beyond the scope of my limited attempts to find out about late-life motherhood, but I deeply hope that in a future woman-oriented society with better values, there may develop greater possibilities for them and their children.

Some Additional Points

There were a number of reasons why the response rate was so high, and paramount among them, I believe, was the fact that I offered complete anonymity to women who would volunteer to complete the questionnaire—they did not have to give their own names or those of their children, and about a third filled out the questionnaires under these terms. For the women whom I interviewed in person, in groups, or by telephone, I promised to change all names and disguise any details that would enable friends or the community to identify a given family. I have kept that promise and the reader is on notice that *all* names have been changed.

In addition, readers should be aware that in cases where two or more mothers reported experiences with their adult sons or daughters that were similar and told in almost exactly the same words, I condensed three or four such accounts into one and allowed one mother to speak for all, rather than repeat the exact words that each woman gave. Words that appear within quotation marks are generally as the mother said them, but in about 20 percent of cases, they represent a composite of almost identical reports offered by several mothers.

Not all women answered all the questions on the lengthy document they were given; if they had, there would have been more than 16,000 separate pieces of information to tabulate, but even so, there were more than 12,000 answers to check. A group of volunteer friends and coworkers helped with this task (see Acknowledgments), which became lengthy indeed because I sought answers to essay-type questions in which the women would be encouraged to write in detail about specific issues in the new relationship.

What I was privileged to learn from so much discussion with so many women is summarized in an epilogue at the end of this book. But before the reader tackles the issues that the mothers said were the major ones in their changing relationships with their launched children, I'd like to raise some questions and outline some hopes.

Professionals and lay people alike approach women as the center of the family from many points of view. Most people who work with troubled families believe that all family life is pathological to some degree in that it is the seedbed of all future disorders and disabilities (see Chapter 2). Others are not so sure about the origins of troublesome personality problems or behavioral difficulties, not to mention extreme cases of malfunctioning. One of the sanest remarks on the subject was made by family therapist John Weakland, who observed:

There are countless difficulties which are part and parcel of the everyday business of living for which no known ideal or ultimate solutions exist. Even when relatively severe, these are manageable in themselves, but readily become "problems" as a result of the belief that there should, or must, be an ideal solution for them.[3]

The women whose voices are heard in monologue, dialogue, and group discussion in this book did not attempt to hide that tension, conflict, strain, and ambivalence were often their lot in the mothering job; many of them sought professional help, others confided in good friends, a clergyman, or a doctor. Others just suffered silently and simmered with hostility and resentment, anxiety or confusion, that they felt helpless to conquer; still others lashed out angrily at those close to them out of fear and hurt.

But the majority of the women who responded to my questions—since they were a self-selected sample—felt that they were dealing with the "difficulties which are part and parcel of the everyday business of living" and it was with those difficulties that they sought understanding and sharing between and among themselves, with my role simply as listener and recorder.

One of the major realities that I have seen discussed very little, but that the mothers I interviewed discussed at great length, is that mid-life women also get some rewards and satisfactions, often very great ones, for the many years of love and caring they have given. Moreover, the current generation of middle-aged women is so much healthier, more active, and more involved in the world than their grandmothers were at the same age that they fully savor the pleasures of their young adults and can share a great deal with them. This was not the pattern just four or five decades ago.

When harvest time comes, according to my respondents, it often offers ripeness, right along with the worry and anxiety that most women have learned goes with the territory.

Since I am a reporter and not a member of any of the helping professions, my modest contribution to the women who shared their late-life mothering stories with me cannot be on an "expert" level, but only that of a fellow mother who can serve, perhaps, as a conduit for women to speak with, to, and for one another. If duly accredited experts in many disciplines can come to look seriously at this new stage of later life for women, if mothers themselves will feel better about what they have tried to do and about what they need to do in the future, and if our adult children look long and hard at the choices before them (using some of the experiences recounted here to help illumine the way), then this effort will have been amply repaid. One cannot ask for more than to add a brick here and there to the bridge that might be built between the generations.

Z.H.G.
New York, N.Y.
1985

1

After the Launch: A New Life Stage for Women

*A*nna P. sits at her secretarial desk early on a gray Monday morning. Her eyes are red-rimmed, her face pale; she sips her coffee slowly. She and her husband were awakened in the middle of the night by the telephone's shrill jangle. Her youngest daughter was sobbing frantically; her husband had just walked out on their eighteen-month-old marriage. She was crushed; could her parents come over?

The intercom buzzes sharply. Anna takes a deep breath and, averting her eyes from the silver-framed wedding picture on her desk, walks into her boss's office. . . .

Fran R. flies into her uniform as a volunteer hospital aide; she is bubbling and jolly, even this early on Monday. Her eldest son, now 23, announced to his parents over the weekend that he was tired of drifting from job to job and was thinking seriously of returning to college. He thought he might finish the preengineering course he dropped out of two years earlier. Of course, this probably means that Fran and her husband will have to dig into their savings to help with expensive tuition. Hmmm . . . those savings are strained right now, helping to care for her 84-year-old mother.

But Fran mentally brushes that problem aside in the midst of her happiness and relief. Jamie is going back to school! He'll graduate with an engineering degree and the new high-tech world will be his oyster! She is whistling cheerfully as she picks up a stack of patient charts; maybe she'll think about getting a paid job, even though she hasn't worked for a salary in twenty-five years. . . .

It is lunchtime on the same winter Monday. Rhoda C., a 51-year-old divorcee, carries her tray to a remote table in the modest faculty cafeteria. Rhoda teaches biology at the community college near her home, but today she avoids the lunch-hour banter with her colleagues and stares thoughtfully out the window.

This is the first day of classes after the Christmas recess and Rhoda is reliving the holiday gathering at which three of her four children were present, along with their spouses, live-in companions, and two grandchildren.

The gathering was rich and marvelous—and tiring—for Rhoda, but today she is having lingering pangs of worry.

She's still troubled that she might have shown too much obvious pleasure in the achievements of one child in particular. One son, the oldest in a family of sober, industrious folks, has, startlingly, gained some fame as a jazz musician. He is becoming visible in national magazines and on TV, and Rhoda knows that his brother and sisters are feeling a bubbling mix of emotions: pride, excitement, and jealousy among them. Therefore, it becomes important: Did Mother pay enough attention to Nancy's quiet, steady climb up the ladder at the insurance company? Did she praise John's fine performance as a father with his new baby? Did she do all those things the way she should have in the midst of all the furor about Doug being on the cover of *People* magazine?

Rhoda sighs. As she heads for her afternoon class, she thinks, "Even when everything is going great, you never know whether you're doing the right thing."

Who are these women and why are they so sad and worried—or crazily happy while going broke?

All their children are in their late teens, twenties, and thirties; they've all left home for marriage, school, or work. Aren't these women just about finished with their stint in the mother business?

The answer is no, they're not finished, they're only beginning.

What they are beginning is a new stage in the life of women and in the lives of families. The postlaunch era of the new relationship they must now start to build with their adult kids is a new thing under the sun and these women—also never before seen in human history—are the pioneers.

The new relationship and the new task for women—second-stage mothering—is part of the revolution wrought by longevity, by lengthening young adult dependency, by the pervasiveness of middle-class aspirations throughout American society, and by a different kind of older generation—one that wears designer jeans and goes back to school at fifty—than was ever known before.

Anna, Fran, and Rhoda are participating in a stage of life and facing a long and different relationship with adult children and grandchildren that is so new it doesn't even have a name in the specialized literature that deals with families.

It used to be called the "postparental" phase of women's lives, the assumption being that when the kids left home, you lived a life that didn't include parenting. Now we know that parents are always parents, however much the relationship must change, and that having grown-up children is not "post"-anything; it's rather more connected to everything than women with young children ever dreamed.

Another popular description was the "empty nest" stage of life when, just three short decades ago, mothers were to mourn their losses in a deep depression when the children grew up and left, because, theoretically, they were now unneeded. Their "careers" were over and they exhibited "retirement" emptiness and sadness.

By now the so-called empty nest syndrome has been thoroughly discredited; students of women's lives have found that relief is the primary emotion women feel when they are once more free to take up at least some of the threads of their own lives after so many years of unremitting child care. Nostalgia, certainly; wistfulness, possibly; but most of all—relief.[1]

"Because of the newness of this phase and our limited language for describing systems, we have no adequate terminology to define this period," wrote one student of family development in a 1980 textbook on the family life cycle.[2]

I would like to suggest that "postlaunch" comes closer to describing the stage women face in later motherhood, but even that seems to imply a leveling off, a diminution of attention and interest (after all, the rocket has gone up—what more is there to do?) because the anxious launch period is over.

But in fact, while everyone else watches the plumes and vapor disappear into the sky, Mom better get back to the control panel because she is in charge of the orbital phase of family life that will now ensue, just as she's been in charge of much of the family's life up to now. The rocket may be downrange a hundred psychic miles, but mothers are just entering the second stage of maternal life.

It is now she who will track the orbits of the traveling children and report them to Dad and each sibling's path to the others; it is she who will often deal with funding for the next launches and the returns to earth via divorce, illness, or work troubles; it is Mom who will have to learn how the launchees now want to relate to the folks back home—close, but not too close; intimate, but at a distance.

Just as a real space-traveling rocket has an "umbilical cord" that ties it to the launch pad and must eventually be cut, so contemporary women and their grown kids stand looking at one another in surprise after the launching cord is severed. There they stand, each with half a cord dangling from their hands!

Abandoning our space analogy, but keeping the concept of young adults in a sort of orbit around the reality of their living ties to their families, we must ask why this stage is so mysterious and new. Haven't parents always had to forge some sort of new relationship with their children when the kids grew up, moved out, established their own families?

Not really—and for a multiplicity of reasons: social, political, economic, medical, and scientific. These new developments in American society have given rise to distinctly new women (while many of the "old" variety are still young and active) who are doing distinctly new and different things in their later mothering life.

First among causes is, of course, the astonishing longevity of American women in the last quarter of the twentieth century.

For millennia, women died young in childbirth or were old at thirty because of ill health and overwork, if they did survive their multiple pregnancies. In the first decade of this century, less than two years elapsed from the time the last child married to the death of a parent in the average family. Now, even with children marrying later, more than thirteen years elapses between those two events on a median scale. It is no wonder that such a concept as an empty nest didn't even exist until after 1900. Research on that "new" stage of life did not begin until the 1950s, and today the notion is already an anachronism. Now, a great percentage of women who live in the developed countries of the world are routinely expected to live into their eighties, four and five times longer than their great-grandmothers did after the last young 'un was thrown out to farm his own land or sell newspapers on the streets of the burgeoning cities.

This means a much longer journey through life with the grown children; a journey that will offer many more joys and sorrows, much more interaction between the generations than was possible for earlier mother-child pairs. This can mean decades more of pain, strife, and hostility in troubled families; it can also mean mothers will be giving support and help to their children through many more of life's crises than before. And a bonus may very well be that women will be able to hold in their arms many more of their progeny than could have been typical a hundred years ago.

One 45-year-old woman I interviewed, whose firstborn son married just recently, has figured out that if the young couple has children quickly (not statistically likely), she probably can dance at several great-grandchildren's weddings.

"I'm laying in a new supply of dancing shoes," she says confidently when the subject of women's increased life expectancy comes up.

Next among the causes of this new second-stage mothering is the ever-lengthening period of dependence that modern young people endure as they require longer and more expensive educations to meet an increasingly competitive and complex world. Even in families where college can't be managed financially, a longer period of support for vocational school, job-hunting, and launching is in the cards for parents. And for those who are college-bound, even the most responsible slaving away at Burger King will not yield all the money needed for today's educational costs. For reasons beyond the control of parents or students, college kids usually need help, and that help, where possible, comes from Mom and Dad.

This situation clearly illustrates some of the brand new complexities that arise in contemporary family interactions, for while it is no one's fault that children today require lengthy and expensive educations, the conferral of money by parents also brings unwelcome parental control. Some of those young adults long to be free of the purse strings, while at least some of the parents would like their bankbooks back, even at the cost of surrendering some control.

And the problem of the very long maturing process that modern youth undergoes—with its accompanying long financial dependency—also spotlights yet another socioeconomic pressure that pushes parents into a continuing relationship much more active than they thought it would be after the launching period. That pressure is the pervasiveness and depth of middle-class aspirations at all levels of American life.

The women I interviewed for this book were the objects of the most intense consumer drive toward the highest material standard of living ever seen in the world. During the "golden age" of the American economy—the long sustained postwar boom years of the 1950s and 1960s—the growing affluence of the average family would have staggered the immigrant forebears of most of these women.

Their children, in turn, are the offspring of affluence, with a sense of entitlement that takes for granted designer jeans at 12, their own phones at 14, and their own cars at 16. For middle- and upper-middle-class young adults, being able to buy books and paintings, to go out to dinner, to know about wines, is taken for granted as part of life, no matter that Great-Grandpa who came over during the Irish potato famines of the nineteenth century would faint dead away at their lifestyles.

And as these children of relative affluence reach their second and third decades, the crucial American dream of home ownership dies hard with the mothers, if not with the young adults. So again help is indicated, lest the young people, in columnist Ellen

Goodman's memorable phrase, "miss the last boat to the middle class."

The bitter realities of today's newly contracting, finite world of limited possibilities—the downward mobility that young people fear, where a new home costs eight or ten times what it did for the parents—comes as a nasty and frightening shock to both generations who have tasted that postwar affluence.

Terror of slipping out of a middle class that takes vacations as a matter of right and casually acquires cameras, ten-speed bikes, and personal computers motivates both parents and adult children to share housing, money, travel, and plans for the future in continuing postlaunch ways that neither had quite anticipated.

One way, of course, is the much discussed contemporary development of returnees—adult children who have left home for work, school, marriage, the service, or just to find new grown-up selves, and who for one reason or another have come to ask for their old rooms back like guests at a hotel.

Parents, but particularly mothers, quickly learn that there is no such thing as an empty nest in those circumstances; children are not sparrows and seldom fly away for good.

In fact, when they return, they come complete with tape decks, tennis rackets, and hair dryers, and they are not infrequently accompanied by a retinue of live-in partners, close friends, spouses and/or children.

They return after painful romantic episodes, failed marriages, job troubles, illnesses, or accidents; they return when the money runs out and they return, sometimes, "just to get my act together," or because home is where the clean socks come around dependably on schedule, there's always toilet paper in the bathroom, and the morning paper is frequently delivered.

The returnees are only the tip of the iceberg (see Chapter 9), because even when the adult sons and daughters are gulping down their own yogurt in their own kitchens, and Hondas with ski racks on top have long since replaced tricycles, they are in an orbit that maternal radar registers sharply at each revolution around the earth.

What women are learning in this later motherhood (a stage which isn't even popularly supposed to exist) is that while all the rules of the game have changed, and they now feel a lot of the same old responsibility and concern but have practically no authority, they are still influential to a degree that is surprising, and are needed in ways they never imagined would continue.

Nowadays, they are finding that when the demands do come, the mothering task remains intense in tone, if intermittent in time. The life stakes now are much higher than when Jimmy didn't make the team or Susie missed out on a part in the school play.

Modern young people don't hesitate to yell for attention or help in a difficult and darkening world, whether they are nineteen or thirty-nine or even older.

They bring their broken love lives and their cash-flow problems and their longings for support—emotional and financial—right to the family doorstep, and when real crises loom, like illness or unemployment, they involve their parents with lightning speed.

Now that the stereo plays "Stardust" instead of rock; now that there are no longer guitars in the middle of the living room floor; now that the refrigerator door no longer clicks relentlessly all day and all night—a very new and a different way of relating to grown children must be found.

Because mothering adult kids today means *being there in a special way.*

Instead of the 2:00 A.M. bottle of infant years, it's the 2:00 A.M. crisis phone call: divorce, drugs, money, job problems.

Instead of helping with homework, it's helping with the sober adult project of buying a home or an apartment, or helping to start a new business, often with parental savings.

Instead of driving small tots to the dentist and music lessons, it's hiring a truck to deliver some of the now unneeded family furniture to the off-campus college digs or the first-job, first-apartment household.

Instead of supervising Boy Scout campers and Girl Scout hikers, it's parents giving up their own precious days of solitude to let the school-weary or work-harried young adults have the cabin on the lake or the vacation cottage.

"You see a lot more of your kids after they leave home," cracked comedienne Lucille Ball, and to many modern mothers, bewilderedly finding their way through these new thickets of

"Help-me-but-leave-me-alone" and "I-need-you-but-don't-get-too-close," the joke seems all too serious.

Mothers of 64 million Baby Boomers, and mothers of the millions more born in the first postwar years, were never told about this new orbital stage. They had no idea it existed, how long it would last, or what it would require from them. Several sharp observers of contemporary family life have noted that there is no clearly marked exit, no termination date, no honorable discharge from active duty for the modern mother.[3]

When today's middle-aged mothers were marrying young, their new roles as wives and, quickly, mothers rang down a flimsy curtain of sorts between themselves and their old-for-their-age parents.

Today, as young people postpone marriage and children to ever later years, their parents abandon grandparenthood dreams in favor of going to the flicks or out to dinner with the same young people who, generations ago, would have been too busy with their own young families to be around.

Mothers of today's grown kids were encouraged by their own mothers, as well as by their husbands and peers, to believe that it was pretty much all over when the children left home, except for a Christmas dinner here or a christening party there, or a nice bar mitzvah reception once in a while.

Moreover, they were told, it *should* be all over if you are a "good" mother and have solved the "hanging-on-or-letting-go" struggle that remains at the heart of all generational relations. If you are a "healthy" mother, ran the dicta of the Sixties and Seventies, you never meddle, stay out of your kids' hair, get off their backs, and do a variety of other acrobatics that all add up to: Stay away!

All this advice, of course, was based on an assumption that mothers were people who were totally child-centered, had no lives but those they lived vicariously in their children, and would hold on forever if not forcibly removed from around their kids' necks. (More on this "horror mother" in a moment.)

But the advice quickly became outdated; it did not keep up with the social reality of what the mother person was becoming: glamorous grandmas who worked out at the gym, career-interested fiftyish mothers who went back to school and work, traditional homemakers who sped out to surrogate careers in

voluntarism and community activities the minute they got
sprung from three meals a day and fifteen loads of wash a
week, or used the time to indulge in long-postponed private
interests of their own.

What has happened now is that it is *Mom* who wants to be out
of the nest, or at least she wants more peace and freedom within
it. "Free the 40 million" read the banners of contemporary
mothers, who, though they remain as deeply connected to their
children emotionally and psychically as ever, no longer feel the
need to live their entire lives only through what their children
do and are.

This Let-me-out-of-the-nest-already mother is herself so new
that we don't have a clearly drawn profile of how she might go
about dealing with the surprisingly long maternal life she will
live with her adult children.

In fact, I believe the less-than-totally-child-centered mother is
actually coexisting (often within the same woman) with the old-
fashioned emotionally grasping mother, and with the interim
traditional mother who is willing to be less involved but is living
a stay-at-home life.

Because the transitional mother is a new reality on the scene
of generational sagas, she has no models, no precedents to
follow. "The psychological work in late motherhood is as ardu-
ous as that of any other developmental stage," points out Dr.
Janet Z. Giele in her book *Women in the Middle Years* (Wiley,
1982), and she also observes: "In just three decades [1950s to
1980s], the social roles of middle-aged women changed drasti-
cally. The [transitional] mother had grown up with the ideals of
her mother's generation, but now has to live with a different
reality."

"And," writes another expert, "the lack of clearly defined
roles for the postparental parent can lead to . . . an uncertainty
as to what is 'proper' conduct. . . ."[4]

It's quite true that middle-class women have ways of "practicing" for their children's leave-taking from home; college
represents an important separation, and mobility toward careers is a middle-class value. In working-class and poor families, the children often live at home until they marry, so that
the mother does not know, even approximately, when the
leave-taking is going to happen. But the mothers of these lat-

ter classes have been touched, too, by the contemporary
women's movement that has been so instrumental in changing
women's horizons and implanting new desires, values, and
goals, as well as by the sweeping rush of all the other social
forces of the past thirty years.

Let's take a close look at the contemporary middle-aged wo-
man/mother who stands with one foot back in her mother's idea
of motherhood and one foot in a new era of maternal independence and freedom from the children—while up in orbit, her
kids are beeping messages to her that she tries to read with all
the love, guilt, and energy she can summon.

Women Young at Middle-Age: A Brand New Sex

The contemporary woman who is pioneering this new stage of
later mothering is herself a kind of woman never seen on the
planet before.[5]

Modern medicine, health advances, and cultural and social
changes mean that today, women in their middle years and
much later are active sexual beings; they have kept youth and
charm and physical attractiveness decades beyond what their
grandmothers knew. Moreover, they have done this as part of a
whole generation, where earlier there were only a few lucky
beings whose genes conferred the blessings now available
through hormonal therapy, lifelong medical and dental care,
new knowledge of nutrition, and a national craze for physical
fitness that touches all ages. Modern obstetrical care was, of
course, one of the biggest items in the development of this
generation, and that science is still progressing apace.

Middle-aged contemporary women are thus almost a new biological subsex, says the redoubtable Dr. Jessie Bernard, an
eminent sociologist and sharp observer of feminist currents in
our society. "She [the young middle-aged woman] was an
unanticipated consequence of modern science," writes Dr.
Bernard.

This then is the new woman sitting at mission control and
looking at the orbiting children. What will her challenges as a
later mother be? What does she face as she tries to peer into this
new part of her life?

Asking women about the centrality of this later mothering, I quickly learned that there is a time lag in this mid-life experience, just as there is in the larger society outside the home.

Just as the world hasn't caught up with its own technological and scientific explosion, so modern, youthful mothers haven't caught up with themselves yet, and still behave and feel much more like old-fashioned mothers than their slim, trim, chic, contemporary selves would indicate.

Most of us still don't know what to make of animal-to-human heart transplants, of satellite dishes on roofs that can bring us 2,000 TV programs tonight if we want them, of computers that beat us at chess; we're still trying to catch up.

Similarly, women who are indeed marvels of modern science —women in their forties and fifties and sixties who ride bikes across Europe and scuba dive in every ocean of the world—are still trying to catch up psychologically with what this new kind of womanhood and new kind of later mothering are really going to be like.

In the chapters that follow, we will be able to track three distinct, evolving styles of mothering that are shifting and changing even as we examine them, and one may even be disappearing altogether.

First is a vestigial "horror mother." She barely exists anymore in this new young middle-aged generation, but she pops up here and there. This is the woman fabled in earlier decades of this century as guilty of "Momism"—the all-consuming, ravening, emotionally greedy woman who lives only in and for her children and eventually destroys them, particularly her sons.

Though some adult children may question these findings (they are perhaps not the most objective observers), I met relatively few of such "vipers"[6] in my survey for two reasons:

1. The woman who has no other interest in life but to metaphorically devour her young—the woman who is not interested in her own love life or marriage, in any kind of paid or unpaid work, in any sort of contract with the outside world, and is also uninterested in friends, hobbies, or other family members—is a disappearing breed, whether one views her sociologically, psychologically, or demographically.

2. Enough modern knowledge about child-rearing has reached even this type of mother that in interviews with me, she fibbed or glossed over evidences of undue control and insatiable demands upon her children. In most cases, however, she withdrew from the survey almost immediately when she learned it was about second-stage mothering with the grown children because, sadly, so many of her relationships with her children are so dysfunctional that it is painful for her to rehearse the sorrows. One can only hope for outside help for both generations in these families so that some kind of peace can be obtained before it is too late.

But this remnant of the forties and fifties is a statistically disappearing style of mothering. ("Momism" first appeared in 1942, created by Philip Wylie in his book *Generation of Vipers,* possibly as an allergic reaction to wartime yearnings for "togetherness.")

By far the largest group of women I surveyed—more than three-quarters of the nearly 500—are clearly identifiable as "transitional" women.

These are the women for whom all the signals changed right in the middle of the game. These youthful middle-agers were brought up to hold husband, home, and children at the very center of their lives.

Three decades later, the notion that there might be lives for them in addition to their families, or that marriage and children are not forever, inform the very air they breathe.

For this is the woman who is playing on the old field by the old rules and at the same time moving into the new field along *with* her existing or remarried or living-together new family structure.

The transitional woman came of age in the 1940s (World War II), the 1950s (the quiescent Eisenhower era), and the incredible early 1960s.

This was enough change to tear at the fabric of even the most deeply rooted human relationships, some of which have taken centuries to reach their present form.

This mother, who is trying to understand her 1980s kids, is one who was a teenage cheerleader in high school and turned into a Pentagon marcher during the Vietnam war. At 18 she pledged a sorority at college; by 48 she was joining a conscious-ness-raising group with other women.

Programmed to be chaste before marriage and monogamous within it, she found that her husband could leave after twenty-five years of marriage and run off with the baby-sitter; her love life today would curl her mother's hair.

If this woman remains married, she is delighted to discover that her sex life with her husband is more and better than when their 3.2 children (the typical-sized family for many of her gener-ation) were at home.

Raised to be solely a homemaker, she now goes back to school, works, has an income of her own, and contributes might-ily to her family's money and to its life-style and aspirations for the future.

There is, in fact, no end to the way the game has changed, but in her maternal soul, she's still wearing the hats for both teams: the child-centered (but not devouring) traditional mother and the transitional woman of the newest era.

It is precisely because the young middle-aged mothers of today are handling so many different currents feeding into the stream of their maternal behavior with their adult children that we find so many contradictions and confusions in this new life stage for which, indeed, there has been little preparation.

Who could have ever imagined twenty-five years ago that Mom would be off chairing a conference someplace when Daughter called to get the recipe for Swedish meatballs because she's throwing a party to celebrate her first promotion? Who would have believed twenty-five years ago that Mom would have sent a check to Son for his birthday with the cheery note that since she and Dad would be on vacation out west when his birthday came around, it would be helpful if he bought his own birthday sweater?

This transitional mother doesn't forget birthdays, and she'll send the recipe by overnight mail if she needs to; she's still on active duty, and feels pangs if she forgets something really im-portant, but manages to accommodate her own life in ways earlier generations did not.

Although this transitional mother represents a very large ma-jority of today's young middle-aged women, there are the re-maining 25 percent of my survey group whom I call "traditional" mothers—in quotation marks. Because while they are traditional in many ways, they show some interesting signs of change as well. These are the women who, if they ever did work outside the home, did so largely on a temporary and intermittent basis, without ever being seriously committed to a career. These are also the women who, while hard to find, still do most of the civic, educational, and social work chores for the rest of society, and also pursue many personal interests.

The change taking place in this group is that this woman is also, like the transitional mother, becoming much less child-centered, *even if she is not working.*

I believe the traditional mother is reflecting a number of contemporary developments: First, the ambience of the women's movement has created a climate in which women are freer to do *whatever* they want, whether it's hobbies, civic activities, gourmet cooking, or sky-diving; they've absorbed the idea—wildly refreshing compared to how they were raised—that it's okay for them to spend time and pursue projects unrelated to the children. Also because of the women's movement, they feel prouder of their homemaking contributions, can put a dollar figure on their worth (thanks to women-instigated court cases), and know that they were working for sure when they were homemakers. The feminist slogan "All women work" has hit home with this group and fewer and fewer say, "I'm *just* a housewife."

Second, since they *are* members of this brand new "young" middle-aged group, they can share more of the friendship aspect with their children. They can go on vacations, go shopping, go to museums and movies with their kids without violating some mythical "I'm the mother and you're the child and we can never be friends" syndrome that used to separate generations when women seemed so much older than even their adult children. (For more on this, see Chapter 8.)

Third, they have a bigger world to move in and that beckons them outside the walls of home. Reading, traveling, gardening, enjoying films, TV, and other entertainment that brings the world in, are all quantitatively and qualitatively changing their lives and lessening the focus on the children's doings. It's certainly healthy and good in many ways and it relieves some of the intensity and overheating of the conventional nuclear family.

But making it all work out—reconciling everyone's interests, keeping family ties strong and the bonds of love and concern active, working out strain and conflict—has, as usual, fallen mostly on the shoulders of even the most modern of mothers, rather than fathers.

In that respect, the traditional and the transitional mother are one and the same—plugged into their kids in ways that are strongly influenced by the past while they struggle toward the future.

2

Guilt, Despair, and Other Good Things That Go Into Mom's Apple Pie

It seems to me at times as if the weight of responsibility connected with these little immortal beings would prove too much for me—Am I doing what is right? Am I doing enough? Am I not doing too much? . . . if I neglect everything else, I must be forgiven. . . .

ABIGAIL ALCOTT, letter, 1883

[The father] made it clear . . . that he considered Lulu responsible for her daughter's defection. This was not, of course, without its own perverse justice—that justice under which mothers are held responsible for everything from life's random negative quality to the genesis of every neurosis developed by those passing through it.

JUDITH ROSSNER, *August*

One hundred years of maternal guilt and anxiety separate Abigail Alcott, the Victorian image of saintly Mamma, from Dr. Lulu Shinefeld, the smart, tough, warm-hearted modern psychiatrist–heroine of Judith Rossner's best-selling novel of 1983.

Yet they are sisters under the skin, not only to each other but to millions of the new "young" middle-aged mothers we met in Chapter 1.

Though these snappy new fortyish mothers may be playing video games with their grandchildren, they continue to play guilt games with themselves in a hangover from the maternal styles that were bred into them decades ago.

For their part, adult children of these women often can be heard complaining about the "guilt trip Mom tries to lay on me." But most such young people have little idea of how much of what they perceive—in both healthy and not-so-healthy mothers—is a projection of the enormous burden of guilt that modern mothers carry about their own *performances as mothers.*

In performance-obsessed America—be it in sports, business, sex, or entertainment—to perform badly is to be virtually un-American. On both a superficial level and much deeper levels, American women are burdened with performance anxiety that is a legacy from the past in which they came of age as mothers.

And this past is different from any earlier maternal generations. Although poor Abigail is proof that mothers' anxiety and guilt go back at least a century, it's probable that some kind of concern goes back to the beginning of history and evolution. Very possibly cave-dwelling mothers burned a lot of animal entrails to the gods to try to assure good hunting for their sons and easy childbirth for their daughters. But if the gods were capricious and frowned, it's doubtful if Stone Age mothers, or those that came later, blamed themselves.

Before the twentieth century, mothers tended to curse God, fate, false idols, luck, inappropriate sacrifices, or the toss of the dice if things went badly for their children.

Although poems and stories from every culture and every historical period show us that mothers grieved and mourned and felt deeply sad or disappointed in times of their children's troubles, few held themselves to be the sole culprit if their children did not win at life's lottery.

But in hearing directly from nearly 500 contemporary women and digging into the maternal stories of dozens of them, what emerges is this: Women who came to maturity as the first generation of post-Freudian mothers spend more time worrying about their responsibilities for their children's lives than can be believed, considering that they are also the first generation to seek, as a whole group, active, involved lives outside the family.

Most became mothers in the first wave of "the psychological child"—the first group of children in recorded time who could be raised according to vast amounts of new knowledge about how human beings grow and develop. The fledgling sciences of psychology and human development, which did not really leap from the pages of history until the late nineteenth century despite the shrewd observations of the ancient Greeks and Elizabethan Shakespeare, came down like a ton of bricks on the now middle-aged women whose voices you hear in this book.

These women grew up, as mothers, convinced that there is a "right way" to raise children to assure super adults—and that *other* mothers have found it! After all, look at their kids, functioning so much better than one's own!

Indeed, to this very moment, thousands, if not millions, of American women believe with the fervor of religious faith that while the "right way" is elusive for them, many other families have solved the major problems and are living painless lives of idyllic harmony; only *they* have disappointment, sorrow, and strain with their kids!

The women whose evolving histories with their young adult children were gathered for this book describe so many different kinds of motherly guilt, experienced in so many different modes (sometimes in a cozy bout of anxiety with the children's father, sometimes starkly alone, sometimes with another mother) that they almost require computerization of categories. But so much confusion, guilt, and worry tumble from their stories that it is best to listen to them directly:

Sandra D., a divorced mother of five sons, mourns that she was raised in such an emotionally "cool" family that she was always discouraged from outward displays of feeling. This, she believes, made her unable to help her sons develop the expressive side of their natures (she ignores the fact that American stereotypes of what constitutes boyishness didn't help her), and even though this problem is at least partially traceable to her own parents and to a lack of help from her ex-husband, Sandra assumes total blame.

"I feel so guilty," she says in words I was to hear over and over until their repetition became nightmarish, "because all the time we were raising them, neither my husband nor I really were much good at letting anybody know our real feelings; in fact all the trouble that can cause was the major reason for our divorce. Now I can see—and it hurts more than you can ever know—that my kids lack the emotional, interpersonal skills they need to go out into the world and try to make good ties with people . . . any kind of people . . . friends, lovers, coworkers; or even communicate halfway decently with people in their own family . . . it's bad and it makes me feel hurt, angry, guilty, defensive—but mostly guilty.''

Another woman, Rose P., the youthful mother of two grown married daughters, both of whom are doing well at love and work, is still troubled by a sense that she pushed them toward maturity too fast, was too eager for them to be on their own and independent of her.

The major reason, she explains now, is that she experienced the responsibility for these little lives as "absolutely overwhelming. I had no idea what I was doing when I had those kids," says Rose, and she was typical for her time. "We never thought about it or questioned it—we just had 'em; and then there they were, and my real reaction was: 'God, what have I gotten myself into?' ''

Despite the presence in the home of Rose's loving husband, who was a father who cared attentively for both his wife and little girls but who was typical of *his* time in being preoccupied with commuting and working twelve hours or more a day, Rose felt the children were completely her assignment.

Now, more than twenty years after the fact, she still remembers how desperately she wanted to be relieved of the incessant anxiety that covered everything from whether she was buying the right shoes for little growing feet to whether she was later allowing the "right" boys to hang around the house.

"Was I pushing too fast, or hanging on too long? I never really knew," Rose continues, "even though we used to say that if our girls came from a good, strong, loving family, everything would be okay when they got out on their own. But was that really true? These were the Sixties and Seventies, remember."

She pauses to reflect, "Well, I guess they were okay. We got through that time without an abortion, though I know they experimented with sex and drugs at times—but they didn't become addicts, they didn't run away from home, we didn't lose them—but I know some families who did, so I guess we got through all right. But"—she shrugs and turns her palms up and outward in the classic gesture of uncertainty—"do parents ever really *know?*"

Rose reports she has shyly discussed her feeling of having pushed her daughters out of the nest too fast with her firstborn, whom she sees as the one most sinned against. It's delightful that the mother has been reassured by the young woman that she has no such perception. While this relieves guilt to some degree, Rose says, "I still think it's a miracle they don't hate me for that."

Another category of guilt among the dozens mothers have developed for themselves might be labeled: "I did what I had to do for my own life, but I think some of it had a terrible effect on my children. Still, what else could I do?"

Claudia B. is the 48-year-old mother of a son now 25, and a daughter 21. When the children were in their late teens, following seventeen years of an increasingly unhappy marriage, Claudia sought a divorce.

"Although Bud and I had a lot of problems between us, we really tried hard to impress on the children that we both cared about them, that we would cooperate together for their best welfare, and all the rest of it," remembers Claudia, thinking back to the time of divorce, "and we thought we were doing the best we could for them under the circumstances.

"Yet," she sighs, "I often wonder how much of it is my fault that Laura's engagement to a very nice guy has been on hold for nearly two years. What did my divorce really do to her attitude about marriage? I know I'm probably being silly—divorce and separation are so common nowadays; but I just can't help wondering whether what I did with *my* life has somehow made it harder for both my kids to handle long-term situations."

If the mother's own divorce gives her the jitters about what she may have done to cripple her children's capacities for commitment, she falls headlong into an abyss of guilt when the issue is the *child's* divorce.

She sees grown sons and daughters who, despite a somewhat

stabilizing national divorce rate at the moment, still seem to her
to be meeting, living together, marrying, separating, and divorcing in dizzying numbers and at breathless speeds.

The mother's view: It can only be her fault. Dad just wasn't
around all that much; his share of the blame, if any at all, is seen
by the mother as much smaller than her own in all but extreme
cases.

"Where did I go wrong? There must be a failure somewhere
if our son married at twenty and divorced at twenty-three. I
don't care what people say about divorce just being in the air or
that young people don't work hard enough at making a marriage
last. I'm telling you that no matter how we try to make ourselves
feel better with that kind of talk, I doubt very much that there's
a parent alive whose kid gets a divorce who doesn't feel at least
a little bit of guilt or blame. Maybe it's because my age people
just can't help but look at divorce as failure—and we might be
wrong, but that's how we were brought up."

Speaking is Janice N., a mid-fifties sparkler of a woman. Two
of her four children have been divorced and now are remarried.

Janice's thoughtful summation is especially interesting because she is the exact opposite of the clinging, overinvolved
"horror mother." She has a strong self-image, lots of outside
interests, a wonderful sense of humor, and an impressive perspective and detachment from her grown children, although she
calls it, with a smile, "only semidetachment."

Janice has been married to the children's father for nearly
thirty-five years and they have, in her view, "come through"
every kind of strain with their kids that both normal growth and
a turbulent society could impose. She is proud of the fact that
both she and their father are still in meaningful and rewarding
touch with all their children, and even with one of the ex-in-law
kids. She also reports the parental marriage was strengthened
when the children left home, even though one or two have
returned to live at home briefly for intermittent periods.

But in spite of all these personal and marital strengths, Janice
says that when a marked trauma such as a failed youthful marriage befalls one of her children, she begins, in her words, to
"climb the walls" with almost the same desperation and sense
of shame and failure as mothers with much less self-confidence
and perspective.

Dealing with divorce, remarriage, and the convoluted families of today, many women reported a variation on the classic guilt symptom: the special dilemma of the stepmother.

Mary N. is now married for the second time. Her new husband, a number of years her senior, was also married before, and brought three children of his own to their recent marriage. Mary contributed her only child, a son, to the new ménage.

Since Mary and her new husband married in middle age after earlier divorces, all the children were a bit past adolescence, each had loyalties to the other parent, and all were living away from Mary and Richard—some in college, some working, and one still living at home with Richard's former wife.

Attempting to integrate the two families through visits, vacation trips, and special times together proved infinitely harder than anyone had anticipated, Mary says, even though the children did not have to live at home together daily under the same roof.

"Nobody ever asked the wicked stepmother how *she* felt about Cinderella," says Mary with heartfelt emphasis, "and I have to say it's one of the hardest things in the world to handle right and I made a lot of mistakes. . . ."

Although relations in the four-child stepfamily are relatively good now, Mary reports: "When I look back on it, I feel rotten. My husband was much nicer to my son than I was to his kids. If I could do it over, I'd be more patient, more giving. One time, his oldest son came to visit and it was a bad time—the boy regressed, messed up our house, wanted attention like a five-year-old. It was so tense and miserable that the next time he visited, he stayed with a friend instead of with his dad and me. I felt guilty about it for years."

Actually, the stepfamily is not as modern as we might think. Generations ago, families often were broken and re-formed, with many stepchildren, half-siblings, and children who did not even have one common parent, all living under the same roof.

But the agent of change in the seventeenth and eighteenth centuries was usually death, not so often divorce. Long ago, it was unusual for men or women to survive to their fifties, and if they did, they seldom had spent more than ten years married to the same spouse. What we now call "serial" marriages were common in an age when disease and the terrors of childbirth carried off husbands or wives.

The difference today is that we will find women parenting children not their own for decade upon decade; they have to be long-term copers where their ancestors were short-termers on the stepparent scene.

Observing both the harried stepparents and the eternally guilty natural mothers, one has to ask how perfectly bright, capable women—now at or near the very peak of their experience and vigor—who are themselves going to school and work in large numbers, surviving divorces, finding dramatic new life patterns, still remain so vulnerable to judgment about their children.

After Freud and Before Friedan

The gnawing guilt and fear of being perceived as a failure or inadequate in the mother role is at least partially, I believe, a reflection of the particular niche these youngish middle-aged mothers occupy in female history: a bit after Freud, a moment before Friedan, and much before the current information now coming to light about *all* the elements that might go into shaping a child.

Later in this chapter, we will examine some of the new knowledge about genetic and environmental factors that influence human development, along with the maternal impact, but first let's try to remember the framework of knowledge about mothering that was operative at the time these women had their usually large crop of children.

Women who are now parents of adult children came of age themselves when the work of two giants in the field of human psychology loomed over the cradle. One of these scientists, of course, is well known to the entire world: Sigmund Freud. The other, who is still alive and is more our contemporary, is Dr. John Bowlby of England. Though his name is not so universally recognized as Freud's, this British physician, Freudian psychiatrist, and distinguished student of the mother-child bond *is* known to professionals in the field of family studies around the world. He has also, like Freud, had the most profound influence on what one modern female psychiatrist has called "the idealization of motherhood."[1]

Between Freud and Bowlby, the women/mothers of the mid-twentieth century were handed a role new to any woman since Eve failed to straighten out the sibling rivalry between Cain and Abel.

The story begins, of course, with the greatest pioneer of human psychology in the modern era, with the towering figure of Freud. In the early decades of this century, American women first encountered scattered news reports of Freud's stunning revelations and discoveries. They heard, usually at third hand, the news that the first adults in a child's life, especially the mother, are critically important to all the rest of his years.

The significance of the caretakers was documented at the furthermost frontiers of science by a daring investigator, and thus at least part of what some intuitive mothers had probably known for centuries was now scientifically *proved*—and this at a time when Science with a capital "S" was the ultimate god.

The story of how today's middle-aged women began to reap a whirlwind of guilt and anxiety based on this kind of news then leaps ahead to 1951, when, at the request of the newly formed World Health Organization (an agency of the United Nations), Dr. Bowlby submitted to that body the results of intensive research he and his team had been asked to undertake.

The world health body had requested Dr. Bowlby to survey the plight of children who had, through war and other disasters, been separated from their mothers. The aim of the survey was to assist in planning for the huge numbers of child refugees and displaced persons thrown up homeless, stateless, and familyless on the shores of war-torn countries.

For the most part, Dr. Bowlby and his researchers encountered these children as they were being cared for in institutions of various kinds. In the light of Freud's earlier findings about the absolutely crucial first years in each human life, Bowlby's conclusions could not be too surprising, but he had—in orphanages, foundling homes, and refugee camps—dramatic illustrations at hand of the main hypothesis: Children suffer terribly if they are denied consistent, continuous nurturing care by a "mother or mother substitute," and their outlook for a healthy future is bleak, if not catastrophic.

The list of miseries that befell these children who had suffered the most extreme maternal deprivation and many other traumas of war, dislocation, and loss as well was so horrendous, their future so disastrous, that the world was forced to take some note.

Silent, apathetic, malnourished in every way, these unsmiling babies who had apparently never learned basic human ways of responding to other humans became haunting, grim photographic images of war's aftermath.

Most of the women I interviewed more than thirty years later had never heard of Bowlby, nor were they conscious of ever having seen photographs of these heart-rending infants.

Yet most of them had clear visual memories of having seen pictures somewhere (not necessarily those from the World Health Organization or from Bowlby's researchers) of what children look like when they have not been adequately nurtured by any mothering figure. In their minds' eye, women clearly see the appearance such children present: skeletal (even when food is available), hollow-eyed, blank, and unresponsive.

Even for women who have no conscious memory of what I have been describing, there is a recognition of these deprived children instantly when they see them in the flesh or in pictures.

Even unsophisticated, less-well-educated mothers of the middle-aged groups we talked with seemed, in their early days as mothers, to have absorbed by osmosis (they did not remember reading it, although they may have received diluted versions from doctors or teachers) the thrust of Dr. Bowlby's main thesis, which was reported as follows:

> What is believed to be essential for mental health is that the infant and young child should experience warm, intimate and continuous relationships with his mother (or permanent mother-substitute) in which both find enjoyment. . . . *Partial deprivation* [italics added] brings in its train acute anxiety, excessive need for love, powerful feelings of revenge and arising from these last, guilt and depression . . . complete deprivation . . . has even more far-reaching effects on character development, and may entirely cripple the capacity to make relationships.[2]

In a short time, the World Health Organization report, followed over several years by a massive three-volume study titled

Attachment, Separation and Loss, had become the seminal work, after Freud's, behind all advice to new mothers.

By now, there was no question that, in Margaret Mead's sweet and common-sense phrase, "a baby needs someone to smile back when it smiles."

But hosts of later child-development experts in many disciplines, including Freud's own brilliant and compassionate daughter, Dr. Anna Freud, continued to do additional research throughout the 1950s, 1960s, and early 1970s that seemed to women (however diluted and fuzzy the interpretation they received) to be saying that there could be no hope of health for their children unless there was a strong, continuous, and seemingly exclusive mother-child attachment.

The concept of mother-child "bonding," though capable of infinite definitions by experts, came through to the now-middle-aged women in our sample in an absolutely clear way, both when they were new mothers and, in a different form and structure, in their new roles as older mothers.

The necessity of this bonding to assure the psychological health of the child is seen by both parents as a *guarantee* of proper development in most ordinary circumstances, and this belief is still central to most child-rearing attempts today.

It is probably difficult for contemporary young mothers (not without some guilt of their own) as they trundle off to work in the morning, leaving their children with other caretakers, to quite sense how sternly the dictum *take care of that baby—or else* became an inviolable commandment to their mothers.

It would not be exaggerating to suggest that the findings of a whole generation of physicians, psychologists, and psychiatrists, inspired by Freud and motivated by Bowlby and others who came after him, had passed into a sort of vast collective maternal unconscious, there to linger and to stimulate almost all women of that era to feel responsible and anxious about caring for all children, not just their own, with a view to preventing the terrible consequences of maternal deprivation.

One contemporary figure in modern child psychology, Dr. Jerome Kagan, professor of human development at Harvard, has an interesting interpretation of the insistence that the caretakers have exclusive ability to help or hinder children's development.

In his startlingly revisionist collection of essays and research reports recently published, *The Nature of the Child* (Basic Books, 1984), Dr. Kagan writes:

> Every society needs some transcendental theme to which citizens can be loyal. In the past, God, the beauty and utility of knowledge and the sanctity of faithful romantic love were among the most sacred themes in our society. Unfortunately, the facts of modern life have made it difficult for many Americans to remain loyal to these ideas. *The sacredness of the parent-infant bond may be one of the last unsullied beliefs* [italics added]. The barrage of books and magazine articles on attachment and the necessity of skin-to-skin bonding between mother and infant in the first postnatal hours is generated by strong emotion, suggesting that something more than scientific fact is monitoring the discussion. If the infant can be cared for by any concerned adult, and the biological mother is expendable (this has not yet been proven), then one more moral imperative will have been destroyed.

But Dr. Kagan's search for some scientific "cool" on an over-wrought subject comes very late in the game for today's middle-aged mothers, who had so thoroughly absorbed the earlier version of the gospel.

How in the world could millions of women, from every kind of class, racial, and religious background, go off the deep end in the guilt-and-anxiety department based on some complex developments taking place way out on the furthermost frontiers of science and coming back to them, often, in highly garbled form?

There are a number of elements in the arrival of the "age of the psychological child" that we must keep in mind.

First, contemporary critics of Bowlby have pointed out that in the initial WHO studies, the children were living in institutions; most were not in anything resembling a normal family environment.[3] This, of course, does not invalidate the notion that early "mothering" in some form from some consistent caretaker is deeply important to the child, but it does offer some perspective, some balance, another angle of vision, which somehow did not come through to the American women who heard vaguely of some of this work. Mothers in this country—those who got any version of the Bowlby researches—jumped (or were pushed) to the conclusion that the children who were suffering such terrible consequences of maternal deprivation were just like any other children, and that included their own.

Second, and most important, it is hard to overstate how badly the serious, important new mental-health information was communicated to inexperienced, uncertain, and anxious new mothers. It came through in a crudely popularized, simplified form in mass women's magazines, newspaper features, and Sunday supplement articles, and in books that put parents in a double bind: "Relax, enjoy your baby, you know more than you think you do"; but this approach was combined with an intense emphasis on inculcating almost professional-level competence in parents, so that they learned that caring is not enough, it is parenting *skills* that count.

Two detailed studies of how, when, and why parents turn to printed materials for guidance—primarily magazine articles and books—have been completed by students of family life in the past decade, one in 1978 and one in 1981.[4]

Both these surveys of how mothers (fathers read far less, though some) get their information help explain why our middle-aged mothers were so ill served by the primers meant to help them. Both studies covered both educated and less-well-educated mothers from the major economic groupings and they agreed on a number of points:

• Parents turn to magazines and books to an astonishing degree to help with the first one or two children. In one sample, 96.7 percent of parents had read at least one book or magazine article; in the other survey, the figure was more than 94 percent. Researchers disagree on why this is so—some say it's because mobility of families has removed grandparents, neighbors, relatives as guides; others say it's just symptomatic of modern life that people turn to experts for help on everything, and that includes parenting.

• Dr. Spock's famous baby book was, of course, the most widely read "Bible" when mothers were given several titles to choose from, but when an open-ended question like "What else have you read on child care?" was asked, the most frequent answer in one survey was *The Better Homes and Gardens Baby Book.*

The 1978 study was able to confirm that reliance on these kinds of materials (not exactly comparable to Freud's published works or Bowlby's three-volume epic) had grown steadily from the 1940s to the present moment.

Both researchers surveying parenting primers and guides were concerned that parents were not being given the kind of information that was intellectually honest or respectful enough of (usually) the mother's capacities.

The author of the 1978 review of child-development information, K. Alison Clarke-Stewart of the education department of the University of Chicago, pointed out that very few popular magazines cater exclusively to the parent audience (as does, for example, *Parents Magazine*), and that "most commonly, articles on raising a child are interspersed with those on planting a garden, decorating a room, planning a vacation, or designing a wardrobe which are found in the popular women's magazines."

Said the author of the 1981 study, "The findings . . . suggest that parents do listen to the advice of those who write books and articles about child care. Because of the significance of the task to which their advice is applied—the rearing of children—authors are encouraged to take their responsibilities seriously. Parents are entitled to information based upon evidence, not merely belief, presented in a manner reflecting an understanding of the significance of their task and a respect for their capability."

From what the mature mothers of today said in their letters and interviews, they received plenty of pressure about how significant the task was, but very little respect for their capabilities in the face of what they perceived as overwhelming directives on how responsible they were for the emotional well-being of their children.

In the 1978 study, the author is even more critical of those who undertake to "translate" complex scientific information into popular parenting literature.

"Perhaps," the University of Chicago educator writes, "it is the tension created by the experts' attempts to both bolster parents' confidence and at the same time promote their competence that makes these books [the popular primers of the day] relatively unsuccessful at achieving either goal."

The middle-aged women we are concerned with here knew all

too well the tensions that came from the oversimplified dicta they inherited in the wake of growing new knowledge.

Virtually none of the sources they consulted dealt with early scientific findings on child development in really substantive ways; most of it was superficial interpretation when it was not sensationalized, as in the case of Freud's discoveries about human sexuality. It is important to note, too, that the studies cited above showed that mothers tended *not* to go to their doctors or friends for this general information on child development, but to use those "people" sources for help with specific problems. What they were seeking was dependable reporting on the expanding body of new knowledge. Sadly, they received simplistic, somewhat trivialized forms.

As could then be expected, few of the details, speculations, qualifications, and provisos that appeared in the original works by the great psychologists of human development were passed on to mothers in anything like adequate form. If they had been, they might have prevented countless hours of worry and anxiety. The problem, typical of many religions, was not in the original thinkers, but in the disciples and less rigorous interpreters.

Dr. Ann Dally is a compatriot of Bowlby's who is not totally persuaded of the validity of some of his theses. She is also a British psychiatrist, the mother of six children, and the author of a book called *Inventing Motherhood* (Schocken Books, 1983).

"To many," she writes, "[the new rules] were an enormous relief. They gave simple guidelines by which an undoubtedly important aspect of infant development could be understood by even dim mothers ("just stay with your children every minute of the day and everything will be alright") and . . . could be used simultaneously to allay the anxiety of mothers; keep women tied to the home, thus making life comfortable for men, and to save the government money that otherwise would have to be spent on children, given the discovery of the importance of the early years." (Headstart programs have funding trouble in the United States, too.)

There have always been women who were either naturally intuitive and sensitive to their children or who were raised in large families where they learned to be relaxed and knowledge-able about infants and toddlers, without ever having read a book on the subject. There are others who are easy-going people who don't get overly tense about anything life hands them, including their children. And there are still others who were so young when they had their children that the babies were more like entertainments or diversions for them, and little guilt or anxiety attended their young motherhood. For all such women, mothering is much easier than it is for the great mass of American women, many of whom have never seen or held a newborn child until their own baby is placed in their arms.

This brings us to the third element in the excessive guilt that saddles so many middle-aged American mothers of young adults. The new knowledge about child development inter-sected with another characteristic American approach to life: the native Yankee belief that anything that isn't working right—including kids—can be fixed if you have the right tools.

And the Freud/Bowlby findings seemed to give new mothers in mid-century a set of specific instruction manuals that providentially arrived right in the same historical packing case as the new baby.

The fresh knowledge about sibling rivalry, neuroses, frustration, aggression—all the popularized buzz words of the evolving science—became the tools with which the newly enlightened corps of mothers could "fix" everything wrong.

Though Freud himself is on record as having said that the goal of psychoanalysis was to enable people to live with more or less normal unhappiness, his disciples held out hope to the new generation of mothers that they could raise children who would function far above that minimal standard: children who would attain the magic status of being "well adjusted," by all odds the most frequently used adjective during park-bench maternal gatherings throughout several decades.

The results of such expectations were overwhelming and col-ored mother-child relations for entire generations at a clip. Now women nervously but bravely believed they had the keys to wholesome, lifelong emotional health for their children, if only . . . if only . . . if only they used these new tools properly. Ah, there was the rub!

Responsibility and anxiety unknown to even the harried Abi-gail Alcott of a century ago became the hourly lot of the women whose voices we hear in this book. They describe themselves as

"locked up" with their responsibilities in the father-empty suburbs or garnering ever more guilt and worry if they worked, for
whatever reasons and on whatever schedule.

Unfortunately, as many women in our sample group described their tussles with this weight of night-and-day caretaking, it became clear that they had lost a number of guilt-relieving
alternative mothering styles when the psychology fairy granted
them the keys to unlock lifelong mental health for their children.

They lost, for example, the "benign neglect" more typical of
the way their great-grandmothers handled several children.
Those worthies lived at a time when few of one's children survived to adulthood or even to full-term birth, so a fatalistic
maternal laissez-faire made life more endurable in the face of
repeated grief and loss.

Gone also were the preoccupations of their own mothers who
were the recipients of new knowledge, too—about the germ
theory. Their own mothers had been given another kind of
magic key: Advances in public health, hygiene, and sanitation
allowed their mothers to become the first generation to conquer
the child-killing and crippling diseases. By the 1930s, most
women not mired in hopeless poverty could plan to raise their
children to adulthood in reasonably good health—twin goals
undreamed of before, and now completely taken for granted.
The victory of getting children through measles and scarlet
fever was no longer a triumph; it was routine and assuaged no
guilt at all.

Moreover, these new discoveries about how human beings
develop psychologically, with their sobering implications for
child-rearing, came well before the current wave of feminist
"networking" and support groups were on the horizon.

The mothers I talked to felt themselves pretty much alone
with their new responsibilities. Their own mothers were unaware of a new mind-set that dealt with things like sibling rivalry
and Oedipal stages of development. Their husbands were absent at work, and the women's movement as a place to turn for
help and encouragement did not yet exist, although of course,
as has been true from time immemorial, women did find one
another in a less formal way and found modest comfort and
sharing in classes, nursery-school parent councils, and play
groups.

* * *

In addition to all this, another element had been piled atop the new psychology and the Yankee tinkerer approach, an element that I suspect will continue to hound not only the mid-life mothers who reported it, but their daughters as well. And that is the American insistence on performance in every arena of life, referred to earlier in this chapter. This shows itself as an intense drive to prove that you have the maternal "right stuff" in order to win the approval of mother-peers.

Were your kids the ones who got thrown out of nursery school because of overaggressive behavior? Were they the last ones in the playground to give up the thumb and the blanket? Were your teenagers just average students who didn't bring home particularly good grades, didn't play the French horn, and did not win athletic letters? In other words, was it all too clear to her peers that Mom had flunked good-adjustment training?

And, say the women I interviewed, it only gets worse as the children get older.

More than one woman, in interviews and letters, claimed that while everyone else's children are getting good jobs, with security and a future, or getting into Ivy League schools, *their* kids are going to schools nobody ever heard of or living with partners whom bemused fathers label instantly "losers."

If Mom works, she reports, her failure to have the right stuff is blamed on that; if she doesn't work, it's because the exhausting labors of the homemaker-manager are not seen as work, and she has failed to provide a role model for either working daughters or sons who will marry working women. Mother-blaming has taken ingenious turns in the day of the Yuppie and the female stockbroker, but it remains a vigorous industry still, women report.

Meanwhile, work-driven Dad, himself raised well before men ever dreamed of sharing child care to any serious degree, most often left the demonstration of the right stuff to his wife. She had the time to talk with teachers and other mothers and to read the books and magazines necessary to find out how this tricky business of raising well-adjusted children was to be done. Suitably impressed and decently concerned, he could only hope she knew what she was doing and that the family would eventually win all the accolades—probably when the kids got into Harvard or won scholarships for grades *and* popularity.

So with the performance ethic in full bloom, with the urge to fix things that don't work, and with the very real and serious fact that children do need steady, caring love and attention from adults, the mid-life woman of today received it all like lashes across her back. These women spent more than twenty years of their lives—whether they stayed home or went out to work or did both—ceaselessly chasing the elusive goal of Perfect Motherhood.

They took all these new orders and marched straight into the "feminine mystique"; once more in history, they had become the patsies who tried to do it all and do it alone—now sans the certain God of the nineteenth century, sans husband, and sometimes, they felt, sans sleep, sanity, or the blessed refreshment of common sense.

New Balm for the Wounds of Guilt

It is ironic, poignant, blackly funny, and hopeful—all at the same time—that at least some of the enormous load of guilt borne by the mothers of today's young adults now is becoming obsolete excess baggage.

New research only recently available to nonprofessional audiences has revealed comforting information about the surprising resiliency and plasticity of the human child and its ability to overcome considerable trauma as well as "ordinary" parental errors and failures.

If even a shred of the new information might help mature mothers handle their guilt better in working out relationships with their grown children, then we ought to take a brief look at what is developing now in this field.

Of all the inquiries now underway, perhaps the one that can speak most directly to the youthful middle-aged women in our sample is the work referred to earlier (see pages 27–28) by Dr. Jerome Kagan, professor of developmental psychology at Harvard.

Dr. Kagan begins by making clear that consistent, nurturing care for infants and young children is still a crucial tenet in his theories of healthy development. "I cannot escape these beliefs which are so thoroughly threaded through the culture in which I was raised and trained," he writes.

But then Kagan goes on, in 308 closely reasoned pages of text, to advance the hypthosis that "the human being is not a prisoner of his past," as one reviewer put it.[5] In the age-old struggle between "nature and nurture"—between the innate qualities of the child together with the maturation process, and the "catalytic" power of social experience—Dr. Kagan appears to be looking anew at the "nature" part of the equation, especially as it works itself out in the process of growth and maturation. He suggests that the outcome of a particular kind of nurturing may simply reflect a biological or neurological "readiness" of the child to take certain developmental steps.

He gives new emphasis to the infant's portion of the infant-mother interaction and suggests that children vary enormously in their "irritability" thresholds, even at birth, and this may be so regardless of specific care-giving techniques.

In *The Nature of the Child,* mothers past, present, and future can study work by other researchers, reported on by Dr. Kagan, including that of one team who studied children who had undergone various types of stress at birth and later during their adolescence. "As we watched these children grow from babyhood to adulthood, we could not help but respect the self-righting tendencies within them that produced normal development under all but the most adverse circumstances," wrote the researchers.[6]

And Dr. Kagan's questioning approach to the "mother is responsible for everything always and under all circumstances" theories that the mothers in our sample were raised to believe is backed up by a number of other contemporary students of human development.

As reported in *The New York Times,* a well-known husband and wife team of child psychiatrists, Dr. Alexander Thomas and Dr. Stella Chess, wrote recently in the *American Journal of Psychiatry:* "The emotionally traumatized child is not doomed, the parents' early mistakes are not irrevocable."[7] In a report of a study following 133 people from infancy to early adulthood, they offer data showing that most of the troubled children grew into stability as they reached adulthood, according to *Times* reporter Daniel Goleman.

Goleman quotes another psychiatrist as saying that "many, many people live through the worst things in life and come out all right,"[8] though, says the *Times* writer, " 'all right' is a relative term. No one leaves the emotional baggage of childhood behind entirely." Both Goleman and other reporters and researchers have noted current work that tends to suggest that there may even be specific periods (notably between the ages of 2 and 3) when the child is more vulnerable than at others.[9]

In a 1983 book from Britain, a team of English psychiatrists and a social worker have done a new study of maternal bonding that suggests that the mother's tie to her child and the child's to her grows gradually over a period of time and that it is seldom that the initial "failures to bond" that so terrify new mothers are really so dreadful in their consequences.[10]

"What emerges," write the English mental-health team of psychiatrists Wladyslaw Sluckin and Martin Herbert with social worker Alice Sluckin, "from cross-cultural studies of varied perinatal practices is that human beings are remarkably adaptable. . . . It is this . . . which has enabled the human species to survive and thrive in all sorts of situations. . . . There is no need for mothers to feel anxious lest this or that practice will have dire psychological effects for years to come. Contrary to a variety of strongly held beliefs, there is no evidence that events around and soon after the time of birth can readily or seriously distort either the development of the infant's personality or interfere with the growth of maternal love and attachment."[11]

The new research agenda seems to indicate that in the future, more attention will be paid to the mutuality, the back-and-forthness, between baby and caregiver, rather than the one-sided emphasis on the mother. In addition, new work is underway on father-bonding and multiple care-givers, and on the process by which parent-child relationships develop. Additional emphasis on factors outside the home such as the society in which the family is embedded, for better or worse, are being looked at by all manner of child-development experts.

What are the implications for women in mid-life of these new trends in thinking about the mother-child bond?

A number of women in an informal discussion group organized to review the new material remained highly skeptical.

They continue to believe firmly in the primacy of the mother's behavior, and the quality and style of nurturance, as the chief determinant of the future adult, even while allotting a portion of both praise and blame to fathers, and to other outside factors.

Two or three women embraced the idea that children might be able to survive a fair number of maternal errors and failures without too much devastation. To this very small group (out of fifteen women) the new ideas came, indeed, as soothing balm for the eternal wounds of guilt.

But one woman, while intrigued by the revisions in approach (so different from how she was programmed to look at maternal influences), shook her head sadly and seemed to be speaking for the group when she said: "I hope all this new research will help some on the "mother-blaming" bit, but I don't know . . . it may have come too late for me. Maybe for my daughter . . ."

Indeed, mid-life women as I encountered them did frequently seem like victims of what Dr. Chess calls "mal de mère"—the tendency to blame all childhood psychopathology on mothers who are, at best, incompetent, and at worst, cruel and neglectful. It seems doubtful to me that the great majority of women taught to be mothers over the past three decades will be able to root this blaming syndrome out of their lives, but on the other hand, these women have made so many incredibly resilient changes in themselves and their relationships that it can't be ruled out.

No Plea Bargaining: Innocent or Guilty?

Now these mature mothers are looking at the results of their handiwork—the adult children, the product of all this concern. What are they feeling and thinking?

Fear . . . and happiness

Anxiety . . . and great rewards

Guilt . . . and intense joy

How they feel at any given moment, they said, depends to an amazing degree on what is happening in the lives of their adult children.

"No mother is happier than her least happy child," explained one experienced mother during a person-to-person interview.

"I can't put my head down peacefully on the pillow at night if something is not quite right with one of them—I feel a sort of unease," wrote another, the mother of four adult children.

Both of these women are busy working wives and mothers, with better-than-average jobs and newly satisfying marriages that got a breath of fresh air when the children left (even if one or two returned once in a while). They hardly fit the stereotype of the weeping clinger who stays all day by the telephone in the hope that one of her children will call.

Yet they find themselves always with a tracking system at the ready. Now the woman who steered her little boy through "separation trauma" at nursery school is heavy-hearted because that same son has just separated from the third live-in companion he's been with in the past two years.

Now the mother who fought the usual teenage battles over lipstick and allowances with her eldest daughter finds herself digging deep into her savings to help the disappointed young adult face the fact that she's not going to wow Broadway and that she'd better go back to school and get some other training.

This is now verdict time for the mothers of grown children, and many women have a built-in, efficient radar that scans the horizon tirelessly for the answer to only one question: Is my kid going to make it? (whatever "making it" may mean to the individual mother). Is my son or daughter on track or off course? For in the answer, she feels, lies the mother's own guilt or innocence by her own lights and her own conditioning.

The verdict comes in against a clear backdrop of wishes and hopes and aspirations for each woman, regardless of her social class, her income, her ethnicity or religion or education. Though the specific goals may be different for each of these backgrounds, women I interviewed by the dozens had certain universal hopes they cherished for their children.

Regardless of how the mother has lived her own life, she confided extremely conventional notions of how her adult children's lives ought to unfold if she was to feel successful in her performance as a mother.

Those desires are actually not very complicated, but they are sought with an eagerness that is touching in its intensity and longing. They want some kind of schooling or training if possible for their children, but if it cannot be had, they certainly dream of a decent job, a stable marriage, a livable home, and, true to their era, "at least" one or two children.

And with a rueful mixture of exasperation and love, the adult kids know it. In Wendy Wasserstein's 1984 hit play, *Isn't It Romantic,* the young daughter answers her mother's call with "Hello, Mother, this morning I got married, lost twenty pounds, and became a lawyer." The waves of laughter that wash over the audience are tinged with the actual pain that mothers feel daily (fathers feel it, too, but more intermittently) if their children seem to be wandering too far away—too off course—from what all those years of work were all about; the guilt can be reactivated in a millisecond.

In my group of respondents, virtually no women were willing to risk estrangement from their children over the young life-styles (although they ranked first on the list of things mothers found it hard to talk to their kids about), but that doesn't mean these wishes and hopes for what constitutes being "on course" aren't the most secret, persistent dreams that mothers cherish.

However each woman may define success for her children, she experiences wild ups and downs of satisfaction and dismay as the children seem to either come near to fulfillment of her hopes or veer away from them.

One mother wrote on her questionnaire, in reply to the simple question (meant to elicit a geographical answer) "Where does your son or daughter live?", the answer: "In his own lovely, big home with a beautiful wife and two wonderful children." Her pride, her *relief* were palpable on the page. She had not failed! The verdict, at least for the moment, was: Innocent of producing a disappointing child!

Another woman wrote: "Even though we've never had a lot of money, we have managed to put five children through college. Some of them even went on to graduate school on their own. Their five graduation days were the proudest of my life." On talking in person with this mother, I found something in her story beyond normal parental pride. There clung to her and to others who described similar feelings an aura of inexpressible relief. All the bone-crushing, gut-wrenching effort paid off! The pure joy is real, but it seems to come *after* the resounding satisfaction of having been tried and not found wanting. If the kids are on course—right where they ought to be in life—that proves that Mother passed the test, that she demonstrably has the right stuff.

Conversely, the anguish and even the shame is heart-tearing when an adult child seems to the mother to be off track. The pain is a daily ache of which she is never entirely free when the young person drops out of school or seems to be dropping out of life, when he or she chooses someone the mother thinks is an inappropriate partner, or drifts, rudderless, from one unsatisfying life situation to another, or is underemployed at far below what her education or skills would seem to suggest.

Several women in my sample confessed that they had cut social ties with friends whose children were getting along in life so well that the gap between those young adults and their own children was just too painful to bear; the amount of guilt this activated for the mother was unendurable.

"You try not to make comparisons. You know you should just accept your kids as they are, even if their life-style is driving you crazy, but sometimes it's just too much," said Kathleen R., with her eyes full of tears. Two of Kathleen's four children are on track with work and personal relationships, one is a wavering question mark, but the fourth child, a daughter, with a high I.Q. and some musical ability, dropped out of school a year ago and has been living at home, doing house-sitting and child care in the affluent suburb where she grew up. Most of her high-school friends have gone on to school or work; she is not dating or socializing, and there is no return to school on the agenda. Both her parents are distressed, but Kathleen's sorrow has deep striations of guilt and personal responsibility, which the father does not feel.

A most eloquent statement of this anguish was given by Tina W., a thoughtful middle-aged mother of two adult children whose lives so far have caused her both fleeting happiness and the deepest of griefs.

Tina's older child, a daughter, suffered through a difficult separation and divorce that seemed to Tina to last for centuries before being resolved. But at the same time, the now-shattered marriage provided Tina with two extraordinarily beautiful little grandsons whose existence gives a glow to Tina's days, even though they do not live nearby and she does not see them as often as she would like.

Her second child, a son, has become a promising young architect and seems to be moving forward professionally, which certainly pleases his parents immensely. But when it comes to home and family, he lets his parents know plainly that he considers marriage, or even long-enduring unmarried relationships, to be traps that he refuses to enter. Tina fears he is on his way to becoming a reclusive workaholic.

Following a lengthy interview, Tina sent me the following letter: "My Christmas mail this year certainly would add fuel to the fire of our discussions about mothers and their adult children. Here is a sampling: one lovely daughter of friends in a psychiatric hospital; another reports a son in jail without bail; another friend's daughter has such severe depression that the parents cannot even write to old, close friends about it; yet another son trying to stay in AA but dropping out, staying in, dropping out; tell me, how can we take it?"

Her letter continues: "These are you-and-me kind of parents that got hit with this in the midst of our 'free' years—who is ever free? Yet," Tina writes, "there was a lot of good news in the holiday letters, too. I heard about one married daughter happily pregnant after six years of marriage, with the prospective grandparents (our friends) just wild with happiness; another son was elected to Congress; another daughter, just a short time out of college, has already opened her own accounting office. The son of another family, barely 25, writes successful movie scripts. Tell me, are the odds 50-50? Who cares about statistics? If you are in the bottom layer, is there enough time and luck left in your life to repair the damage? What does it take to relieve the despair?"

Tina's cry from an anxious heart has echoes of both the Victorian Abigail and the modern Lulu, as well as echoes from the subconscious unease of every contemporary woman whose kids ever flunked out of school, lost the first job after they left home, or asked for money to start an ice-cream business at the North Pole.

Guilt, we can see, is certainly the beginning of these women's stories, but it is by no means the end. At the moment, it is a backdrop, part of the space in which the children's orbits are tracked. Guilt, I learned in the interviews that follow, may change its shape considerably in the future as the relationship itself grows and changes. But whether women can shake off the "mother-blaming" syndrome or whether they leave that knife between the shoulder blades, they know one thing: As long as they live, they have to get on with the tasks of later-life mothering.

How women remain in touch—or can't; how they show love and continuing concern—or don't; how they referee their kids' continuing sibling battles—or disguise them; how they handle the other growing-up issues of money, family loyalty, new friendships with their kids, and the inevitable crises of life—these are the subjects we will explore with mid-life mothers in the following chapters.

3

The Wired Nest: The Telephone as Electronic Bond

Mass communications make a new kind of [family] unit feasible, one composed of dispersed membership based on perceived emotional proximity and interaction rather than face-to-face contact; this is now possible through . . . telephone calls, letters. . . .

Changing Images of the Family, edited by Tufte and Meyerhoff

"Talking to her on the phone is like taking her temperature. I just need to know how it is with her . . . and if she sounds down, I can't get off until I've worked to get her up."

BERNICE L., 49, describing a phone conversation with her
daughter

"E.T. called home, but his mother was out."

Child after seeing the movie *E.T.*

*M*iddle-aged American women are often shown in the media as scared of machines, baffled by cars, fearful of electricity, and paralyzed by a leaky faucet.

This nonsense is belied by many realities (including the millions of households daily buzzing with half a dozen gadgets and appliances), but chief among them is that these alleged technological illiterates demonstrably and briskly use every sophisticated communications device available to stay in touch with their grown children who've left home.

They use video and audio tapes and all the equipment needed to activate them just to catch a glimpse of faraway sons and daughters. They eagerly push for huge expenditures for still and moving pictures—often taken with many fancy and complicated lenses—that will stamp the images of family members on retinas forever. And they're learning to hook up computer networks to exchange messages on an electronic family bulletin board.

But the preeminent tool for mothering grown-up children—scattered to school, work, marriage, new lives of their own—is the telephone.

This extension of the family's brain, heart, and nervous system is so taken for granted, so ubiquitous in American life (it's been with us for more than a century), that we no longer are aware that the modern family could not exist in its present form without the telephone.

It has replaced nearly all the earlier ways families got together —the barn-raising, the sewing bee, the potluck supper—and has even replaced later contact channels: the telegram, the long auto drive, the rare emergency plane trip.

If love and fights, jokes and tears, caring and worrying continue at all in mobile American families—and mothers emphasize that they surely do continue—it is because of the insistent ring of the telephone and the beep of the answering machine.

This technology has become the glue that, day to day, keeps members together and underlines and illumines the uniqueness of each family.

The shaping influence of this technology has not escaped notice, of course. There are at least three separate groups of specialists in our society who monitor how this glue is manufactured and how it works within the traditional family which once proceeded mostly by face-to-face contact.

One group is made up of the social commentators termed futurists. John Naisbitt, author of the popular *Megatrends,* is an example of the folks who've been looking for some time at how communications technologies will change all human institutions, including the family.

The profit-makers, such as AT&T's advertising department, have certainly taken note. Their famous ad campaign to "reach out and touch someone" is, however, but a pale version of the emotional freight actually carried on those buzzing, expensive wires. AT&T's bland ads suggest that most phone calls will be affectionate and promote understanding—a notion that real mothers of real adult children greet with wry amusement at best.

The third group is comprised of professional family-watchers —sociologists, communications experts, family scholars and therapists, and cultural historians—who have begun to analyze and describe the new intrafamily communications patterns evolving in the wired nest. However, these descriptions are geared primarily for experts in a variety of disciplines.

But there is another group that has had perhaps the greatest amount of direct experience with the telephone as an extension of deeply personal (not business) relationships.

It is quite possible, I believe, that the largest amount of firsthand data on how today's communications systems affect the family is now being compiled not by experts but by ordinary women. These are the mothers of adult children who have established separate residences, whether those living spaces are as transient as a college dorm or as permanent as the first apartment or home, whether near or far, whether inhabited alone, in a group, or with a partner.

It is now Mom who is expected to have the most up-to-the-minute area codes and phone numbers of each family member ready to provide instantly to the others, even if one son or daughter just reported to the new job or moved into the new apartment five minutes ago.

It is most often Mom who is called first with problematic news, or requests for money, to be relayed later to Dad, and it is usually Mom who senses when it is time to pick up the telephone and speak to one or another of the absent kids whose silence requires a divining rod *now*.

It isn't that fathers don't talk on the telephone to their grown children—of course they do. But in frequency of calls, length of conversation, ability to "listen with the third ear," and responsiveness to modern telephonic mores, fathers are less active.

"The communications linkage . . . is generally stronger along the female line" writes Rutgers University psychology professor

Lillian E. Troll. "Many men count on their wives to keep them in touch with their children and their parents and the loss of a wife can almost sever family communications for older men."[1]

It is the mother, in short, who functions as mission control for the entire family in the electronic era.

Conventional wisdom and social stereotypes lag well behind these new family realities. General psychobabble holds that the family is disintegrating, the rise of the single-person household spells terrifying human isolation, and technology is making us love our machines more than we love our kin. But the communiqués I have gathered from the "mother front" in the supposed battle between cold machines and warm people report strikingly different information.

The tales told by mothers of gone-from-home young adults reveal that the grown kids hang on the phone endlessly and are the exact opposite of isolated—they're so in touch, it's exciting, interesting, and exhausting.

An elaborate study of teenagers conducted by social scientists at the University of Chicago showed that girls and boys from the ages of 13 to 18 spend one-third of their waking hours conversing with others. Researchers said this was "by far the single most prevalent activity in their lives"—and that 13 percent of that conversation was via telephone. The survey, using electronic pagers to beep the subjects at different times in their day, began in 1977, and its results were released in 1984.

Mothers of "older" young adults—those between 20 and 35 —say their sons and daughters carry those adolescent talking-and-telephoning patterns over into their new life stage even more strongly in an effort to defeat the distances that separate from them those who are important to them.

The young adults may be wed to their Walkman earphones and personal computers, but they have by no means lost all interest in their friends, parents, lovers, ex-spouses, siblings, grandparents, and fellow-workers, and the folks at mission control have the phone bills to prove it.

Far from fragmenting the family, say mothers, the round-robin conference call, extension phones, tape message machines, call-forwarding features, and other refinements make it possible to organize get-togethers, holiday visits, parties, and vacation trips with the minimum of trouble and delay, as well as

joint outings to movies and sports events and dining out together.

It is the mothers of adult children who give the lie to AT&T's
rosy, sentimental electronic fables and who grimly describe the
knock-down, drag-out fights and bitter, hurtful quarrels that
also can take place on the telephone. These often end with one
party hanging up in a rage, frequently to apologize or receive
apologies in yet another phone call.

Or a telephone exchange can leave both mother and adult son
or daughter in a heart-aching misunderstanding that can be
repaired only by many additional phone calls or a face-to-face
visit or searching letter. Sometimes the misunderstanding cannot be repaired at all, and simmers for a long time, telephone
or no, just as it used to in preelectronic times—but there are
some modern differences.

"It isn't all sweetness and light when I talk to my daughter,"
says Toni L., the 50-year-old mother of a son and daughter who
both live beyond driving distance. "She's quite often sulky and
petulant on the phone—she's mixed up, I think, between wanting help and attention from home and yet wanting to be independent. I understand all that and I try to be patient, but it's just
so much easier, sometimes, to talk to my son. He's just a different personality and is more open and clearer about when he
does and when he does *not* want emotional support.

"But," continues Toni, "talking with my daughter once a
week or two or three times a month is very, very important to
me all the same—*at least we're in some kind of touch.*"

There seems little doubt that this latter point is the over-
whelmingly important consequence of the ease of telephonic
communications as far as mothers of adult progeny are concerned.

The United States Census Bureau recently reported that more
than half of all Americans over the age of five moved their
residences between 1975 and 1980.

This dramatic proof of the continuing mobility of Americans,
together with the demonstrated importance of keeping links
strong among family members, raises a number of practical and
philosophical questions about how and whether the family can,
in fact, keep itself in working order in the face of so much change
and shift, such barriers of time and distance.

Accordingly, I asked 175 women to analyze the form and frequency of their contact with their collective group of 560 roving adult children, 14 of whom were in foreign countries at the time of the interviews, and the remainder scattered in every region of the United States, in small towns and cities, in suburbs, in exurbs, and on farms.

"Your children are now launched on separate lives, most of them living away from home more or less permanently. How much do you actually see them, talk to them, write to them? How often and in what way do you have contact with them?" were typical of the questions that I asked them to consider in detail.

The results were astonishing.

They showed a persistence in staying in touch, and an amount of time, money, energy, and feeling spent in contacting one another by a variety of methods that was mind-boggling for a human unit widely perceived to be on the edge of extinction.

Fathers, of course, were included in many of the contacts, but mothers did not keep an accurate count of when the fathers were present and when not. But mothers had no difficulty in recalling fairly accurately the average number of times in a day, week, or month they were in touch with their adult children.

Here is what they reported:

• Nearly a quarter of the young people—approximately 23 percent—were in contact with their mothers *daily*, either by telephone, personal visit, letter, or other channels.

• The average amount of contact for the majority of adult children was once a week. More than 50 percent of the young people either talked on the phone, dropped in for a visit, had a formal outing with their parents to a sports event, dinner, or the movies, or sent some kind of written communication, however brief. A minority within this group (fifteen young adults) averaged two, three, or four contacts a week. (One mother wrote, in response to this question, with rueful humor: "I can absolutely certify there is no truth to the dastardly rumor that 100 percent of all contacts with the adult kids involved a request for money. Sometimes they want to borrow the car or my clothes, instead.")

• More than three-quarters—77.5 percent—of the 560 young adults were in touch with their mothers *more* than once a month.

(This figure reinforces a similar finding made by a *New York* magazine survey in 1979, in which 75 percent of 500 young adults in the Boston/New York area were reported to be in touch with their parents more than once a month.[2])

• The mothers reported that the channel of contact was the telephone in nearly 80 percent of their "touching" their distant kids.

This telephonic, but somehow very human, contact has given rise to whole new ways of experiencing the realities of family life.

The New Household Necessity

For starters, the long-distance phone call that was once an unimaginable luxury has now become a household necessity. Mothers (much more so than fathers) have rationalized the absolute requirement of costly phone bills to keep the family members in touch.

Where once a car was a great sign of family status, where once the new TV set marked folks as an avant-garde family on the block, and just as washing machines and electric coffee pots became necessities or very-desired amenities, so now has the bulky monthly phone bill detailing calls to virtually every state in the Union and overseas become routine in millions of households.

Otherwise unremarkable houses on plain residential streets now can show the most exotic toll listings if a son or daughter is in the service or studying or living abroad. Mrs. Smith may look just like another suburban housewife as she shops at the supermarket, but at home on her desk is a phone bill for two calls last month to Morocco, North Africa; her daughter is in the United States Foreign Service. Mrs. Brown lives in Portland, Maine, but the phone company knows that Santa Cruz, California, takes at least thirty dollars a month from her family budget; her only son out of a family of five children is in college there.

Mrs. Smith's and Mrs. Brown's grandmothers—who indeed placed long-distance calls to announce deaths and births—

would have fainted at twenty-dollar tolls for one call, placed any time it suits either party's convenience, rather than frugally waiting for low-cost calling hours to be in effect.

Surprisingly enough, these costs appear to have been interiorized by less affluent as well as middle-class mothers, just as a TV set gradually became a necessity in 98 percent of American households regardless of income.

In fact, one of the most enduring visual images of the mature modern family is a picture of Mom on the telephone with one or another of the adult children for many long minutes (even hours), while Dad dances agitatedly in the background, pointing to his watch, miming a cash register, or just shrugging his shoulders in annoyance.

One mother of five daughters, three of them married, all living at some distance from home, reported sheepishly that her husband threw in the towel, and for birthdays, anniversaries, and Christmas, started giving her stock in various telecommunications companies after all efforts to cut down long-distance bills failed.

Another woman snapped at her husband when he chided her about the cost of two-hour conversations with a son, daughter-in-law, and grandchild three states away, "Listen, I don't buy myself many new clothes. This is my little treat—let me have it in peace."

Even families of very modest means—the ones that a generation ago utilized long-distance calls only for extreme crises—now have more or less accepted the expense as a necessary price of keeping the family connected.

A mother whose disabled husband's income was severely restricted and who herself worked at a low-paying job as a sales clerk in a small neighborhood clothing shop reported that when the younger of two sons was in the service, he was stationed in Australia. But, she said, he called home regularly once a month for a virtually unlimited talk with his parents, siblings, and other relatives in Ohio. He would then carefully deduct—"to the penny," proudly reported his mother—the cost of his three-dollar-a-minute visit from his army paycheck and send it home to his parents.

Endless collect calls, too, are almost always taken by the parents if that is the only means of contact available. Several mothers pointed out that they regarded the first long-distance phone call the son or daughter did *not* place collect as a milestone of maturity, a marker on the rites of passage toward adulthood.

"The first time Jim called us long distance in a normal, direct way without our hearing the operator ask us to accept a collect call, I knew we'd passed through an era," said Samantha R. "More than his graduating from college, more than his first job, more even than when his live-in girlfriend became his wife, this business of finally not expecting Mom and Dad to bear all the cost of staying in touch told me he'd arrived—he was a grown-up!"

It is this acceptance of the cost as a standard and necessary way for parents and adult children to stay in some kind of emotional touch that explains the appreciative murmurs and knowing chuckles audible from coast to coast when the recent hit movie *Terms of Endearment* was shown.

In a key scene, mother Shirley MacLaine embraces daughter Debra Winger as the younger woman, with husband and child-laden car, is about to depart for the husband's new job far away. "You know," says the mother, hugging her daughter tight, "our phone bills are going to be enormous!"

An aspect of the film that marked it indelibly as belonging to no other age of family relations but our own was that nearly half of all the mother-daughter contact (the heart of the movie) was shown as taking place over a span of years and distances mostly by telephone. These included calls placed or received at the most intimate of moments—when each woman was in bed with husband or lover! Audiences thoroughly accepted the telephone as routine handling of family operations.

When Was the Last Time You Called Your Child?

A second new development in family relations bears on the emotional climate between mothers and adult children in the 1980s, a climate that will very likely become even more flexible in the Nineties.

Based on old stereotypes, all this expensive and pervasive staying-in-touch activity could be interpreted as supporting the all-too-familiar image of the horror mother—the one who is greedy, grasping, unbelievably needy, and yet impossible to satisfy. Perhaps it means that the nightmare lady is still demanding far more time, attention, and love than adult children, busy with their own lives, could ever wish to grant.

But according to the respondent mothers, that is not the scene at all, for they report that they share equally with their children the task of initiating contact and making sure they're in touch.

Not only did a majority of the mothers say that the responsibility is shared about equally in most cases, but a substantial minority of adult children—26.4 of the total group—took "most" or "all" the responsibility for the work of initiating contact through phone, letter, or visit, and this included both sons and daughters. Despite popular perceptions, mothers reported children of both sexes participated in contact-seeking.

Typical of the evolving mother of the Eighties who tends to leave behind the whining supplicant of comedy routines is Harriet B., 52, who lives in a modest suburb of Trenton, New Jersey.

Harriet, assistant manager in a supermarket, has four adult children, none of them living nearby. Her son is in a foreign country in the service, and the three daughters are scattered in other parts of the United States, two of those three being married and having moved in response to job opportunities for both themselves and their husbands.

"It's kind of a sixth-sense thing," explains Harriet. "We just seem to know when it's time, and one or another of us will just pick up the phone and get back in the swim. No, we don't take turns—we're nowhere near that formal. It's sort of casual. We just kind of know when we need to be in touch. The kids talk to each other a lot, too—even to Ross in Germany—but often we don't even ever know anything about it. My husband's a bus driver and he works different shifts, so he can work out the time difference to talk to Ross better than I can, but most of the time, the calls go up and down [in number] depending on what's happening in everybody's life at the moment . . . mostly they get through to me rather than my husband, most of the time, yes, I would say so. . . ."

More than half the 175 mothers reported this equality of

effort in initiating contact, while another 31 women (roughly 19 percent) conformed closer to the old-style mother when they said they did "more" but "not all" of the calling and visiting.

The most traditional of the reporting mothers, a very small statistical minority—six women, or about 3½ percent—said they did *all* the work of initiating contact.

Regardless of their individual patterns, most of the 175 women did not find it surprising that in only a few cases did the mother bear the entire burden of keeping contact going. To them it seemed quite natural to be sharing the "reaching out" task, since many of them, just like the adult children, are also leading extremely busy lives.

Many middle-aged women today are part of the now-famed sandwich generation, concerned about their own aging parents as well as their young adult children. They're working or keeping house or both, while continuing lifelong patterns of friendships and activities in church, club, or civic groups. They're pursuing hobbies, health projects, and a wide range of other interests. Many also have gone back to school to update earlier job training or for personal growth and enrichment.

"My kid always call with a crisis when I have a big paper due or am studying for an exam," grumbled one mother who is getting a degree in psychology, never having attended college before having her family.

The viperish mother of Philip Wylie's earlier excoriation is being replaced by an evolving, new-style mom who doesn't have to look so completely to her children for justification of her existence, but to whom it is still extremely vital that she be in relatively frequent touch with the kids (see Chapter 2).

Since family life, like marriage, is so overidealized in the United States and is expected to provide much more emotional fulfillment than any human institution possibly could, any forms of contact among family members that furnish connection without smothering may prove beneficial in the long run.

Mothers believe the telephone may be that flexible and adaptable medium that permits them to run a quick check on the tenor of their children's lives without unduly disrupting the young person's daily schedule—and perhaps turn down the thermostat a little on the sometimes overheated nuclear family.

Voices as Weathervanes

There is a third startling intrafamily pattern that is being born in the incubator of the new family: the use of the human voice as complete psychological barometer.

In other eras, mothers said "How wonderful to see you" when members of their brood were available face to face, and the deep feeling with which it was said often was a sad measure of how infrequent visits over long distances could be.

Today the normal greeting is "Good to hear your voice."

This salutation is not just politesse, it constitutes recognition that both mothers and adult children are becoming supersensitive to matters of pitch, timbre, and volume and to their emotional and relational meanings.

This sensitivity, though more sharply developed on the maternal side, is not unknown among young adults. It comes into being because in the eternal phone exchanges, there obviously can be no eye contact, no body language, very few nonverbal clues at all except sighs, laughter or tears, or silence—the latter often very eloquent.

The exquisite "tuning in" that mothers and adult kids do to each other's voices would do credit to a skilled musician or an expert accoustical engineer, as witness the testimony of the mother of an only son:

"I can tell in the first three words exactly how things are with him—whether he's tired or ill, irritated, bored, angry or reasonably okay, or maybe just has a case of the blahs," says Ruthanne L., whose son is an intern at a medical center three hours' drive from his parents' home.

Says another mother: "When one of my daughters calls up— she's the one who just got married recently—I can tell from the first word that she's got a lot she wants to talk about, a lot more, of course, since she's married and keeping house herself now, so immediately I sit down in a comfortable chair."

"My son just says 'hello' and I know pretty much what's what," reports the 46-year-old mother of one son and one daughter, "and when I hear the first word, sometimes I think to myself, 'Uh-oh—what now?' "

Polly P., 48, the mother of two adult daughters and a grown

son, was trained as an actress, and feels, perhaps more keenly than many, that her children's voices on the telephone are tangible, physical extensions of their bodies and therefore almost as embraceable.

She talks weekly for hours to two of her three, and somewhat less often with the "difficult" one (who seems to be found in many families), and she says these conversations are quite a satisfactory substitute for seeing and hugging the children in person, although almost all women say nothing can beat an in-person visit.

Polly explains that she was "telephone trained" early in her own life by parents who were affluent enough to travel frequently. They left the children with other care-givers, but called home very often from whatever parts of the world they were visiting. This, combined with Polly's own speech training, has made her a superstar in the voice-interpretation process.

"When my dad died a year ago, losing his voice was one of the worst parts of it for me," she says softly, "and though I still can reproduce his voice to some extent inside my own head, I know that may fade someday and I dread the time I can no longer hear him on my inner telephone—maybe that's why I keep wanting to hear my own children's voices so often. It's a form of connecting that is extremely important to me."

Some of the adult children, while used to being on the receiving end of this audio attention, also are developing their own new consciousness of how their mothers sound on the phone, too.

"I sometimes answer the phone in a low tone of voice if I'm tired or upset, and both my kids grab it right away," marvels Marian R. " 'What's wrong, Mom?' is the first thing out of their mouths if I haven't sounded exactly right to them. To be honest about it, the bother of always sounding 'up' for them is a pain sometimes; I don't say every phone call is a total joy, but most of the time I'm real glad to hear from them."

As in all communications, mothers and kids are often angry or irritated, or feel misunderstood, each by the other, and as part of their electronic operating procedures they have developed ways to use the telephone as an aid in whatever quarrels they're pursuing or whatever "editing" of information they wish to project.

Ellen A., 51, mother of two sons and two daughters, says about one of her sons, "I think Fred uses the telephone to manipulate me. If he's annoyed with me or afraid I'll disapprove of something, he just won't respond to my messages on his tape —or take forever to answer. He can sound colder and more rejecting on the phone than he usually does in person."

Other mothers said they think they handle anger and irritation better on the telephone than in person, and one woman confessed gratitude for the cover the phone provides when she is having marital problems with a new husband who is not the children's father. "There's no need for them to know about it and we can instead talk about other things much easier than if they were right on the scene," she says.

For Verna T., the 60-year-old mother of six widely scattered grown children, only two of whom live within relatively easy visiting distance, the phone call is quite simply an important symbol of family love.

"Verbalizing love as such isn't important to me," says Verna. "I look for it in symbols. The *fact* of writing letters, the *fact* of their phone calls, the 'What do you think, Mom?' The fact that they can turn to me—mostly on the phone—for advice, help. I take it for granted all through life that they love me. . . ."

Verna continues, "My daughter is a junior in college now and she calls a little less often than she used to. Once she called four times in ten days about changing her major. "But," sighs this veteran, "no matter what hour of the day or night they call, they expect you to focus totally on them. They'll call at midnight and expect you to get out of your good book and make the transition to where they are and understand what they're thinking."

The Split-Level Communications Bridge

What Verna, Ellen, and Polly, from their different angles of audio perception, are describing are elements of what the experts call the "content/relational" nature of human efforts to reach one another.

Looking at all communications as essentially a process of one person trying to influence another, we can see that two things happen in a talk between mothers and their adult kids:

Some neutral information is passed ("Can you give me your

recipe for spaghetti sauce?" "Yes, here it is") and some relationship between the people is implied, such as "Now be sure you
don't cook it too long," suggesting that the mother is skeptical
of the son or daughter's competence, or "I'm sure it will be
delicious," meaning a vote of confidence.

No matter how we may try, say communications experts, we
can't eliminate some aspect, however minor, of a relational nuance in many phone conversations, even if overtly the talk is
about the weather.

The group of respondent mothers who were willing to try to
examine their phone contact with their children from the con-
tent/relational viewpoint described this in their own words as
"split-level talking."

The split-level mode they say they have developed consists of
two channels—one atop the other—in which information is divided in this fashion:

On the top level is a big load (estimates vary from 50 to 80
percent of all messages) of what mothers say are everyday matters—routines of work, school, health, friends, requests for advice or assistance on mundane items, a joke or a comment or two
on the outside world, and a brief word, perhaps, about other
family members.

On the bottom level is carried the emotional load of feelings,
thoughts, dreams, hopes, troubles, worries—what the grown
kids call "heavy stuff," and what mothers call "telling me something important or I tell them something deep about how I feel."

Of course, report the mothers, these two levels of conversation in real life are not so strictly separate; the feelings,
thoughts, and worries spill over into the neutral, informational
top deck, where most ordinary conversations take place.

But most mothers believe that most of their telephone talk is
heavily replete with a "dailiness" that is not noteworthy. The
children, they say, would sound like this: "My roommate split,
the boss is nice, I got a bargain in a raincoat." From the mother,
it might sound like: "Do you need boots, I saw some on sale,
how's work, Dad's fine."

By far the largest majority of the respondent women (nearly
80 percent) were unaware that even in these kinds of practical
matters, they and their children are acting out a whole set of
feelings and attitudes about their relationship.

This unawareness of the relational content may be, experts conjecture, the root of the unhappiness or dissatisfaction that many mothers say they feel once in a while after they've hung up the phone.

"The more anxious I am about a particular child, the more likely it is that child will strive in a phone call to prove that everything is fine and the less likely it is that he will reveal himself," shrewdly observes Shana N., mother of three sons. Shana's boys experienced much of the turmoil of the Sixties and gave their parents many sleepless nights during that period, but they have righted themselves in the past five or eight years and are well afloat with school, work, and friends. Although Shana's concerns are founded on realistic history, she is trying to convey less anxiety and more confidence in the frequent phone conversations; she is one of the few who understand that all the exchanges bear *some* emotional weight.

Francine K., 55, is another of the few women in the mother's group who could describe explicitly some of her own communications errors with her children. She reports her biggest problem (experts say it is one of the most common) is sending mixed messages—saying something to her kids for the sake of outward appearances that the children probably know she doesn't mean.

"For instance," says Francine, "our two daughters are both in graduate school. They're achievers all right, maybe overachievers. Yet I find myself in an awkward spot because even now, with one working on her master's and one on her doctorate, they have anxiety attacks about their work. They carry on about grades and passing and failing to such an extent that I can hear myself saying, 'Oh, c'mon now, whether you get this damn degree or not just isn't the end of the world. You've got enough credentials for a good job, for sure."

"But," she says gloomily, "as my younger daughter pointed out, it's a little late in the game for that. All through their growing-up years, scholastic achievement was deeply important to us. Both my husband and I were cheated out of college by the Depression and then the war, and even though my husband went to night school later, he never was able to graduate because of family responsibilities. We probably sent all kinds of messages to the kids for years that school *is* terribly important, yet when I'm trying to help them over a tough spot now, I'm saying it isn't so important. I can see how that would be a double bind. But it's hard to unscramble those messages now, believe me. . . ."

It's clear that in spite of all the ease and quickness, spontaneity and immediacy that electronic contact can provide, there is no new nirvana of understanding on the maternal/adult child horizon, any more than peace has come to the world's nations because of instantaneous satellite television communications between them.

The way human beings bypass one another in their communications efforts ("I don't think we mean the same things by the words we use at all," wailed one unhappy mother after a nasty phone quarrel with her son over money) is a story as old as human interaction, even though laser-beamed voices have replaced the shouts and grunts of the prehistoric cave.

But out of the communications complexities that exist for members of the human family, mothers emerge with one clear message to themselves: *Family ties must be maintained,* whatever that requires.

The Basic Bond

Almost 100 percent of the mothers interviewed said that no matter how unhappy they might be with one or another aspect of their relationship (and their communications) with their adult children, they consciously and steadfastly followed one golden rule:

Ties must not be severed.

This is the unwritten, unspoken, but crucial commandment that underlies *all* of most women's ordinary contact with their grown children, whether it be by telephone, tape, letter, or in face-to-face visits and family gatherings.

This maternal law totally controls the subjects chosen for discussion, the emotional tone given to each topic, and the length of time devoted to each. This imperative also lies behind each woman's determination to use whatever technology comes to hand—no matter how hard to master—to overcome gulfs of time, distance, and misunderstandings.

The collective concern that mothers of grown children feel on the issue of possible estrangement (since ties are now much more freely chosen than when children were small and dependent) is reflected in these statistics:

I had contact—either written, telephoned, or face to face—with nearly 500 mothers of more than 1,200 young adults over a three-year period. They covered most of the regions of the United States, reflected all income groups, and comprised a diverse but not scientifically representative sample of different ethnic, racial, religious, and cultural backgrounds.

In this whole group, only one woman was truly estranged from her child in the deepest meaning of the word. (It must be borne in mind that this is a self-selected sample of women whose relationship with their grown children was functional, if troubled in some cases. Women who were not functioning in the usual maternal sense with their children—for whatever reasons —opted out of participation in the survey.) This mother had not been in touch with her daughter for a number of years, did not know her whereabouts, and was resigned to a permanent loss of a living child. The mother hinted that the rupture had been at the daughter's instigation and that she had gone along with the girl's wishes for a total separation.

This was so rare in the group willing to discuss their relationships that the only other case resembling it was reported by the divorced husband of a woman whose four children lost contact with her when she entered a religious cult based in the Far East.

These two instances must be seen in sharp contrast to reports from a substantial minority of mothers who reported there had been *periods* of estrangement from one child or another or times when contact was so minimal it could be considered an estrangement, but the cord was almost never completely severed, and in all the cases that women were willing to discuss, the relationship was resumed (occasionally on a better basis) later. In most instances, these temporary estrangements lasted under a year, but a few went on as long as four or five years, before ties were repaired.

Divorce, death, loss, life changes of the most intense and soul-shaking sort, do little to change most women's determination to remain in contact with their children.

It is this fierce belief in continuing ties among family members that exerts the strongest influence on choosing *what* is talked about in these millions of phone calls and in other forms of communication.

Sociologist Jesse Bernard, author of *The Future of Motherhood,* discussing technology and motherhood, notes the two-edged quality of communications, which can disrupt or mend, irritate problems or solve them.

For example, Dr. Bernard points out that any two-way communications device that can let mothers and adult children interact with each other holds the potential for dismay on both ends, and may not be greeted with universal acclaim. The adult child may think, "Will I never be free of her interference?" and the mother may think, "Will I never be free of their demands?" during the time they are actually talking about the family dog. But Dr. Bernard and others have also noted the other side of the coin: the potential for integrating and reinforcing family ties.

"The strong pull of family feeling," writes Professor Lillian E. Troll of Rutgers University, "induces careful avoidance of difficult issues that might cause conflict. *Conflict is not absent* [italics added] but is restricted to issues that will not sever relations.

"Most parents," she continues, "who disapprove of important aspects of their children's behavior carp instead about the way they dress or clean their house; they do not emphasize errors in marriage or career. Most adult children who are annoyed by the values or life-style of their parents criticize them for spoiling the grandchildren, or fussing about cleanliness, not about things they hold sacred. Each generation may complain to friends . . . about their more central angers concerning each other, but ties must not be broken."[3]

It is the force of this truth, plus another cultural convention, that makes mothers in the respondent group say repeatedly that "mothers should keep their mouths shut" when dealing with controversy with their adult kids.

The cultural habit that mothers have developed—whether for good or ill isn't quite clear to family therapists—is obeisance to the forceful injunctions against "meddling," "interfering," or "invading the privacy" of the young adult.

Thus many modern mothers often withdraw and narrow down the channels of communication—along with the possibility of helping or advising—out of an intense wish not to be seen as meddling or interfering.

But when the wish *not* to meddle collides head on with a wrong turn in the child's life or with the child's need for help (whether clearly stated or not), the mother's feelings and her dilemma are painful to behold.

Robin B., the attractive, youthful 48-year-old mother of two married daughters, describes such a scene:

"I know that when my younger daughter comes over to see me [the daughter lives an hour's drive away], she always brings some bit of crewelwork or knitting or other chore she wants me to do. I'm aware that she's 'using' me in some sense, as well as wanting to have a visit. But her shopping chores she does near my house and the sewing and cooking I do for her are, to her, the major thing, I think. On one hand, I'm glad to do these things—I think I should do them—but on the other hand, well, yes, I'm a little annoyed, I guess, a little resentful. I guess I don't want to ask myself which is most important, seeing me and getting a chance to talk, or having me do these things for her. We have a strange kind of contact. Sometimes, it's very close, and other times, for a long period, she withholds any really important information. I know, for example, that her marriage is not going so great and she may even be having an affair on the side. She doesn't know I'm aware of all this and I don't let her know I know. If she wants me to know, or ask for my advice, she'll eventually tell me. Otherwise, I keep quiet and keep on knitting."

Robin's story echoes a fact that came up repeatedly in answer to the question "What subjects do you most (and least) discuss with your adult kids?" The *least-discussed* topics, regardless of who initiated the conversation, are money and sex, according to the mothers surveyed. Money (see Chapter 3) is losing some of that taboo quality, but sex still retains it strongly. Adult children, said their mothers, will discuss "relationships" ad nauseam, but not specifically sex, except in rare instances. More than 90 percent of the mothers said they "never" initiated conversations about their own sex lives with their adult children. These taboos arise from many traditions and much family history, but one of the elements is, again, the mother's wish to avoid anything so overloaded with feeling that it might cause a real rupture.

Kay T., 54-year-old mother of three, cites another case of pursuing the commandment: Thou shalt not cause trouble that could lead to severing of ties.

Says Kay: "My son has a weak self-image that makes him do crazy things like gamble or buy gifts that are too expensive, to try to impress people. At this point, I really don't know how to tell him that I dislike that kind of stuff."

She mourns, "He's 24 now, and if I criticize that kind of behavior, he just gets mad and storms off or hangs up the telephone and it really doesn't get to the cause of the problem, anyway. I don't know what to do because I don't want to nag him or meddle or interfere with his life, so I just keep quiet— I don't talk about it—I feel like I'm walking on eggs all the time."

Answering questions about their hundreds of conversations, mothers reported four topics they discuss but handle most gingerly with their grown kids:

• Life-style (usually meaning drugs, unmarried cohabitation, or other contemporary patterns difficult for some mothers to handle).

• Inappropriate choice of spouse or live-in partner, as viewed from the mother's own cultural, religious, socioeconomic, racial, or ethnic background.

• "Drift"—the young adult's inability to focus on long-term commitments to school, work, or personal relationships. For middle-class mothers with aspirations toward at least middle-class lives for their children, as well as lower-income families hoping to see their children rise, "drift" is the issue most difficult to handle without estranging the young person. Mothers may cry when they tell friends or relatives of their children's lack of direction, but they hide those tears on the telephone and "walk on eggs" again when in direct contact with the young person.

• The fourth topic on which mothers tend to keep silent or that they disguise under other quarrels is the emergence, in their child, of serious character flaws. If the mother sees the adult son or daughter behaving cruelly or thoughtlessly or exploitatively too often, or notes a persistent immaturity in dealing with the world, or encounters excessive moodiness or self-centeredness, all these can bring on a profound, disappointed silence from the mother.

There is a joke making the rounds that a mother is a person who never stops expecting improvement from her middle-aged children.

In reality, though, mothers say sadly that character flaws make them freeze up into uncommunicativeness. To some degree, this is because of maternal guilt about what part they may have played in producing what they see as serious defects.

There are some other silent angers, not as frequently recorded as the four above, but which mothers try to control and often cannot, thereby evoking new fears of estrangement.

These, listed in the order of frequency mothers reported them, are:

• "Why don't they help around the house when they visit?"

• "I wish he/she would stop smoking. I'm really worried."

• "I'd like them to be more tolerant of *my* lifestyle, including men friends other than their father, or a job that's okay with me, even if they look down their noses at it."

• "I don't want to talk about the mistakes they say I've made —some of which they are right about, but some of which they're all wrong on."

• "I hate it when they sound so bored and irritated on the telephone—they're so eager to be rid of me they can't even be polite. It doesn't happen all the time, but enough times to hurt. I never say anything, though."

Communications between human beings can be therapeutic or destructive, and everyone, surely, would like to emulate the candid, open communications that students of family life have identified as one of the components of a healthy family.

But mothers and adult children have been in vehement, intense intimacy for twenty or thirty years, and their communications patterns are complex enough to include both love and hate, both affection and dislike, both acceptance and rejection. The pressures of the outside world have also infiltrated their responses to each other: The parents must face earning a livelihood as well as self-actualization and aging; the young people must endure growing pains, peer pressure, and the challenges of young adulthood.

This was put touchingly by actor Michael O'Keefe, when discussing the role he was playing in *Split Image,* that of a young man who was trying to examine his relationship with his family. The young hero's thoughts went like this: "There was one moment when he thought he could love everybody. In most families, strangely enough, they don't talk about love that much. The emphasis is on other things, getting to work, getting to school. It's 'I'd like to tell you I love you, but I have to get up at seven.' "[4]

The I-have-to-get-up-at-seven syndrome—which has blocked much parent-child interaction over the years—bothers many mothers and also many communications experts who are eager to assist people to improve their message-sending and -receiving.

Escape From the Tower of Babel

The distilled wisdom of some of the mothers who thought hard and long about how they pursue their telephone links with their absent offspring, together with general observations by experts, resulted in a set of communications recommendations as follows:

• Focus on the *person* who's talking, not the words you're hearing from the other end of the wire. Sure, it's just your familiar, known son or daughter (or mother or father), but it's also a man or woman of a certain age, in a certain place in the world, doing certain things, not all of which you may know about. The person you think you know so well (either parent or adult child) is only *partially* the person you're hearing on the telephone.

• Be aware that *everything* you say, no matter how casual or how significant, pushes the conversation toward either acceptance or rejection. Because so many women want to avoid open conflict, they try to go in the direction of acceptance, but find it difficult if they really disapprove or are worried or anxious.

• This leads to mixed messages, and those ought to be cut back wherever humanly possible. Some tactful candor may be better for the long-range health of the relationship than con-

stantly pretending everything is okay when it isn't. It just isn't
in the cards that mothers will be equally pleased with everything
their kids say and do, and some honesty, rather than saying one
thing and feeling another, might be in order.

• Don't be afraid to ask a question for greater clarity, and learn
the knack of restating or reframing what the other person is
saying and then check that back with them for approval to make
sure you're getting what's meant to be conveyed, and not some
other message.

• Try not to interrupt. It may sound just like eagerness to let
the other person know you are fully "with" him or her, but it's
almost always interpreted as more rejecting than accepting.

• Situational context is important, too. You can't possibly
know whether you've called in the middle of a marital spat, at
the end of a dreadful day, or at some other inopportune moment, so just ask—and be ready to end the call, hoping for a
better contact another time, if it's possible to do so.

Families in the Telecommunications Future

We've been looking closely at the new realities of mothering that
have emerged in the modern information revolution, but that is
merely prologue to what the futurists say is in store over the next
couple of decades of telecommunications growth.

Electronic engineers, government planners, and research
scientists are getting ready for a communications future that
could include, at the very least:

• Mobile person-to-person communications anywhere on
earth. Each person will have his personal telephone number and
Dick Tracy fantasy-style wristwatch-sized receiver that could get
calls via satellite and advanced switching systems. Young adults
in the Peace Corps in Nigeria will be able to call mothers in
Cincinnati without phone lines or overseas operators.

• Electronic mail will send copies of the company's announcement about Susie's promotion at the speed of light between
California and New York and all points in between.

• Several developments seem to be returning the home to an earlier role as the center of family activities. Chief among these is teletext, a system of interactive TV shopping, voting, making hotel, plane or theater reservations, and accomplishing other chores the woman of the house traditionally did by driving to shopping malls and offices. Already the home is where the computer is installed, the video games are played, and thirty-five regular cable and pay-TV channels are available in some cities. Also sure to be utilized in a different way as the population ages are variants on closed-circuit TV and the telephones that permit you to see the person to whom you're talking. The latter has been available for some time, but did not enjoy much market acceptance since the average phone talker didn't necessarily want to see or be seen while phoning. But as more and more parents, grandparents, and great-grandparents remain on the scene, a videophone may permit younger generations to check regularly the well-being of elders through this device.

Thoughtful observers have raised questions about whether citizens of developed countries everywhere can adjust—psychologically, socially, and politically—to the rapid changes that such technology will introduce.

In terms of the impact on family relations, the late René DuBos, eminent biologist and professor emeritus at Rockefeller University, may have had the most prophetic word. In a 1974 article, Professor DuBos said:

> Sociologists publicize the breakdown of familial ties, but . . . telephone wires are kept busy by long-distance calls between children and parents. All the social and technological futures we invent turn out to be reformulations in contemporary context of the tribal ways of life in . . . the natural paradise we have lost. . . . Fortunately, human beings have displayed a remarkable ability to change the course of social trends and start on new ventures . . . and thus serve as catalysts in an endless act of creation.[5]

Money Matters: The "Big Chill" or a Warm Gift?

Of all the icy blasts that blow on love, a request for money is the most chilling and havoc-wreaking.

GUSTAVE FLAUBERT, *Madame Bovary*

In the psychiatrist's office:

Patient/Gambler: "For me, gambling is a question posed to Fate: Am I loved?"

Doctor: "Assuming you were right, why do you challenge Fate time and again?"

Patient: "I want to be sure."

EDMUND BERGLER, M.D., *Money and Emotional Conflicts*

"My husband's folks helped us buy our first house back in the Fifties. Then we were just lucky—inflation helped us, we bought two more houses, and now we've been able to get this very expensive house plus a weekend place, too. I only just wish they were alive to see how much they helped us with that first little stake. Naturally, we'd like to do the same for our kids, too, if we can."

KELLY M., mother of three, grandmother of two

*C*ontrol and dependence—or love and help?
Money is all those things and more in the complex role it plays

in the relationship between mothers and their adult children. Dads are involved, too, of course—perhaps more involved than in many other facets of the relationship—but the mother remains interpreter, buffer, mediator, and general translator of money's many meanings.

Money as symbol—of both love and control, the heart of the dependence/independence struggle—also means conflict, tension, and disagreement that illuminates some of the most fundamental goals and aspirations of American families.

Neutral and indifferent in itself, money spells security, success, achievement, and status in the society at large, and these are values American women live by as completely as anyone else in the culture, both for themselves and for their children.

Consider, then, what the women in our sample report:

• Of the more than 200 women who wrote and spoke openly about their financial dealings, *more than half* said they had already lent their adult children "substantial sums" of money.

• On a list of fifteen topics that caused the most disagreements between mothers and adult children, money ranked second. The first-ranked topic, life-style, and the third-ranked topic, lack of children's motivation, also were linked with differences of opinion about money.

Why is money so fraught a matter between the generations after the children have presumably left home to make their own way in the world?

In addition to the classic American success drive mentioned above, there is the reality of an erratic economy that makes it hard for young people to get launched and see the clear path ahead that their postwar-boom parents saw spiraling ever upward during the family's early years. Many mothers said they thought that the children seeking financial help, and the parents giving as much as they could, was not necessarily a desire for either parental control or evidence of dependent children, but rather a realistic evaluation of a troubled national economy with cloudy skies for the future.

A number of women described parents today as bulwarks against a set of crumbling economic possibilities for their children, and are stalwart about helping.

"It's a lot tougher world out there for our kids—more of them competing for fewer jobs, housing so expensive and hard to get, companies doing layoffs even in good times—you bet we'll help all we can."

Speaking, albeit a trifle grimly, but with much certainty, was Marilyn S., whose own financial situation isn't all that strong. Her husband was disabled after a work-related accident last year, and Marilyn herself has only modest pension expectations after more than twenty years as a clerical assistant working for a large corporation. She and her husband already have gone into their life savings to help their son begin a solar energy business ("We believe in him and we believe in the business," she says), and they are also caring part-time for their grandson, the child of their divorced, working daughter, in order to help the young woman save child-care costs.

The economic realities behind Marilyn's decision to help her son and daughter may be the reasons why a recent national poll found that the most money-conscious of all age groups in the nation are young adults between the ages of 18 and 25—the very adult children whose mothers speak in this book.

Psychology Today surveyed 20,000 Americans of all ages, trying to find out just what money does mean to people, and they found that today's young adults are worried about not being able to get the things they once thought they'd have as a matter of course. The *PT* report showed that young adults think much more about money, in general, than any other age group, including retirees and those over 60.

Financial transactions between the generations are also complicated by the most intensely difficult issues of loving and giving, gratitude and understanding.

All these are reflected in the story of Amy T. and her husband, who lent their daughter interest-free funds that enabled her to get a degree in veterinary medicine. After less than a year working as a new member of a group vet practice, the daughter mentioned casually that she was planning a European vacation, but she did not discuss resuming payments on her college loan. Since the money had been clearly identified as a loan, she initially had begun repaying it while still in school, but drifted away from discussion of the matter after graduation.

It was difficult for Amy (impossible for the father, who left the execution of their joint plan to his wife) to write to her daughter after the European trip was announced, but she says, "I just forced myself to do it; I wrote her that I thought it was time to resume regular payments on the college debt. I didn't mention the trip, but of course, that's what was on my mind. I felt we'd be subsidizing her trip, and I just felt that was wrong somehow."

Contemporary young middle-agers, in our interviews, shied away from using the word "gratitude," though a few of them commented that they felt that Amy's daughter should have been "grateful" for the help her parents had given her toward a higher-income future than her nonprofessional parents probably ever will attain.

But gratitude, as a psychiatrist who studied the emotional patterns behind money hang-ups pointed out, is a sign of maturity, of having grown beyond the small-child stage where the world exists only to gratify one's wishes.[1] And most mothers in our sample agreed that the maturation of their young people— though now in their twenties, thirties, and some nearing forty— was a sometime thing, especially where money was concerned.

It seems to be the one area—more than work, more than interpersonal relations—where young people hang on to the old dependency patterns, expecting their parents to continue to "feed" and nurture them as in the old days.

Eva R., for instance, feels that immaturity is behind the "wrong" way her daughter, one of three children, spends money.

Eva is troubled that her married daughter, a schoolteacher who as yet has no children of her own, and who is married to a white-collar husband of moderate income, buys gifts for her friends and family that Eva believes are far too costly, even for the young couple's joint income. Eva and her husband are embarrassed about receiving such expensive items "sometimes for no reason at all—not a birthday, not Christmas, or any particular reason.

"I don't like to think," says Eva unhappily, "that she might be feeling she has to buy her friends' and her family's love. It bothers me, but *I don't want to quarrel with her,* so I just stay out of it."

While discussing her daughter's financial immaturity, Eva inadvertently stumbled on an issue that among mothers aroused some of the most active and passionate discussions in the area of money. Feelings were intense, almost violent, about when to speak and "when to keep your mouth shut" when money matters involve grown children.

One mother, Adele Z., told the group she has a simple rule: "If it's my money—if I lent it or gave it outright—I want to retain at least a little of a say over how it is spent. If it is *not* my money, I keep quiet, no matter how foolishly I think they may be spending it."

Money is always an exchange, and family life is also always full of exchanges, so the temperature heats up when the love and care, the support and help that money spells to parents is viewed differently by the young people, who see it as sometimes too controlling. Because most of the mothers interviewed *do* see money as an offering of love and help, they are not nearly so clear as Adele on when to speak up and when not to. Most in our sample fell off the fence on the side of *not* speaking up when they have objections or mental reservations, because they see it as invalidating the help part of the offer, as giving a gift with strings attached. This violates their basic sense of why they are offering the money in the first place, I learned.

For example, by far the largest share of respondent mothers quite specifically stated that they feel they should not voice any opinions about their grown children's handling of money unless asked for advice. The unanimity of this was startling: 85 percent said no to the question "If you have lent large sums of money or provided baby-sitting or other services to help your grown children save money, do you think you have the right to speak up about how the child handles finances?"

This skittishness, this sense of traversing an emotional minefield, runs through most maternal conversations on money, partially because they never know exactly what is, as in any minefield, about to blow up in their faces.

The exact opposite of the financial "leaner" among young people (those who never quite get that last toe out over the doorsill of the nest, economically speaking) is the one who has such an intense drive for independence that he or she refuses help when it is really very much needed.

Because mothers indicated that they see financial help as basically a way of keeping family ties strong—a kin assistance unit as old as time—they, too, have immature struggles with the question of control, letting go, and not insisting on helping, even when it very plainly would be enormously useful.

Carol T. has been caught in this dilemma more than once. Carol feels that her youngest, a 24-year-old married daughter with a new baby, is "overdoing the independence bit" because the young woman, her husband, and the little grandson are living in an old abandoned farmhouse without central heating. The young husband is an unskilled carpenter who finds it hard to get steady work; the young mother is also unemployed.

"We worry about them constantly," Carol says, "but they won't let us help, little as it would be. It's a matter of fierce pride with them, and we have to respect it, though the thought that they might be cold or hungry just haunts our sleep." Carol says she fell silent under the sadly calm statement delivered to her privately by her daughter: "Mom, I know Tom isn't a good provider. But if I couldn't take it, I could always leave." Money in this situation, Carol feels, is so loaded with so much emotional freight, she is terrified of making a misstep and being coldly rejected by her daughter as seeming to be unacceptably hostile to the young husband.

Carol salvaged a small slice of humor from the situation as she described how careful she and her husband try to be with their son-in-law, attempting to show respect for the couple's independence and sturdy tries at getting by on their own, without help from either family.

"When we are there or they visit us, we handle Tom with gingerly tact and try to be kind," says Carol with a tiny grin, "but I'm sure every time he looks at us, he sees an imaginary sign going on and off over my forehead, spelling out 'Why don't you get a job?' I must look funny with that flashing sign sitting on my head, but there it is . . . there's no real way I can disguise those thoughts, I guess."

When adult children who are otherwise managing on their own—living apart, earning their own paychecks, and so on—continue to drag out some economic dependence after the money tie (like the umbilical cord) should have been broken, or, conversely, when they make a huge issue out of refusing even badly needed help, there are clearly some dependence/

independence struggles going on again, but mothers report themselves often confused and unable to see the issues that clearly.

For example, Bernice J. feels herself poised precariously right at the very spot where dependence and independence are almost exactly evenly balanced for her son, Paul, who is trying to break into the murderously competitive world of the New York theater (the family's home is in Wisconsin), and who needs his mother's helping hand in the form of occasional checks from home.

"I not only approve, I'm really proud that he is trying to become a serious actor," she says a mite defensively, while explaining that her husband forcefully *dis*approves. "And when Paul gets work of any kind, he's good about trying to pay me back a bit at a time. He's had good training at the drama department of a fine university, experienced people have said he has talent, he's not a goof-off. . . ."

Bernice's voice becomes a little tremulous: "But everybody knows that more kids are always *out* of work in the theater than ever do find work there. So the question is: Am I really helping him by keeping him afloat in this way?" She asks softly, "Would I be a better parent if I refused to lend any money and let him learn more quickly that only a very, very few people ever make a steady living in the theater?"

In this setting, Bernice feels that she is doing five jobs simultaneously: She (1) worries whether she's helping or hindering her son's career, (2) fends off her husband's threatened cutoff of funds, (3) pleads for more time for Paul to try to make it, (4) fears that underneath it all, she and her husband may just be trying to retain control over their son's life, and (5) enjoys a great thrill when her son gets even a walk-on part with no lines.

Bernice's dilemma is replicated in every detail by many other parents whose adult children are trying to break into almost any aspect of the arts or entertainment. Whether it is film, dance, photography, writing, music, theater, painting, or sculpture, these are not activities that society generously rewards. For the young adults trying to get a toe in the door of resistant producers, talent agents, or editors, it is the parents who try to help reconcile a materialistic society that does not attach great economic value to the arts with their children's needs for three squares a day and rent money.

"Even kids without college, but who manage to latch on to a good trade—say plumber or electrician—can make their fifteen to twenty thousand or more a year when they get experienced, if they are not lazy—and my Ginny is not lazy—but my daughter is averaging about six thousand dollars a year as a waitress and part-time office temp while she tries to break into TV. How long do we go on subsidizing this effort?" chimed in Niki Van O., mother of a daughter and a son, when she heard Bernice's story.

This dancing on the razor's edge between helping and controlling may confuse parents horrendously, but it doesn't dampen their intense desire to solve the problem in some way that will fulfill their primary goals: keeping the kids on track in their life course, and reaffirming family ties as supportive and helpful, not destructive and adolescence-prolonging.

The mature women in our core group stressed that it is family love they want to express in giving money, even though they know the money brings an automatic degree of control.

According to a number of women, they differ strongly with their husbands in viewing money as a backup in times of trouble for their kids. They say their menfolk tend to use money with the children in a different way: as a measure of whether the child is reaching a desired level of maturity and is functioning well outside the sheltering circle of home. A substantial minority said they quarrel often with their husbands over when, whether, and how much money to give the children, because the mothers find it hard to look at money as an objective yardstick of the young adult's maturation, seeing it more as a very ordinary kind of direct help when needed.

However, the legendary tyrannical father of nineteenth-century novels who stormed about threatening to cut children out of his will or used money in stagy, highly visible ways to keep control turned up only once or twice in my sample. He is basically an outmoded type. Modern fathers tend to be more subtle, using a carrot-and-stick approach to get the influence they may seek in their children's lives.

Susan N., the mother of one son in college and two daughters trying to earn enough money for secretarial and computer-programmer courses, summed up the prevailing maternal confusion about the real outlines of the problem when she said:

"Everybody we know in our age group is just intensely preoccupied—in some form, though they may not say it in just so many words—with one tricky question when it comes to money. And that question is: When does giving or lending money become a barrier in the way of the kids' growing up; when does it mean parents are hanging on too tight too long, taking too much of a hand in how the kids' lives are working out? Or when is it just that temporary, crucial helping hand at the right moment that gets a young person off to a good start and then they can do fine on their own—sort of like helping them learn to ride a bike—they waver and fall off and get on and fall off and finally they just ride away? Do you know which it is when you do it? I myself am never quite sure—we go back and forth on it."

The Fine Art of Giving, Lending . . . and Saying No

Two women in a discussion group represented opposite extremes of maternal reactions to requests for money from the adult children.

One mother said: "I don't lend, I give. If they need it, I give it—no questions asked, no strings attached. They are part of me, not a business deal."

At the exact opposite pole, a mother of four said: "I don't like to make loans or gifts at all after they reach a certain age. We worked hard to raise them and gave them as much schooling as we could afford. Now it's up to them. I'm sorry if they can't buy a house right away—we waited sixteen years for ours."

Most of the mothers—about 150 out of the core group of more than 200—fell somewhere between a long-term "yes" and "I've paid my dues—let them pay theirs."

What became clear after many thoughtful hours of discussion was the difficult course that lies ahead *after* parents have made the decision to help out with money.

The problem then becomes, mothers report, to decide whether the money is a gift or a loan. It is right at that point that a large number of respondents confessed failure and ambivalence—that is, they themselves could not decide firmly which it was! If it was to be a gift, that very decision left them uneasy. A gift seemed too "unbusinesslike" an attitude to many mothers, at the same time that they really wanted to achieve the sense of something freely given. But gifts also made them uneasy for another reason. Many feared that outright gifts didn't teach the children enough about the "real" world with its harsh demands. And behind many money gifts often stand a slightly skeptical set of parents who simply wonder vaguely if they aren't just being "conned" by manipulative children.

If it was decided the money was a straight loan, then a new set of questions arose. How much of a strictly business deal is appropriate, or feels right to parents, notably mothers? Do you charge interest? Do you draw up a legal contract or put something formal in writing? Many women were appalled at such a notion, yet admitted that it might save a lot of heartburn at some point.

"It just seems so cold, so impersonal—no, I couldn't do it that way," wailed Gerry B., mother of two sons.

Of the more than a hundred women in our sample who had lent "substantial sums" of money to their children, only seven had anything at all in writing and those documents were far from legal contracts. In most cases, they were letters exchanged in the normal course of events, with many other items contained in the letters in addition to some references to the loan. Three of the seven had hasty notes scribbled by one party and signed by the other, and one mother had a "mock" legal document written as a parody by a son in law school concerning the loan his parents were making. More than three-quarters of the lenders said they either asked for no interest on the loan or asked for an interest rate well below what similar loans at banks would cost.

"God," said one mother discussing the tricky loan/gift problem, "do I want my kids to think of us as business people or as loving parents? I don't see how the two can be reconciled, really."

The problem of first identifying the money as either outright gift or loan is simply fudged in many families, we learned through this exchange of stories. Parents leave the status vague and the children often are content, also, not to have the status too clearly spelled out. Gifts bring undue obligation, the children often feel, and loans imply repayment, which isn't great either from the adult child's point of view.

The latter point represents yet another issue mothers view as gigantic: If the money is clearly labeled a loan, how does an affectionate parent go about specifying repayment?

Some women were stern on this point, feeling that parental need and reality should dictate repayment as rapidly as possible and the children should have that laid out very clearly when the money is given.

But the handful who were ready to say, "I want it back and fast —I need it!" was smaller than I had anticipated. In our group were a good many women whom divorce, widowhood, bad luck, or ill health had left far from economically secure—yet this seemed to have relatively little to do with whether they firmly asked for repayment or not. In other words, realistic need was not the guiding force; it seemed to have something much more to do with the mother's attitude about a "giving" role and about the level of responsibility and maturity the child had reached. For example, three of the mothers who felt strongly that the loan repayment schedule should be arranged right along with the money at the time it was given were all working, all with husbands present and working, and while not wealthy, could not claim real need. Yet they felt it was important to each party's dignity and self-respect to ask for the money back as promptly as possible.

The majority, however, continued to act out ambivalence, even when the money was identified as a loan. They asked for the money back "when you can" or "whenever convenient" or "in some reasonable time" (unspecified).

One mother told her son clearly that $1,800 to help in a business venture was a loan, but she did not discuss repayment at the moment of sending the check. When, a year later, he had made no mention of repayment, she asked about it and was told he had simply forgotten. Small payments began to arrive irregularly after that.

Especially painful is the loan parents make to help adult children start businesses, and then the business fails. This involves parental misery on a number of levels at once: The adult child is clearly not following the success scenario the parent so much

hopes for, the not inconsiderable fact of lost money is a head-
ache, the remorse on the adult child's side and the loss and
resentment on the parent side are all hard on the fabric of
affection. Sometimes the family suffers a period of estrangement
(depending often on the degree of financial disaster involved)
and often there are angry quarrels and much disappointment
when everyone's judgment is called into question.

But anger aside, what can a mother or a father actually do,
what steps can or should they take after an adult child has lost
some of their money in a business failure?

"Just bail 'em out if you can possibly do it—what recourse do
you have?" wrote one mother philosophically.

"Let 'em take the consequences—that's the only way they'll
learn," said a maternal disciplinarian.

"You might want to cut your losses and get out, but can you
let your children and grandchildren starve?" asked another
mother with just a hint of hyperbole. This woman, the 51-year-
old mother of three adult children, backed her son in a gift shop
he opened in a neighborhood not affluent enough to support
the steady purchase of small luxuries. He lost a painful, though
not catastrophic, amount of his parents' retirement money.
Luckily, both parents were working, had no immediate retirement plans, and could anticipate fair, if not lavish, private pen-
sions from their respective companies.

But the loan/gift dilemma arises from many other kinds of life
events besides business failures. Dinah B.'s 23-year-old daughter is having serious marital problems. Dinah found out through
another family member who lives nearer her daughter that the
husband (Dinah's son-in-law and the father of her adored only
granddaughter) has undergone a religious conversion and
joined a church that requires its members to tithe 10 percent of
their incomes.

Dinah recounts sadly, "They're already having a hard time
making ends meet with a little one and another on the way. I can
just imagine how hard this is for Josie, but I can't talk to her,
because I'm not even supposed to know about it. I have to wait
for her to tell me and it's probably hurting her too much."

Another typical life event that is what one another called "a
real can of worms" is the problem of fairness among the sib-

lings. If parents gives loans or gifts to one child, must they then be absolutely evenhanded to all the others, even if the children's needs, place in the life cycle, careers, and income potentials are all different?

Nothing in this world spells more trouble than giving one child and not another a gift or a loan of money once they have all passed the college-tuition level, explained several women in the money discussion group.

Norma F. and her husband were so concerned about not showing favoritism among their three children that they took an unusual step. After giving one son $500 for an investment that a friend recommended (which later flopped), they decided to cancel repayment on a $500 loan they had made to their oldest daughter for unexpected medical bills, and they initiated a new $500 gift to their other son. Neither of the other two children even knew about the gift for the investment that their parents had made to the middle son, nor had they asked for any money, both being set in reasonably secure jobs.

"But," explains Norma, "we just felt we wanted to treat them all the same." Norma's checkbook reflected the try, but students of the sibling bond could have saved the parents some money because perceptions of favoritism by the adult children are often not based on reality at all, but on a complicated life history and a whole set of other considerations (see Chapter 5).

The Working Mother: Cash Flow as Chicken Soup

As we have seen from the foregoing reports, giving and lending money to adult children carries a great many relationship overtones, which are themselves overlaid with social and cultural drives for success and status of one's children. The problems seem numberless.

But there is one brighter spot in the picture that reflects clearly the very different way today's young middle-aged mothers operate in economic terms with their adult children compared to the way their own mothers of two generations ago were able to operate.

And that is the considerable pleasure mature working mothers get from earning money of their own to spend as they please

—minus any paternal veto—on their children and grandchildren. Although their own mothers, born in the late nineteenth century or the first years of this century, were often extremely clever about worming household money from sometimes tight budgets for just such pleasureful spending, they seldom had sums of the kind working women can now offer. Such sums help with serious projects like education, home buying, or entrepreneurship, and also with "frills" like summer camp for the grandchild or a special evening out for the adult children themselves.

Some of the mothers in our group have been back at work for over a decade or more, and recall fondly the special delight it was to be able to make a real contribution to enriching their children's educations with junior year abroad for middle-class youngsters, or for helping with a second-hand car for less affluent 20-year-olds.

It is well known now that a little more than half of all of American women over 16 are in the labor force, but less well known is that more than 47 percent of those millions of women are over the age of 35.

And even among women 55 to 64 years of age, there's a steeply rising number of work returnees. According to various government reports, this age group had 18 percent of its members working in 1940, but 42.1 percent of women in that age bracket were working in 1972, an increase of 140 percent. Projections call for nearly half (45.8 percent) of women in second-stage motherhood to be working by 1990.[2]

What this translates into for adult children is a mother who is on tap not only for TLC, but also for that green launching fuel that helps youngsters get started on their paths more easily.

Although there are about six million working women (of all ages) who make more than their husbands do, middle-aged women as a group make considerably less than their husbands because of often lengthy absences from the work force.[3] Their generation tended not to resume full-time training or work until the last child was at least in higher elementary grades, if not until junior high or later.

But the demographics play into their hands in another way, because, on the average, they are a few years younger than their husbands and thus often are in the work force for a while after their husbands may retire.

Regardless of how long they work, women on the average still earn less than men, overall, so the sheer dollar amount that late-life mothers are able to contribute to their sons and daughters is limited compared to the father's income. Still, several women described how the mother's contribution often subtly changes the whole family's life-style expectations.

"It's really because of the good tips I earned over the years that my kids learned all about having dinner out and going to the movies a lot more than I ever could as a kid," explains Edie S., an experienced beautician who was always able to work, when she wished, in expensive salons. Edie has two children, and while her husband was a hard-working construction helper who made good money when he worked, there was also no doubt that her extras—the new color TV set, the trip to Disneyland—made life more enjoyable when the children were growing up. Now that her son and daughter are launched—the son an accountant, the daughter a dress buyer for a large department store—she plans to work full time and save for both her retirement and hoped-for grandchildren.

The extra money working mothers have brought to the family has come just in the nick of time, too, for as financial columnist Sylvia Porter writes, "What 'everybody else' has today is a lot more and a lot better than what anybody else ever had before."

The constantly rising aspirations of Americans coexist uneasily with the fact that the economy doesn't blossom endlessly for today's young adults; in many cases, the optimism and hope are kept alive by the extra margin, the "cushion," that the late-life mother provides.

The transitional mother's financial contribution to the family's standard of living has eased some tensions, made both parents a little freer with small luxuries, and earned the mother some welcome respect and a delicate new identity as a worker separate from the father, mothers said.

The advent of the working mother has also led to another new development: much more open discussion about money around the family table.

The Vanishing Taboo: Money Talk

There was a time in the United States when no one talked about money.

It was considered bad taste in some cultures, too revealing of private matters in others—and that reluctance is still quite evident in some families today.

But generally speaking, money has joined alcoholism, child abuse, and homosexuality as topics that can be shouted in headlines, dramatized on TV, and discussed ad infinitum in the public print. *Money* magazine, which didn't exist 12 years ago, now has 1.5 million circulation; columns of financial advice and TV programs on money management are almost as popular as "Dear Abby" lectures on sex and child-rearing.

Both working mothers and traditional homemakers said that they often were the bookkeepers for the family and did all or a portion of actual day-to-day money handling and tracking, most of the time in close, conferring partnership with their husbands or companions. A minority (about 22 percent) reported that all money decisions as well as actual handling of family finances were in the hands of their husbands and they simply doled out money as it was needed for personal and household expenses.

But working mothers described themselves as much more conscious of how and where the family money is going, now that they have paychecks, and that this leads them to varied and numerous financial interactions with their grown children.

The taboo against speaking about money is vanishing right at the telephone and the dinner table, said working mothers, and, to a somewhat lesser extent, stay-at-home mothers agreed.

Respondent mothers said the money talk between them and their adult children is generally a two-way flow, though in terms of volume not at all an equal one.

Going in one direction, the parents generally tell the children as much as they want them to know (and it's usually quite a lot) about the parental financial picture. In the other direction, the parents ask for—and the children occasionally volunteer—some information about the children's financial situation.

The way this works out in practice, said the mothers, is that the parents divulge a good bit of substantial information, but the kids tell much, *much* less!

The background of the imbalance is this: Mothers, playing a dominant role in financial negotiations as they do, tend not to relate to their children's financial problems in the abstract; they are caught up in the specifics of who needs what, who is worrying about money and why, which child owes what debts, and so on. Fathers are genuinely involved, sometimes with deep anxiety, but often leaving the actual telephoning, writing, or talking face to face up to the mothers.

Thus, in carrying out these front-line challenges in the money wars, mothers report they must share quite a lot of information with their grown kids for two reasons: first, so the young people will know the well is not bottomless (a notion that children acquire automatically with the blowing out of eighteen or so candles on the birthday cake); and second, to serve as an example to the young adults of how important it is to plan their own financial futures wisely.

This latter need to be a role model of sorts in the financial area often takes the form of elaborately casual introductions of the subject at quieter moments at family gatherings, or discussions of future financial plans at retirement or other milestones, and sometimes includes details about wills and inheritances.

In some families, the parents just put into an ordinary letter a few key things the kids need to know in case of illness or death —where the savings bankbooks are, whether there is a lawyer or an accountant to consult, and similar matters. These attempts at prudent planning for the sake of the children have the effect, whether intended or not, of giving the kids at least an outline of their parents' financial situation, if not every last word on it.

And some mothers reported they try to protect and defend the children against money tangles by taking the opposite tack —by withholding information out of concern for the children.

Phyllis N. is the 48-year-old divorced mother of a grown son and a college-age daughter. Phyllis went back to school after her divorce, and is making a moderately good salary as an executive secretary.

"No," she says, "the children don't know much about my personal finances. I don't want them to. I never discussed the settlement I made with their father; I don't talk about my bonuses or salary on my job. The reason is that I feel the most important thing to them is to know that I can take care of myself and they don't need to worry about me. If they had too much information, they might not agree that I really can handle things myself. If I remarry, that'll maybe be a different thing, but right now, the main thing is that my daughter has to finish college and my son has to get settled in a job and I don't want them worrying about me while they're trying to do that. I just want them to concentrate on what they have to do for themselves right now."

This approach also was taken by two widows in the group of mothers interviewed. One of them said, "They want to think I'm a rich widow—so let them. Their father left quite a bit less than they think, but as long as I can manage without too much problem, I'm not going to interfere with their peace of mind; at least not for the present."

However mothers choose to handle the subject, the fact is that, as a group, the adult children often tend to share much *less* money information with their parents than their parents do with them.

For example, regarding topics that mothers reported their adult children would initiate conversations about, money was at the bottom of the list, just barely above sex, the last subject grown kids will open a discussion about with their folks.

Work, friends, travel, sports, hobbies, even intimate day-dreams, hopes, aspirations—all are way above money in the frequency with which young people will volunteer information to their parents, according to the mothers whom I queried.

Asked why they thought money talk was often so minimal at the young person's end, these were among the answers given:

• "I think they fear my judgment about how they spend their money and the less said the better. That's okay with me, as long as it isn't *my* money."

• "It really has to do with life-style. Their father and I are champion gratification-delayers. We put off expensive pleasures to make sure the basics are covered; I hope it will work for us in our old age. But our kids, like most of their friends, don't want to wait for the things they might, by squeezing a little, be able to enjoy now. Travel is one thing I could mention. My husband and I didn't take the trip out west we'd dreamed about since we were kids—the Grand Canyon, cowboys, all that stuff—until our silver wedding anniversary. Our three daughters, who are nine-teen, twenty-three, and twenty-four, have each traveled a little bit outside the United States already. Believe me, I'm not saying they're wrong—and they sure did it cheaply, biking, backpack-ing, and all the rest—but still it's different and it sure leads to some loud silences on money and how it is spent."

• "I think our two sons and two daughters have the normal amount of ambition and I think they are a little sensitive if their jobs aren't going anywhere very fast and they don't want to talk about money because it's a dead giveaway that they did or didn't get a promotion or did or didn't spend too much time between jobs—things like that slow down what they're willing to bring up on their own."

Not all young people, however, are reticent about money; quite outspoken are a number of adult children who have an attitude that upsets their parents and is a source of considerable strain in almost 20 percent of the sample group. This attitude, according to mothers, can best be summarized as: "Parents, give me some money; I've got it coming to me, you 'owe' it to me."

This peremptory tone causes intense stress in some families and exacerbates the already difficult question parents struggle with throughout the financial history of raising their children: What financial support *is* their responsibility and what kinds of money grants are really outside of normal parental obligations?

We investigated this a little with our sample group of mothers and found that the two traditional obligations—paying for a child's wedding (nowadays this could include either a son or a daughter, not alone the latter) and financing undergraduate college tuition—still lead the list of what parents believe they do, in truth, "owe" their children.

But also high on their list were: giving or lending money for large purchases (81 mothers out of 208); paying for graduate school tuition (61 mothers); and helping a child buy a home or a business (55). This reflected a growing emphasis on their adult children's newer areas of need.

Mothers explained that they do, indeed, believe they *always* will have an obligation to help financially in cases of need and see it as part of their "duty" in a variety of ways. Many said they were glad to give money, even when it caused real sacrifices for themselves and their husbands.

"I feel as though when they get to a certain age, there really isn't much you can do to help them with the problems of their lives except to give them money," explains Marcia D., a 47-year-old mother of two grown children. "At least it's *something* you can do when you can't help with busted romances or lost jobs."

But even women who see their financial responsibility to their children as continuous under some circumstances are hurt and angry at the "you owe me" syndrome some young people exhibit.

"I get really mad at their definition of what they 'need,'" exclaims Agnes L., mother of three. "Helping with unexpected medical bills or something like that is one thing when they're not married or working, but I don't agree that they 'need' two-hundred-dollar boots or cashmere sweaters and I just damn well draw the line at that kind of 'need'; I won't subsidize that under any circumstances and it makes me mad to be told they must have those things. Leads to a lot of trouble."

In a discussion group, several mothers tried to analyze the source of this appalling chip on the shoulder that some young people display when they truculently demand "what's coming to me."

Some of the explanations offered included these:

• Some women said they understood that such demands represent an immature dependency, that the young person was asking to be taken care of like a needy child for a whole variety of intrafamily reasons, including "getting even" with a sibling they may have thought more favored by the parents.

• It was clear to some mothers (by no means all) that money, like food, is a symbol of nourishment. As an answer to the question "Do you love me?" or "How much do you love me?" or "Do you love me as much as you love my little sister?" it's hard to beat money or expensive gifts that shout, "Look at all the money I've spent on you." This becomes additionally complex when the parents' financial status changes over the years, so that the first children sometimes have noticeably fewer toys, trips, and clothes than do later children.

• Another cause, said some mothers, is that the parent is now facing the consequences of having overindulged the children as they were growing up. The new affluence of the 1950s through the early 1970s meant that many parents whose own backgrounds lacked an ease with money were able to provide their children with many more material goods and chances for leisure, entertainment, and travel than they had ever had.

Especially among Depression-reared parents, this often created a feeling of "I want my kids to have everything I was never able to have" that was touching, but ultimately not good for the children. This feeling of showering children with comforts and conveniences remembered as bitter deprivations in parental childhoods has been a problem forever, psychologists point out, but seldom have as many people at one time had the means to fulfill scarcity fantasies as the current group of middle-aged parents.

Several women in the money discussion group even admitted that while they complain of their children's demanding style in money relations, they are, somewhere deep in their souls, rather proud of having raised children accustomed to the best of everything and to living in a certain style. To these women, often themselves children in the 1930s and prewar 1940s, the fact that their children imitate the truly rich is a sign that both parents and young adults have escaped the gray, grim joylessness of the Depression years and will never have to submit to that kind of life again.

Not all mothers share this sheepish and embarrassed pride, however; some described themselves as deeply hurt and sad at what overindulgence has wrought: children with no realistic sense of the value of money, children who are infantile in demanding continued financial "feeding," and adult children who are careless and negligent about emotional gratitude or financial obligations, seeing debts owed to parents as "not really debts," as one mother reported.

"We are reaping what we sowed," said Elena T. sadly, her voice breaking and her eyes filling with tears. Elena and her husband both had come from poor families where shoes for the children to wear to school represented a major investment of the family's meager resources. After World War II, her husband took advantage of the G.I. Bill and government-backed home mortgages to get training as a technical expert in electronics and to buy a modest home. Later affluence meant three successively bigger homes to shelter their growing family, with a three-car garage, a TV for each child, and family summer vacations every year. "We never insisted they work at part-time jobs, we constantly increased their allowances, they had only to ask and we bought," recounts Elena. "Our two daughters had charge accounts at the local pharmacy; they bought lipsticks and shampoos by the case load and our son had his own car the minute he was old enough to drive . . . it wasn't good, I'm telling you, it wasn't good." Of Elena's three children, none completed the expensive private schools and colleges they attended, one daughter was married and divorced by age 19, and their son, after nearly seven years of dropping in and out of school and clinics for drug-related problems, now, she reports thankfully, "has straightened out and is working hard at his own business his father helped him start."

Two women said their reaction to privation in their own youths was to hang on to money perhaps too tightly, which evoked different kinds of rebellion in their children and complicated the money relationship in ways different, perhaps, from the overindulgers, but still quite complex.

One of the major difficulties in this area of mother–adult child relationships is that while money confers power, freedom, and mobility ("It isn't what the rich man does but what he *could* do, that others envy," said one philosopher on money and power), it can never be "an adequate mediator" between human beings in their emotional transactions with each other.[4]

Money remains too colorless, neutral, and anonymous in its own existence to really accomplish anything either positive or negative in how families operate, but it is this very colorlessness and neutrality that make it the perfect *symbol* of whatever is both strong and weak in the family linkage.

For example, mothers bring to the surface a great many deep emotions about what they think is money, but is really a version of all kinds of both intellectual and emotional responses in themselves and their children.

Dismay and chagrin, for instance, over how the children spend their money really has to do with values and priorities in life; guilt sometimes has to do with acknowledging favoritism or unfairness in the way parents distributed family economic resources, or with "making up" for parental absence or neglect.

But more consistent than all those feelings, said mothers, was *surprise* that they are still so intimately bound up in money transactions with their adult children at this point in their lives.

Thinking to inquire about another subject, I asked the core group of 208 whether their children "wanted or expected of them" anything that surprised them when the children were leading their own lives away from home.

Their responses came directly around to money in an astonishing display of unanimity.

"Yes, the amount of financial assistance they needed was a big surprise" was the most frequently given answer. "Nobody told us this aspect of parenting would go on so long," said one mother. Another said, "They expect much more advice on job decisions and finances than I ever thought would happen, plus the ability to borrow—often."

Other answers included these:

• "Yes—continued support for large expenditures and medical bills."

• "Yes. They expect to be able to depend on me for financial backing—especially child number two, who manipulates."

• "What has surprised me the most has been the more or less constant need for loans and gifts of money; I really thought that would end after college debts were paid."

• "I'm always amazed at how differently each of my two kids handles money; one is a frugal saver and the other is profligate in ways I just can't understand. But both of them don't hesitate to ask for financial help when they want it and sometimes (not so often with the saving one) their requests are not at all need, but for things my generation would classify as luxuries." (This mother told how agonized she felt about being asked for money to buy a motorcycle for the younger son, and described the

intensity of her relief when he finally decided against the purchase—before she had been able to choose between giving him
what she considered a lethal weapon and denying him his heart's
fondest wish.)

After these kinds of surprises were outlined by many women
(well over half), there was a vocal minority who wondered aloud
in money discussions whether money acts to tie parents and
adult children together forever.

"Does the time *ever* come when you don't help your kids if
they need it and you have it?" asked one mother rhetorically.
"You bet!" answered another vehemently. "There just has to
come a time when you have to sign off! If you don't, you keep
them dependent forever. For me, that time would come when
my husband retires and we have to think of taking care of ourselves."

In the face of so many varying responses to the money question, there seemed reasonably clear agreement among a majority of mothers (57 percent) on only three points:

1. Most mothers continue to hope they will have sufficient
resources of their own to be able to help their children in cases
of *what the mother defines* as real need. They listed these as accidents, catastrophic illnesses, unexpected unemployment after a
seemingly secure work picture, or other unanticipated disasters
that foresight or planning could not prevent.

2. They volunteered—in interviews, letters, and group discussions—that they have probably been less aware than they should
be that money hassles generally represent something other than
the stark arithmetic they seem to be about. Many women said the
discussion groups helped them to understand that money is
seldom money—it's about love, sharing, helping, or about rejection, greed, overindulgence, or excessively materialistic values.
That money could be a stand-in for sibling rivalry, the old
dependence/independence struggle between the generations,
or even, perhaps, the parents' hidden wishes to continue to
exert control came as a thought-provoking new framework for
thinking about money transactions between mothers and their
adult children.

3. On the most practical level, most mothers agreed that a first concrete step toward defusing the often distressing issue would be to make very clear whether money is given as a gift or a loan, and if the latter, to spell out clearly the repayment expectations. ("Easy to say—hard to do," said one mother, echoing many others.)

Many of us present at the group discussion concluded that the question of money seems to have a life cycle of its own within the mother-child continuum. Postlaunch years initially feature a lot of money contact between the generations; then there seems a period when it is less in the forefront of the relationship; and then, as parents age (see Chapter 10), money once again becomes—so much more than money.

5

Queen Solomon: The Mother and the Adult Siblings

*J*anice was the golden girl while the children were growing up. She was the firstborn, she was pretty, she excelled in school and at the piano. She even won the lead in her high school's senior class production of *Romeo and Juliet*.

The two other children did well, too, says Alice M., 55-year-old mother of the three siblings, now ages 27, 22, and 20. But Janice was a formidable example, whose achievements cast a pall over their triumphs, which were either second best or second time.

Right out of college, Janice landed a glamorous job traveling the world for an international fabric company. She visited her family between fashion shows in Paris and fabric fairs in Italy.

Her legend, both in the family and with friends, grew apace when she married a successful Italian businessman and set up housekeeping in Rome, still managing to visit the family often and always showing up with wonderful gifts for her parents and siblings.

"Her sister looked at me with an icy glare after one of these visits—a visit when I thought we had all had a really good time together," recounts Alice.

"Wendy said, 'Well, I guess Janice is just about perfect now, isn't she?' and I mumbled something about 'Don't be silly, life isn't perfect for anybody,' Alice recalls, "but even I can remember that I didn't say it with a lot of conviction."

Then Janice met with failure. She experienced disappointment and loss in two crushing blows: Her marriage fell apart under many stresses, including culture clash, and her career took a downturn when she abruptly returned to the United States after a painful divorce.

Brother and sister rallied to her side. They visited often, they filled in with phone calls and letters between visits. They saw their sister hurting, they hurt for her, and they offered their support openly and lovingly, says Alice.

"They seemed to know—even though Mike was only eighteen and Wendy was twenty at the time—how hard a time this was for Janice. They spent so much time hovering and clucking and fussing over her. It comforted me to see them support her so wholeheartedly."

But watching her children interact, Alice recognized another emotion operating, too. "They took a small pleasure in Janice's misfortunes. I had to face the truth: They were a bit glad to see her finally fail at something. Suddenly, she wasn't so perfect anymore. And Mike and Wendy were glad to be in the role of 'good' kids—the ones who were doing everything 'right.' You know, getting into college, having nice friends, all those things that mothers usually approve of."

Summing up the seemingly contradictory emotions her grown children acted out, Alice mused, "I think it was one of those typical situations among brothers and sisters where the love and warmth are genuine, but there's also the all too human pleasure in being able to say, 'Yeah, but you blew it on that one!' "

Alice's vision of what her children were displaying—both sibling rivalry and sibling solidarity, with Mom as the pivot on which that seesaw rose and fell—is one of the most difficult and, paradoxically, one of the most rewarding aspects of second-stage mothering.

What mothers see, they report, is their young adult children relating to each other in a dual pattern woven of both competition and loyalty, the latter sometimes so intense it is almost irrational and is labeled by psychologists the "Hansel and Gretel syndrome."

Mothers report they can see both resentment and love; a conflict-ridden struggle to separate and be individuals, and yet at the very same time, a new willingness to recognize and accept each family's unique bond, and also to gain specific strengths from siblings.

Alice's protest to her younger daughter that Janice was *not* perfect, and that no life proceeds without trouble and disappointments, sounded feeble even to her own ears when Janice was riding so high.

Alice's maternal confession reveals the anguish and delight that are mixed in the souls of mothers who know perfectly well that they played a significant role—though not an all-determining one—in the development of whatever relationships the adult siblings now are working out.

Sibship: New Contender for the Family Spotlight

"Despite the importance of parental behavior, the mere existence of a younger or older sibling in the family is a salient force in the psychological development of the child," wrote Dr. Jerome Kagan.[1]

Yet this force has, until recently, been little studied by family researchers, who have concentrated vastly more attention on the parental, and usually the maternal, influences on the child.

Family therapists who see each member of the family as part of an interactive system have probably come the closest to probing "sibship," but their discipline is relatively new, and the overwhelming focus of expert attention has generally been the shaping role of parents.

Recent studies, some of them only a few years old, have begun to take a hard look at how important and influential sibling relationships really are in people's lives.

This new attention may help the mature mother of adult siblings to recognize the heavy weight of the brothers and sisters in each other's lives, and to better understand her own influence on the scene—an influence that very well may go on to the end of the mother's life, so strong is Mom's role as pivot among the sibs.

Among the contemporary sibling facts of life in our fast-changing era is that brothers and sisters may turn out to be the only people modern men and women can keep as close companions over the whole life span.

Due to high divorce rates, custody battles over children, and the inevitable aging and loss of parents, Americans may find that their nearly-same-age brothers and sisters are mainly the ones who stay the course with them through all their years. Even the geographical separation so common among sibs in mobile America seldom severs the tie completely.

Siblings represent a surrogate parent or a coping resource for each other in times of trouble that researchers are only just now beginning to chart.[2]

In many cultures and in different countries, the presence of siblings can mean actual physical survival for children whose parents are too victimized by illness or poverty to care for them adequately.

But aside from siblings as effective parent substitutes, the poetry of the sibling relationship seems to have to do with stirrings of the self, some memory of their own growing personhood that individuals retain.

While mothers of multiple children seldom articulate this, they often say and do things that show that they sense their stewardship of the group as a fearful and exhausting responsibility. It is the persistence and strength of sibling relationships throughout life that impresses their role on mothers and continues to make the mother influential literally forever.

A leading team of sibling researchers put it this way: "Even though by adulthood most siblings have gradually separated and gone their different ways, the knowledge of each other's core identity remains as a legacy and a reminder of one's childhood past, submerged, unverbalized, and only partially forgotten. *To meet one's brother or sister, even after many years, is to recapture the bittersweet memory of one's own essential childhood self, unmoved by the passage of time.*"[3] (Italics added.)

Looking back to that time of the mother-influenced formation of the essential childhood self, I asked the sample group of mothers to reminisce about that period when they were almost the sole conductors of the sibling orchestra and directed the group's activities from dawn to dusk. (Very often, for women who are middle-aged today, the father was absent at work, creating a child-rearing task sometimes too large for the mother alone and driving the siblings even closer together.)

As mothers recalled that noisy band of small squabblers, they perceived the causes of rivalry among their young children to be (in descending order of importance and frequency):

1. competition for parental attention and approval
2. battles for space, privacy, and/or material possessions
3. competition in school
4. jealousy and envy of one sibling's talents or gifts
5. competition in sports or physical skills

The most important conclusion to emerge from this remembrance of things past was: *Mothers as a group believe that the sibling rivalry continues throughout life, but on different battlegrounds. They say that the competition for parental attention and approval remains the number-one claim for each son and daughter, even when many conflicts are muted and much rivalry is dissipated by time.*

The Ghost in the Works: Favoritism

Many people remember comedian Tommy Smothers's complaint to his brother in their television routines when Tommy would say to Dick, "Mother always liked you best," to explain some daffy quirk. Responsive audience laughter frequently included personal memories of real sibling rivalry, I'm sure.

In part, these memories surface strongly in adults because in an America famous for a spirit of fair play and a liking for the underdog, parents meet contradictory signposts on the road to child-rearing. Along with the keen traditional desire for even-handed justice, team effort, and equal opportunity for all, there are also visible remnants of the old frontier values of rugged individualism, cutthroat competition, and an "only the strong survive" kind of ethos as well.

Because of these cultural contradictions, plus the reality that there are few standard models for socializing children for satisfying sibships, both parents (but more strongly the mother) send these kinds of mixed messages when the children are growing up[4]:

- Be close, but distant enough to be separate and distinct individuals.
- Be loving, but don't become intensely or sexually involved.
- Be cooperative, but don't become dependent on each other.
- Be loyal, but not in preference to caring about your parents.
- Be admiring, but don't let your sibling take advantage of you.
- Be competitive, but don't dominate.
- Be aggressive, but not ruthless.
- Be tolerant, but defend your own point of view.

Imposed on this chaos is another influence, the mother's own sibling history. If she regards it as warm and rewarding, she will try to reproduce it among her children. If it was traumatic or less than satisfying, she'll try to field the team in such a way as to avoid what she remembers as negative, in spite of her attachment to values of family unity and loyalty above all.

In addition to the lack of helpful standards for sibs (Cain and Abel are not exactly what most mothers have in mind), women said that a far worse problem for them is the difficult reality of their tendency to favor one child over another.

Virtually every mother interviewed reflected in some way the feeling that she had been fighting a lifelong battle to avoid the appearance of favoritism (even if she actually was drawn more to one child than another).

By far the largest majority of the group (close to 70 percent) declared themselves to have failed at one time or another in the impossible task of always dispensing fairness and justice to each sibling.

While psychologists and family life experts study the favoritism phenomenon clinically, women themselves carry a pitiable load of sadness and guilt when they think favoritism has adversely affected their kids.

"I always felt that my daughter was my husband's child—she was so like him—and that our son was more mine—he was so cute and appealing—but it was wrong to let the kids feel this. I know it was bad—wrong, wrong, wrong," mourns a 59-year-old mother of two who now sees deep unhappiness in her daughter's personal life, with drugs, divorce, and alcoholism all included in the young woman's emotional landscape. Sensibly or not, the mother feels that her favoring the son does, to some degree, make her the one responsible for the young woman's difficulties. At the same time, the mother is able to derive considerable solace from the fact that now, as two adults close in age, the unhappy young woman and the favored brother have quite a warm relationship, and there is even the possibility that he may be of considerable help in her struggles with her personal demons.

There is little doubt that parents, teachers, sometimes grandparents or aunts and uncles, have played wicked roles in comparing, favoring, threatening one child with another, planting and encouraging bitter feelings of rivalry that sometimes last throughout life.

Many sibling researchers, while not condoning or excusing such behavior, have pointed out that the concrete reality of each child being so different in appearance, style, personality, intelligence, skills, and talents should—instead of intimidating and confusing parents—help them adjust to the truth: Each child is markedly different from each other child in a number of ways that are not under the parent's control.

One way is the manner in which the roll of the genetic dice dictates that one child shall be beautiful, another plain, one child have a physical defect, another be stunningly whole.

Another critical way in which each child is bound to differ from its siblings is that the parents (especially the mother) are actually different persons operating in a different family environment as each child comes along. No matter how similarly each mother thinks she is behaving with each child, she is actually at a different point in her life and in the family's history with each. The real picture was outlined by psychiatrist Alfred Adler when he said: "The situation is never the same for two children in a family and each child will show in his style of life the results of his attempt to adapt himself to his peculiar circumstances."[5]

The peculiar circumstances that spring from each child's order in the birth hierarchy were responsible for one of the most surprising conclusions in the whole discussion with mothers on the favoritism problem: *Mothers reported that they found their children's birth order to be* **more important** *in their relationship than the gender of the child.*

This would seem likely to contradict the widespread and rather mushy notion that mothers can, say, talk more easily about intimate matters to daughters than to sons or that, conversely, they tend to favor sons over daughters. The women interviewed in this sample said the questions of whom they confided in more easily or whom they favored had a lot more to do with the child's own personality and spot in the family constellation than whether the child was a son or daughter.

About 67 percent of the women interviewed said that they thought firstborns were often more difficult to understand than their younger siblings, that last children often had a slant to their personalities different from earlier ones, and so on. In other words, a large majority of the mothers felt that birth order, and all the maternal experience and feeling that come with it, was highly significant in shaping their relationships.

An extreme version of this was acted out in what might have been an amusing situation, but turned out painfully for a set of sons who are fraternal twins.

From somewhere (their mother, Alexandra L., is not sure to this day where they got the information), one twin, Sean, learned that his brother James was born first, a very few minutes before himself. For Sean, this meant that Jim was the "oldest" and therefore would be, according to some twin lore he picked up, the strongest, the smartest, the most favored by their parents.

"For years," recounts their mother, "we could see that Sean was giving himself an inferiority problem with Jim, in spite of our treating them, we thought, quite equally. In fact, just because they are twins, we thought it was a snap to treat them in

identical ways. To us, they *both* were firstborns, especially since
we had a single child a few years later who, to us, was clearly the
second-born.

"But no," she sighs, "life doesn't let you get away with anything so easy. The twins managed to establish a birth order
between the two of them, and Sean was in junior high and deep
into adolescent turmoil before we learned what he'd been carrying around all those years—and by then, there wasn't much we
could do to reassure him that we never thought of Jim as being
'ahead' of him in any way. He left for college eventually and the
best thing for him has just been the ability to go to a different
school and work out a separate identity from his brother."

Alexandra is an exception to most of the mothers interviewed
in that she doesn't feel excessively guilty over Sean's self-
imposed second-born status (which children frequently translate into "second best"), but she does admit that she and the
twins' father probably placed too much reliance on the accident
of twinship to avoid birth-order problems of jealousy and rivalry.

Since children do vary in temperament, abilities, and personality, parents would be far better advised, say sibling experts
Steven Bank and Michael Kahn, not to try to hide those truths
from themselves or the children. Instead, they should strive for
balance in their praise and censure of each child, choosing what's
best about each at different times and in differing situations.[6]

One of the most discouraging truths that's been revealed by
current sibling investigations is this: No matter how parents
struggle toward that holy grail of perfect justice and fairness,
and even when they occasionally achieve unusually even-handed
handling of the sibs, each child will still *perceive* the parents as
favoring one of the others, anyway![7]

This finding from sibling research should encourage parents
to realize that "overall fairness" is the best that a parent can
hope for, say Bank and Kahn.

The mothers who discussed this part of the problem agreed
that balance was a goal they found easier and more effective to
pursue now that the children are adult, because the differences
in life-style and patterns are clearer, and life directions are
becoming more specific for each child (see "Sibling Cohesive-
ness," pages 109–112).

Mothers as "Conflictophobes"

One thing was forbidden. Any fighting among ourselves was
punished consistently and severely—no listening to "she did
this" or that. We were to protect each other, they seemed to
say, for who else would? So we bit and scratched each other at
night in bed under the covers, hiding the marks from our mothers.

JOAN CHASE, *During the Reign of the Queen of Persia*

Another problem—or perhaps a different facet of the favoritism
guilt—is that a very large group of women in the respondent
sample of mothers were and remain "conflictophobes"—
women who greatly fear conflict and overt fighting among their
children.

Mothers report this was true when the children were little and
remains true now that they are adult. The mothers struggle
ceaselessly to mute the rivalry and support any emerging signs
of friendship, and they are often deeply sad and sometimes
panicked at the sign of serious quarrels—or even just spiteful
needling—among their children.

A good many mothers—more than 60 percent—confessed
themselves surprised, in varying degrees, that indeed the primal
issue of "Whom does Mom love best?" still underlies quarrels
and strains among the adult siblings and remains a question they
must continue to deal with.

The weariness mothers feel in the face of their self-imposed
demand to continue fighting against favoritism and to balance
attention and praise is partially based on what they had already
been through when the children were small. "Settling fights
among the children" was listed by 58 percent of the mothers
queried as one of the heaviest work loads of mothering when the
youngsters were little. Mothers said that fighting among the
siblings caused as much hard work as "caring for sick children"
or "managing to give each child enough personal attention,"
both of which were at the top of the list of the hardest mothering
jobs.

One of the main reasons women take this assignment so seriously is because they interpret sibling discord as a sign of im-

proper mothering. If the children fought when they were youngsters, why did not Mother develop loyalty and harmony in the
household? If they compete when grown, she sees it as her
failure to manufacture the family glue.

Many women hinted, while others said straightforwardly and
candidly, that their worst nightmare was that after they were
gone, the siblings would abandon one another or drift apart,
uncaring and unmindful of their past, their special tie. Mothers
dread the notion that the children would be indifferent to their
life's work—the building of the family.

Sadly, the "peace at any price" atmosphere many mothers
insisted on when the children were small often does make the
siblings drift apart later because there are too many unresolved
conflicts and it seems too difficult to begin to work them out in
later life.

The fear of this failure can make the mother redouble her
efforts to quell favoritism and rivalry, but in the face of continual
and inevitable defeat in the battle against favoritism, many
women handle their fear of sibling conflict by simply denying
the fact of sibling rivalry. The denial, both to herself and to
others, is frequently phrased: "My children are not rivalrous or
competitive; therefore I have not failed in any aspect of fostering
the proper sibling relationship."

In fact, six women in the group said that their children had
never had any kind of rivalry at all, while all the rest noticed
some form of competition, however mild.

Of the six who reported that no such thing as sibling rivalry
existed in their families, four were special situations in which the
children either were raised in remote rural areas with few or no
outside playmates or were living overseas in foreign countries.
In these strange cultures, as in early immigrant families, the
siblings were forced to cling together for comfort and familiarity
in a strange place.

Two mothers of the six had no particular explanation for how
their children avoided rivalry, but were nonetheless firm in saying that they had never witnessed any competitiveness among
their multiple children.

Most experts are convinced, however, that a total absence of
rivalrous feelings—even if only occasional—is unlikely or extremely rare.

Mothers who can be classified as "conflictophobes" are often so frantic to avoid quarrels between their children that they even anticipate them ahead of time, and whether consciously or not, they actually amplify conflict by jumping into the fray just as it begins.

Experts who have observed conflict-anxious mothers say they are actually driven by two forces: one, a discouraged sense of defeat and failure in the face of the impossible tasks of trying to be eternally and forever fair and just; and two, a subtle but real feeling of hostility toward one child or another.

So the conflict-amplifying mother just gives up the struggle to be Queen Solomon and, whether aware of it or not, gives vent to her feelings toward one or another of the children in a way that underlines the perpetual struggle among the children to find out whom Mom really does love best!

Three mothers in the group confessed openly to favoring one child over another and to having contributed to quarrels and struggles among multiple children. Most women interviewed, however, consciously believed themselves to be constantly attempting to smother the flames of conflict, even though teachers, camp counselors, and others had told them that it is normal and maybe even helpful, in many ways, for siblings to work out their problems alone as long as health and safety are not endangered. One of the saddest aspect of the life of the "conflictophobe" mother is that she may be worrying about fantasies and ghosts; sibling rivalry may not be nearly so serious a problem as she may fear.

Contemporary observers of family interactions have said they think there is a tendency to overstate the role of rivalry as a negative force and that what looks like competition may just be dependency or the need for an intense relationship with a brother or sister, since sibling struggles do add motivation, spice, and continuing contact to each sibling's life.[8]

Though this calm and plausible approach to sibling rivalry may sound sensible, there were very few mothers in the respondent group who could bring themselves to accept and act on the notion that sibling rivalry may not be as seriously negative as they think; they said they thought they would always monitor closely the eternal triangle of which they know they are the third side.

This lifelong triangular relationship—Mom between two siblings or two teams of siblings if the family is large—is always visible to the mother because she has been the closest observer as toddler fights over toys and candy give way to adult competition in new arenas.

These new battlegrounds to which Mom must shift her attention include competition in the areas of attractiveness, popularity, ability to choose a "suitable" (whatever that means to mothers) mate, career and financial achievements, and the founding of the son's or daughter's own family.

Clearly, for *all* mothers, whether they fear conflict or not, the rivalry now is distinguished by the camouflage of decorum, "adult" behavior, and sophisticated psychological games. Indeed, whole battles can go on over Mom's head without her hearing so much as the click of a trigger, so easily do adult children now outmaneuver her alertness to signs of tension or strain among the kids.

A good illustration of this is how one mother was "set up" in the continuing battle among four sisters: The two older sisters had formed a loose alliance against the two younger, particularly the third daughter. All four were constantly looking for Mom to be "on their side," but as the adult years stretched out and the eldest was nearing 40, it most frequently seemed to be a pitched battle between the older twosome and the younger twosome, despite an earlier history when the first and second daughters scrapped between themselves.

The two older daughters, as they grew into their thirties, each suffered unhappy, childless marriages and then divorces—events that served to unite them and make them even more sharply critical of how their siblings fared in this important area of life.

They began to specialize in needling the third sister, who had adopted, a bit ostentatiously, the role of "earth mother" for the whole family, having four babies in a short time, staying in an intact marriage, and thus presenting a suggestion to the mother that at least one daughter was doing things right.

When the third sister had her most recent baby, she chose to have it at home, without the conventional physician in attendance and with some family and friends present. In addition, she informed the eldest sister she was going to use her money gift to plant a fruit tree in the new baby's honor, also planting with the tree the placenta she and her husband had saved when the baby was born.

The eldest sister, not unaware that this would strike their highly conventional mother as an inappropriate use of the money (though the act is not unknown among younger parents), carefully reported the placenta/tree plan to her mother. As expected, Mom was manipulated into trying to explain and defend: "There's something wrong with those two younger ones," she said on hearing the story. "It must have been the cesareans!"

The eldest reported this to her ally sister with glee, and the two of them so enjoyed the triumph of getting Mom on their side once more, that one could only guess that Mom had been ambushed in the sibling wars.

But quite a few women among the interviewees reported that in this second stage of motherhood, they are learning more quickly and a little more clearly their functions as catalysts for the competition and are beginning to get a feel for who is shooting at whom and sometimes even why. Even if Mom misses a few of the frontline skirmishes, she follows the general progress of the war; she learns to follow the shifts of alliances and the reasons behind the flare-ups of tension.

"My daughter Gail, who's twenty-three now, loves her two younger brothers, who are eighteen and nineteen, like mad," confides Thelma G., a fifty-eight-year-old widow and mother of three. "When she talks to them on the phone, you can tell they really like and enjoy one another—that they are getting to be friends. But when they're all home together on a visit, it doesn't take long for the sniping to start. Suddenly she doesn't like the way Billy chews his dinner or she'll say to Mark, 'Have you washed that sweater in the last ten years?' She becomes a real pest."

Thelma says she thinks she is beginning to understand a little of what's going on beneath the petty nit-picking.

"When the boys come home, I love to cook their favorite dishes for them," Thelma explains. "I spend my life in the kitchen whenever they are around. But Gail is always on a diet, which means she can't enjoy the food, and so she gets left out of that part of the mothering I still can do for the boys. I have to work hard to find ways of making it up to her, and believe me, she's very aware of the score. I hate cats, but one time I told her I'd babysit for her cats so she could take a weekend ski trip with some friends. She said to me, 'Gee, you wouldn't even do that for Mark!' "

Thelma's alertness to her daughter's score-keeping is, at its root, part of her fondest hope that Gail and her brothers will always remain close and that she will in no way encourage any rivalry or rift among them.

A different version of this concern is obvious in another mother's story as follows:

Sandra and Judy, the 26- and 29-year-old daughters of a successful businesswoman, Jane R., told their mother on a bright spring day that they were about to launch a new family venture: they were making plans to go into business together, following in their mother's dynamic footsteps in the beauty and fashion field.

They had a great idea, they said, for a new kind of beauty boutique, and they described it with bubbling excitement to their mother at lunch one day.

The young women said they thought they could swing the venture without financial help from their parents, but would seek advice and suggestions. Sandra hugged her mother warmly and said, "After all, Mom, you're the pro and we're just novices."

Facing the flushed, pretty faces of her two daughters—pink from luncheon cocktails, skillful makeup, and their own high hopes—Jane, also the mother of a 30-year-old lawyer son, found herself oddly reluctant to join in their buoyant enthusiasm.

Was it hidden competitiveness she felt with her daughters? She seriously considered the possibility, but discarded it because she was more than satisfied with her business success and had actually been thinking recently of easing up and returning to lifelong interests in art and music.

If not a hidden personal reason, what could it be? She hid these puzzling feelings of uncertainty and joined in the planning with what she believes her daughters accepted as interested participation.

But later she mused aloud: "Why was I feeling so unsure? I thought it all out and realized that it was *not* concern about a business failure. They were young enough so that wouldn't be devastating, and each has a degree in business administration so they'd probably always have a decent job. The money wasn't a problem either. So why was I dragging my feet?"

Jane describes the light dawning: "It came to me in a flash as I walked back to my office. I was afraid the venture, if it didn't work, would hurt or maybe even destroy one of my fondest joys: the really loving relationship my two girls have! I couldn't bear the idea that anything might drive them apart or make them less loving and caring for each other—nothing, nothing would be worth that to me. No business success, or even the lessons of a failure, would be worth it. What if they quarreled, had a falling out over business matters, or didn't speak and became estranged? I'd be heart-broken."

Jane and her husband worried the problem for a couple of weeks while Sandra and Judy, unaware, steamed ahead on their new project. The parents finally decided to discuss their concerns in some gentle, understated way with both young women at an opportune moment.

Such a moment did present itself not long after, and to Jane's immense relief and a joy so deep it overflowed in tears, both daughters explained quite calmly and with a soothing certainty that they had discussed that possibility and had agreed that even if a quarrel or a falling out did take place, their mother surely knew that it could not be permanent, and that eventually their tie would reassert itself. "Even if we got mad and didn't talk for a year or had a lot of clashes of will or personality, still, in the end, we'd be back together. You know that, Mom!" said Sandra. "I'm surprised you could even think it would ruin us *for good,*" said Judy. "You know that wouldn't happen—aw, c'mon Mom, *you know that.*"

Comrades in the Trenches: Sibling Cohesiveness

The profound sense of *safety*—nothing would destroy the circle of five that Jane had put before her work, even sometimes before her marriage—was part of the flooding happiness and relief that Jane felt after her daughters' response to her gingerly handling of the conflict issue.

Her feelings of safety, relief, and joy are typical of what women report frequently as they reach the stage in life where they can observe the gladdening new things happening between the children: They are becoming comrades and friends in life's battles.

Once the siblings have been away from home for a couple of years or longer, the mothers begin to see that the brothers and sisters often show signs of starting to like one another, to notice things about one another for the first time. They "begin to understand each other as people, not just nuisances, rivals, or part of the furniture," as one mother put it.

The mothers see their adult children getting out into the world and discovering its dangers and challenges more directly, and as this happens, report the mothers, the children become kinder, more sympathetic, and more understanding, one to another. They begin, in short, to form the age-old kin network of mutual support and assistance that can operate for them for the rest of their lives.

Several of our middle-aged interviewees who have either lived through a divorce themselves or been witnesses to their children's divorces, or both, became aware in recent years that this mutual assistance unit the siblings are forming may become ever more important as their children struggle with the new households and convoluted remarried families of the 1980s and 1990s.

Edith L., the 60-year-old mother of four children, was worried that Tom, her second son, might be facing a painful and bitter divorce as his marital woes mounted and his small daughter began showing worrisome symptoms of stress from the tense family atmosphere.

"So you can imagine how I felt," says Edith, "when one day, after Tom had been visting my husband and me and his closest sister, Prue [Tom and Prue are the middle children in the quartet], he was walking out to his car, looking dejected and troubled at having to return home, and I saw Prue run after him and hug him good-bye again, and I heard her say, 'Now, remember, Tom, you know I'm here for you. If I can help, just call. Don't give me the stuff about not wanting to bother me with your troubles—*just call me,* hear?' "

Even though the vignette Edith saw and heard had occurred

two years earlier, it was emblazoned on her memory as vividly as though she had seen and heard it a moment before, and she wept with bittersweet joy while retelling it.

These scenes are particularly precious to the second-stage mother because the earlier days when the children fought so bitterly remain fresh scars to her.

One mother watched with bewildered pleasure while her two sons, who had fought over every bike and hockey stick for years when they shared a bedroom, and seemed to genuinely hate each other every minute they were at home together, began to call each other after college and make appointments to play tennis or have lunch together.

Another mother watches an older son whom she once believed would gladly have donated his little sister to the Salvation Army begin to take an interest in her secretarial school training and to give her advice on job-hunting.

The mother's journey toward understanding and accepting the idea that solidarity can surface as fast as rivalry was described clearly by Katherine S., a mother of two daughters now 26 and 31.

"It was awful!" she says. "They were always scratching and biting—even up to the early teen years. They were nasty, naughty little girls to each other. Later, they just got nasty with their mouths. Now, when the girls are together at our family gatherings four or five times a year, they get along okay! They even seek each other out and spend time alone together. It makes me so happy, I'm just delirious—I can't tell you how good it makes me feel. I think it's wonderful, too, that it's happening while they're young."

The sheer exuberant joy and forthright pride that mothers can feel when they see friendship and affection between their children is echoed in these comments:

"Wow!" wrote one mother. "That's how I feel when I look at them together. Look what my husband and I have accomplished —they're just such great people!"

"As the years go by, I see more love and understanding and far less competition," wrote another, and a third said, in a group discussion with other mothers, "You know, sometimes I get scared—I have an old-fashioned, superstitious shudder of fear when I see them all together with their wives and husbands and

their own kids. I feel they're so beautiful and such fun together
—even with the needles they zing at each other sometimes—that
I get afraid they'll make the gods jealous!''

Who's on First? Friends and Rivals Among Sibs

> Even siblings who prefer not to confront their ambivalence
> probably do not wholly escape its effects. Whatever its nature
> in particular cases—warm or cool—the sibling relationship re-
> mains alive in some sense. . . .
>
> *Psychology Today,* June 1981

We asked a number of mothers which was stronger as their
children move into their twenties and thirties, the rivalry or the
solidarity?

"Well, I'm not sure," says Lorraine M., 55-year-old mother of
two sons and a 24-year-old daughter. "I'd like to think that just
in the past year, the solidarity, the friendship, has gained the
edge, but . . ." her voice trails off, then she adds, "after all, it
can't be an accident that the boys are essentially in the same
field!"

Her two sons, Richard and Jerry, are both schoolteachers.
Rick, 31, is an assistant principal in a small suburban school and
Jerry, 29, is a math teacher in a large city public school.

"Whenever Rick would call us up for a sort of telephone visit
[both sons live in the Far West, the parents in Chicago], he'd
always refer to Jerry's teaching in a kind of quasi father way. He
seemed to be saying, 'Hey, Mom and Dad, look, I'm bringing
Jerry right along and he's doing fine.'

"But then," says Lorraine, knitting her brow and frowning,
"when Jerry got that National Science Foundation scholarship
to do some advance math work at a big university one summer,
Ricky would make the kind of kidding jokes that made me wonder if he was worried about his brother catching up and passing
him somewhere along in the world of school that's important to
both of them.

"And then, too," the mother points out, "the battling also
continues; they snipe at each other over choice of cars, live-in

girlfriends, and even clothes. But then, just when I'm feeling blue about what seem like nasty little quarrels between them all the time, and fear of each other's competition, something wonderful will happen. They'll come home for vacations or a visit or Christmas and they'll sit with us in front of the fireplace, discussing, sharing, talking, seriously exchanging ideas about their work and about education in general—they make us so proud! They know a lot, they respect each other, they each seem able to make a real contribution. It makes their dad and me just feel so great, it's fantastic!"

Rick and Jerry's younger sister, Dorothy, has handled her competition with her brothers in what her mother feels is a complicated but on balance rather healthy fashion. Lorraine was one of the few mothers who would claim even a modest amount of credit for this for herself, saying only that she had "worked hard" at the task of helping Dorothy keep from feeling overwhelmed by the boys. Lorraine says this job was greatly aided by Dorothy being the only daughter, and each family member taking their own pleasure in her femaleness.

With both brothers planted firmly in the world of education and academics, Dorothy opted for the creative world of theater and dance, where advanced degrees and time in the classroom are not so imperative.

"She hasn't withdrawn from competition completely," explains Lorraine, "because she fully expects to gain recognition, maybe even fame, as an actress-dancer, but she's chosen a completely different battlefield for the sibling wars and one on which the boys do not compete. Interestingly, the theater was an early love of mine, and she knows she is more fully acting out *my* fantasy life than the boys ever did, because neither I nor their father ever aspired to our sons' world.

"Dorothy talks about her own choices in a rather direct and cheerful way," reports the mother. "She'll often say something like 'Well, it's a good thing the boys are in a pretty secure kind of work so they can be helpful to you and Dad when you get older, because you know how long it takes to make a dime in the theater, Mom.' I think when she talks like that, she's really saying, 'Well, I may not have as much steadiness as a schoolteacher, but you'll be proud of me one day, anyway.'"

Perhaps because Dorothy's choice of work is so very different from her brothers', or perhaps because she's not a same-sex rival, the brothers seem able to take a wholehearted pride in her attempts to break into the tough world of the theater. Their mother reports they are interested in her friends and life-style, and seldom burden her with the day-to-day sniping that was so typical of their lives at home as young children.

When Lorraine reviews all this, she sighs and says, "I don't know—let's just hope!"

Another mother, Lucille T., when trying to separate the strands of affection from those of envy that entwine her two sons, 31 and 28, said: "I think the rivalry and the friendship are almost equally strong, with one winning out one time and one another. Sometimes it makes me feel like a Ping-Pong ball batted back and forth between them."

The ambivalence many grown children show is partly a reflection of how they read their ups and downs in the graph chart of mother's attention, esteem, and approval. It becomes particularly pointed when there is a major event in the family's life, such as the birth of children to the young adult generation. This milestone offers a new and peculiarly satisfying arena in which siblings may indulge this ambivalence, to compete and yet not endanger their comradeship at the same time.

A sibling, I learned from some of the interviewee mothers, is never so righteous or lofty as when criticizing a brother's or sister's handling of his or her own children. Yet, wonderful to behold, this criticism does not have to interfere substantially with sibling solidarity because the critic seldom makes the complaints to the brother or sister—it's usually to Mother!

In the written questionnaire they filled out, several of the mothers said they usually avoid discussing critical differences of philosophy about child-rearing with their grown children so that key differences in approach would not become a constant source of tension.

But, reported the mothers, other siblings sense when the mother is concerned and they cunningly play on the maternal fears that one adult son or daughter is not handling his own children correctly.

Even though several of our mother interviewees confessed

they listen with "more than half an ear" to the way in which one sibling downgrades another's parental performance, still most mothers said they felt intuitively that the criticizing sibling was not truly concerned that nieces and nephews were actually going to be warped beyond repair or made unfit to live in society. No, suggested one mother, "It's more a case that sister X has given brother Y another perch from which to take a couple of shots."

A good example of this was an incident that one of the respondent mothers wrote out on the back of her questionnaire. Adele K., mother of two daughters, one of whom is married and has two little boys, describes a classic case of one daughter being unable to pass up a chance to take a crack at the other, even though the sisters are close and loving.

"Joanna, the elder, always makes a fantastic Easter feast for us all because I do Christmas," explained Adele, "and this year she outdid herself with gourmet dishes—a glazed ham with decorations like you see in the magazines, a souffle like air, and homemade pastries from different countries. We had a wonderful time, but I have to admit that Joanna's two little sons are holy terrors. At four and five, they simply cannot sit still and no dinner where they are is ever very peaceful.

"And this Easter was no exception. The little boys tore the place apart. It was hard to concentrate on the good meal on the table, though Karen, our younger daughter, their aunt, tried to distract the boys and calm them down. But we all know how active children this age are, and we didn't think too much about the noise and spilled milk that went along with the great dishes Joanna was putting on the table.

"But as we were driving Karen back to her apartment afterward," says Adele, "Karen just couldn't resist sniffing, 'If only Joanna could control those kids better and wasn't so permissive, we'd all appreciate the gourmet cooking a little more.'

"I had to smile to myself," wrote Adele, "because I knew she'd never say that to Joanna. She adores those boys, loves being generous Auntie, and is truly proud of her sister's cooking skill. It was just a chance to catch Mom's ear at a tired moment when I had my guard down. I don't let it bother me—most of the time."

Judge and Jury Forever

What do mothers feel now as they continue to try to mute the rivalry and encourage the solidarity among their adult children? The mixture of feelings mothers reported included these:

• Plenty of ambivalence on their own part about how much, when, and whether they want to be involved in sibling tensions.

• Fairly considerable emotional fatigue, based on years of refereeing.

• Residual guilt about real or fancied favoritism.

• Profound relief and sweet pleasure when the solidarity emerges without their needing to push it along.

Often, as the rivalry ebbs and flows, shifts in intensity, and focuses on different issues and events, a mother learn from this changing pattern a great deal about how the children feel about themselves, their life choices, their shortcomings, and about what they continue to need from her to keep their self-esteem intact.

In spite of feelings of exhaustion and depression that continued rivalry can cause, she also values the feedback and the glimpse into her children's lives provided by the varied manifestations of the sibling situation. She discovers things about the roots of long-standing jealousies she once was too distracted by the more immediate physical tasks of mothering to see, and now she can begin to understand how those translate into her children's adult lives, reflecting their picture of themselves back to her.

A poignant look into this mirror was given by Fran W., the mother of four children, all well past the first year or two of separation from home.

"About a year ago," she says, "I was going to give my corner china cupboard to my son Dave, twenty-five, and his wife. I didn't want it in my dining room anymore, and I thought they might like to have it for their house. Bob, twenty-six, got very upset. He said I shouldn't give it away, and that if I did, Dave was the person who least deserved it of the four children because he is the one, Bob said, who does the least for me. I was quite surprised. The cupboard is not anything special; you can buy one like it anywhere. Bob didn't want it for himself. He just didn't want me to give it to Dave. Well, since I hadn't yet mentioned it to Dave, I just kept it myself. But the incident told me something about my children."

Fran explains the underlying feelings this way: "All four of my children have gone in very different directions so far in life. Bob has impressed us all by heading for the priesthood at a fine Jesuit institution and is now getting an advanced degree in philosophy, but Dave was quite different. His way of being the 'good son' was to go into the family auto business, get married, and give us the only grandchildren we have—two beautiful little girls. The other two, Carl and Mary, are also doing well. When Mary finishes school, she'll probably have her own place, too. But at the moment, all the children envy Dave those lovely little daughters, even though when Mary looks at Dave's married life, she sees tedium."

Fran believes that Dave's daughters are part of the key to the corner cupboard mystery. "It occurred to me," she says, "that the ordinary cupboard was a painful symbol of the things that Bob's own life choice does not include if he continues in the priesthood—domestic living, autonomy, and children of his own —all things that win a great deal of motherly approval for Dave."

This motherly approval is getting easier, though, in second-stage mothering as each child shows the world—and the mother —more activities and accomplishments, even if it's just giving up smoking or learning a new skill, not to mention major steps in work and family life. It becomes easier for mothers to reach that elusive goal of balance in the sibling wars and to find more things in each child's life to praise and enjoy, now that the group is not piled atop one another, all shouting at once for maternal attention.

After all, mothers have been the yardstick of success for children since before memory: They served as the judge in the everyday contests through all the childhood years. Women find now, that even though their children are in their twenties and thirties and forties, they are still not allowed to step down from the bench.

As long as she lives, the mother's approval continues to be the yardstick by which children measure themselves against one another, and she learns, she says, that she must dole out her love and approval, her praise and criticism to her 30-year-old and her 25-year-old as carefully and fairly as she parceled out cookies and finger paints to her preschoolers.

When Parents Die: The Sibling Choice

Perhaps the major reason mothers take so seriously the job of strengthening the sibling network is that, among other reasons, it frees them for old age and death.

The mothers talking about this issue all were perfectly aware of the fact, commented on by monitors of social trends in this country, that in mobile, individualistic America, each sibling is completely free to choose whether to stay within his family network or not after the second parent dies. While the parents, or even one, is alive, most siblings still see their son/daughter/brother/sister roles as closely linked.

But their roles as children—albeit adult children—end when both parents are gone.

The mother worries: What then?

Each son and daughter can choose: Shall they go on as a cohesive set of comrades, recalling family ties and their unique legacy, or drift apart, or stay apart because of past hurts and troubles that were never resolved?

In the respondent group of women, many hinted that though they can't really think directly of their own deaths, they do feel a sense of unfocused relief when they see signs of sibling solidarity. In addition to keeping the family intact, it seems to suggest that whatever happens, their children will not be left to wander alone in an empty world.

By far the largest majority of women (more than 80 percent) said they felt a "strong probability" that "in the crunch" the children would not abandon each other or let any real harm come to their brothers and sisters if they could help it.

But mothers remain so tense about this great freedom of choice siblings will have when they are gone that many think it their responsibility to strengthen the friendships, support the assistance networks, and mute the rivalry—even beyond the grave!

It was this kind of responsibility that made Rowena J., mother of a son and a daughter, tell how she had been asked by her son whether she would be buried with her diamond engagement ring.

"When he asked me that," says Rowena, "I realized that the children were becoming aware of what you might call the estate, mighty modest as it is, and I told him absolutely not, that the diamond would go into a chalice for the church. I don't want my kids fighting over material possessions when I'm gone. It's a problem I've discussed with lots of my friends. In fact, it's one of the leading topics lately among those of us in late middle age."

Rowena's fear that her children might quarrel over her belongings after her death was an echo of all the years of the triangle we examined earlier, and that fear found a strong response among many of our interviewees.

Most of the mothers readily understood that an inexpensive piece of jewelry or a pair of tarnished, battered candlesticks could have as much meaning as possessions of greater intrinsic value in the eyes of sons and daughters, depending on their symbolic worth.

One of the respondent women told a story of how her Russian immigrant grandmother had given away the family's prize copper samovar, with matching tray and cups, to the metal scrap drive in the United States during World War II.

"She said she did it," reports Sarah F., who was her eldest grandchild, "for patriotic reasons, to show how Americanized the family had become, but you'll never convince me. I think she did it to avoid what she feared would be a bitter fight after her death! The fight among her three children for her approval had been so strong throughout their lives that even when the three siblings were in their *seventies,* they still had sharp words over who did the most for Mamma!

"I know," concludes Sarah, "because my mother was the only daughter and I heard the words whizzing overhead throughout my childhood and right up to the funerals of my mom and her aging brothers and their wives. They had a really bad case of the 'sibbles,' as my married son calls the fights between his two little ones."

A Footnote

Among the recent research on siblings that tends to show that mothers may be worrying too much about the destructive effects of sibling rivalry is a study of the less-known brothers and sisters of famous people.[9]

It was found that the siblings of high achievers have not at all, for the most part, been destroyed by their sibs' accomplishments, but describe instead the inspiration and "pride of clan" they've enjoyed, along with perfectly ordinary fights and reconciliations with siblings.

"I believe people have avoided studying grown siblings because they expected the outcome to be negative—on the Cain and Abel model," says Professor Michael Lewis, director of the Institute for the Study of Exceptional Children at the Educational Testing Service in Princeton, New Jersey, "but the college students I've talked to convince me that siblings make profound positive effects on our lives. These effects can range from teaching younger siblings to tell time to helping them make friends and shaping their own self-image."

One mother who talked about her three daughters' relationship enthusiastically agreed. She believes that the way the young women taught each other about makeup, hair styles, and good grooming habits during their early teens helped each of them to weather the stormy insecurities of adolescence much better.

"And let's face it," she says wryly, "even when they fought among themselves, they always knew who the real enemy was: It was me! And when they needed to, they stuck together as thick as thieves and presented a solid, united front I couldn't coax or force apart. I usually gave in and let them have the black dress that was too old even for the oldest!"

In this area of family life, as in so many others, the heavy weight of the sibling pattern lodges somewhere in the middle of the mother's soul. It enriches her while it worries her; it is the source of some of her deepest satisfactions and profoundest rewards, while she keeps a wary eye out to dampen down any rivalrous flames.

It is one more reason why most mothers know that the door banging after the first departure is not at all the end of the story; she knows they'll all come home again, often together, to share their secret knowledge of each other's deepest childhood self and to restage, as long as the mother is alive, the eternal triangle.

BROTHERS AND SISTERS
by Kathleen Cushman

Big, and Little, we were two camps under the same command,
jealous of privilege, rations, uniform, but marked
by the brands we all shared: a last name, bones,
freckles, our mother's voice, the same books
. . . And, suddenly,

we are all the same age—all grown:
bearing the marks of each other's teeth, stretched out
into crazy patterns still branding us, our alliances
shifting, old enmities subdued and new ones born
to burn fiercely into the family flesh—

       no one else
is to know all this but us; even love
will not initiate the outsider; it is a closed club,
speaks its secret language,
the password less than a flicker of the eyelid,
knowing, impenetrable, beyond influence.

6

The Family Gathering: An Anxious Harvest

*W*hen women gather their adult children around them for holidays or a family reunion, a wedding or a funeral, they enter a magnetic field of heightened intensity different from the emotional coloration of everyday life.

In these more vivid moments, women experience a sharp swirl of emotions:

Anticipation. Won't it be wonderful to see our sons and daughters, to touch and hug them, and see the expressions on their faces, so long denied on the telephone?

Apprehension. They've gone so far away, physically and mentally, how will I know them? How can we connect again on a different level? Will they regress to being kids again and will I regress to bossing them? How in the world do I entertain them?

Practical concerns. Where will everybody sleep? How many cars will we need to meet everyone?

Joyful jitters. Here they are! My badge of honor, the dividends on my investment, and a minefield of possible worry, disappointment, or guilt!

What mothers feel at such moments is their own peculiar maternal version of responses common to all human beings when significant rites and ceremonies loom up out of the ordinary run of days.

Today's mature women stand much more often (because of their longevity) at gatherings where pride of family meets religion, patriotism, personal rituals, and a host of other mythic occasions.

As a result, mothers of adult children generally are the priest-ess-celebrants of the symbols and the dramas through which humankind eternally has tried to understand the mystery of existence, to make sense of the world, and to imbue life with meaning and value.

Not only are mothers the keepers of the keys that unlock each family's home for the great return when the children come back, but they are also the main carriers of the family's racial, ethnic, religious, and cultural customs, even as they typically embroider these customs with designs of their own invention.

In discussions and interviews, and in long thoughtful letters, mothers described the knowledge they've gained through years of family gatherings, a body of knowledge that professional anthropologists have confirmed over decades of field studies.

The main vision women report about these mythic times when the family is reunited is that the occasion functions as a shield, a fortress—however temporary, however costly in time, energy, and money—behind which can be strengthened and affirmed the existence of the family with its special flavor, history, and character. Even noncommunal rituals, specific to only one family, serve this fleeting function.

"The common aim of ritual," wrote one anthropologist, "is to make manageable that which is unknown, frightening, over-powering."[1]

The mother whose adult children are once more under her roof—whether for feasting or grieving during the key events of life and death—again falls under the spell of an ancient maternal illusion: that she can once more attempt to defend her life's center against the forces of dissolution that always threaten—death, distance, indifference.

There are two major groups of rituals in which even the most modern and liberated of mothers, those perhaps the least child-centered in their lives and hearts, usually feel a strong emotional and physical (not to mention financial) involvement.

One is a rite of passage in which one of her adult children changes his or her status—becomes married, becomes a parent, or, younger, becomes a member of the adult community through First Communion or bar or bas mitzvah ceremonies.

When these rites of passage occur, the mother's ordinary daily existence is permeated with an unusual life-giving quality.

Leslie B., the mother of two daughters, described the letter she wrote to faraway friends and relatives unable to attend her firstborn daughter's wedding on a sunny, fairy-tale June day in the garden of the family home.

"I described the whole scene," she remembers fondly, "and of course it did have a kind of storybook air to it, but the most important thing in the letter was not how charming the brides- maids looked standing under the trees, but rather that my hus- band and I felt for a moment that we really understood a little of what life is about—a bit of a glimpse, just for a second—of a hidden reality that we generally don't ever even think about."

The second kind of ceremony that captures mothers is what social scientists call "rites of intensification." These are the ritu- als that the whole community shares, usually in response to a major historical or religious event, or natural changes such as the turn of the seasons, harvest, and solstice.

These would include the huge national holidays shared over the groaning Thanksgiving board, or set down by the family hearth at Christmas, or enjoyed in summery backyards when family reunions take place over July fourth.

It is at these holidays—marked by whole clans and nations— that women's sense of themselves as living in a web of relation- ships that stretch from their front door around the world is strongly affirmed.[2]

On such occasions, women both delight in their own family and take comfort and reassurance in belonging to the larger society; it is a time when they turn inward and outward simul- taneously.[3]

This was touchingly and amusingly explained by Maggie W., the mother of three grown children, two of whom live within visiting distance. One, married and with a child, lives too far away for frequent visits.

"Thanksgiving is our most important holiday, since we never

had a formal religious affiliation anywhere," explains youthful, attractive Maggie, who at 47 has a new job as an administrative assistant to a sales manager of a small manufacturing company after years of being home with the children.

"Even though my husband and I were both raised as Methodists, it just never 'took' somehow—we haven't been in a church in years, we weren't even married in a church. Somehow, I feel, Thanksgiving is the perfect holiday for people like us. You're not punished if you don't go to church, but you can if you want to . . . we happen not to.

"For me," she continues, "the same feeling as church was when the children were still home, when they were little and then later when they were teenagers. It was that time in the late morning of Thanksgiving Day when the turkey was roasting in the oven, and my husband was gathering up all the kids, finding their boots and gloves and sweaters and getting the car out so they could all go the local high-school football game. I would stay home and enjoy the quiet, baste the turkey, and move dinner along. I loved that quiet moment, the smell of the food, and the way they would all look when they came back from the game, excited and hungry.

"For me," says Maggie eloquently, "that was church."

And now?

"Well, we've moved away from the suburban town's football team they followed for years, but it's just as much fun when I call them away from the television football game. Maybe my feeling of happiness and peace when they're all safely here is even better—it's richer. I know more than I did when I was a young mother, just learning what a family was. On one hand it's nice to feel part of the big American holiday of Thanksgiving—Pilgrims and Indians and all that—and at the same time, if I slip in a little chocolate cake among the pumpkin pies and mince pies —just because chocolate cake is Terry's favorite in the whole world, regardless of the holiday—I celebrate our own family, too."

Precisely because rituals really are about relationships—of family members to each other, of the family to the bigger nation or tribe, of man and woman to God or nature—they represent what one family therapist called a "hinge of time" on which many events can turn quite suddenly.[4] When the emotional currents in the family run strongly, as they do at special times, feelings can be redirected or, if buried, can reemerge—sometimes explosively, sometimes in ways that are just quietly, deeply enriching. Unresolved emotional issues can be worked on; memory is updated; adult children learn more about the context of their own lives and how they came to be.

Because family gatherings do take place in this atmosphere of keyed-up emotion, two distinct communications phenomena were reported by the respondent group of mothers I interviewed.

One is the "indelibility" factor—the strange truth that conversation, comments, or dialogue that take place during a family gathering are remembered far longer (sometimes for life) than ordinary talks during ordinary contact.

Almost everyone in the core group of mothers had a story to tell that began in this vein:

"I remember on the day of my mother's funeral, her sister, my Aunt Dorothy, said to me . . ." Often the remembered remark was made many years previously.

In another instance, a mother reported: "I'll never forget that when my son was married, an aunt of my husband's made a crack about religious mixed marriages to the minister. I didn't speak to her for years." Pressed for details, this woman admitted that the remark itself really was not so terrible, it was the timing, *"on my son's wedding day,"* that made it hurt.

The flowering of feuds, the reunion of long-separated family members—all demonstrate the power of the key event and its symbolism. One woman told of an estranged brother, from whom she'd been apart for twenty-four years, turning up at her husband's funeral and becoming reunited with his siblings and nieces and nephews he had never seen.

This "forever" memory is similar to the national indelibility factor that makes Americans remember clearly where they were and what they were doing when Franklin Roosevelt died, when the first man walked on the moon, and when John F. Kennedy was assassinated.

The second phenomenon reported at family gatherings in a consistent pattern was the "everybody on their good behavior" syndrome that operates noticeably in situations where families are widely separated by geographic distance and where get-togethers are less frequent, each one more emotionally charged.

In these gatherings, several women reported that there was a certain artificiality in the way everyone tried to smooth over difficulties for the sake of not being the one who would blow the reunion sky-high.

Gloria A., mother of four children, remembers one big celebration when she and the children's father were observing their thirtieth wedding anniversary. Two of the adult children who live within travel distance organized a gathering of all the children and their spouses and companions, two of whom lived a considerable distance away.

"This was during the Vietnam war," recalls Gloria, who is now in her mid-sixties, "and we had a lot of the strains that you had then. Bob, our oldest, was talking about going to Canada as a draft resister, and his dad, a World War II veteran, was scared and angry at the same time. To tell you the truth, I was wishing the two who live nearby had never tried to get this party together and that the third and fourth had never agreed to it.

"But what actually happened," recounts the mother, "is that after the first hour or so when everyone was kind of whispering around and handling Bob and his dad as though they were made of glass, Bob finally broke over and said, 'Hey, guys, I'm home —this is Mom and Dad's day—c'mon, now . . .' and after that, everything was okay."

Another interviewee, April N., mother of five children, says she is the biggest good-behavior advocate of the whole family when the kids are all home together again. "I know it's a little fake," she says, "but the kids seem to catch it from me. No one wants to rake up old troubles or fights—they really try hard to make everything nice, and believe me, I appreciate it."

Author Paul Wilkes wrote a book about a year in the life of an average American family, and the tensions between the parents and one dropout son, who left home to drift around the West without a job or other ties, are described in revealing detail.[5] Yet, at Christmas, the strains are glossed over and temporarily shelved during a family holiday gathering, for which the errant son makes a special effort to get home. Once home, he participates in the holiday as fully as the earlier estrangement will permit, without completely reversing his feeling that his parents do not understand or accept him.

This most extreme form of the best-behavior approach reflects, to some degree, the experience many mothers report during reunions and special holidays, especially when family members come great distances.

Interestingly, the question of distance is thought by family therapist Edwin H. Friedman of Washington, D.C., who is also a rabbi, to be a much more complex issue than it looks on the surface. Friedman believes that family gatherings, especially if they are focused on highly significant events like births, deaths, or weddings, have an "absolutely transporting quality, able to transcend great distances. . . ." He does not believe there is a "necessary correlation between the degree of physical distance or frequency of previous communication between family members and whether or not they appear at a given family ritual."

The reason for this unpredictability, believes Rabbi Friedman, is that family ties are usually buried, rather than destroyed, under the weight of time and distance, but can surface rapidly when belonging to the circle becomes important again to each person, for reasons and in ways no one can guess or foresee.

A substantial number (more than two dozen) of the 208 mothers in the respondent group told of children coming home unexpectedly who had been absent at family gatherings for quite a while, almost regardless of how close or distant the mother felt they were emotionally.

"Home is where, when you have to go there, they have to take you in," wrote poet Robert Frost, and this plain statement of the immutability of bonds was echoed in different words by a sizable majority of the hundreds of women I contacted.

Within the respondent group, there were, of course, many women who did not enjoy perfect relationships with each one of their adult children, but that did not stop them from plunging into hope, nostalgia, or dreams at the idea of a family gathering.

Something about the possibility of righting old wrongs, renewing the attempt to reach one or another "difficult" child, strengthening the tie between brothers and sisters—all these can spur women on to veritable orgies of effort when it's holiday time.

For those fortunate (and hard-working) women whose relationships with their adult children are reasonably satisfying, the family gathering is an unparalleled occasion of sweetness and reward, fun and pleasure, even with its accompanying stress and fatigue.

The Major Holidays: Tenderness and Trauma

As we begin to understand the role that ritual plays in people's lives and to look at some of the major events through the mother's eyes, it is useful to know just which family gatherings are up front in the maternal psyche, which are the most symbolically important to her.

According to a survey of nearly 500 women (from whom the core group of 208 was drawn), the two most widely celebrated holidays are Thanksgiving and Christmas, with Thanksgiving actually receiving a few more votes than Christmas. Whether Turkey Day edges out Christmas because of the generally waning influence of religious holidays as such, or whether more mundane considerations such as crowds and the expense of holiday travel account for it, is unclear. Perhaps the very heaviness of the expected emotional interaction is a bar for some families.

Next most important to them, say the mothers, are the two great springtime holy days of renewal—Easter for Christian families, Passover for Jewish. These were identified by mothers in even highly secular families as occasions when they often tried to bring all the adult children home and all the extended family together.

After these major holidays, it appears that most families are creating their own personal rituals and celebrations, unique to each. The birthdays of family members, the parents' wedding anniversaries (especially milestones like the twenty-fifth, thirtieth, or later), summertime vacation trips, or traditional family reunions on annual holidays like Labor Day—all were reported by mothers to be highly popular observances.

In one family, a big backyard picnic on July fourth brings together the extended family for ethnic dances and songs. In outdoor-loving families, the advent of the winter ski season means get-togethers for an occasional snowy weekend, in addition to the major national or religious holidays. In homes where there has been divorce or death (about 20 percent of America's children live in a home with just one parent), single parents work particularly hard at establishing personal rituals with their children that may sometimes be only distantly related to the community's observances.

One divorced mother squirrels away gifts all year long for her two grown sons and exchanges them with the young men on New Year's Eve; the custom has grown to include girlfriends and wives, and now, grandchildren.

Some social observers have said that American disappointment with totally nonreligious, totally secular life may be partly due to a feeling of impoverishment as traditional religious rites disappear.

If this is so (and not everyone agrees that Americans are feeling let down by secular life), certainly one answer widely reported among energetic mothers is: Make your own rituals! Ceremonies derived only from one particular family's ways of living and loving can be extremely satisfying, if begun early enough and pursued by the parents (although the mother usually leads the way) assiduously enough.

Stephanie T., mother of three adult children aged 20, 23, and 25, gives a memoir of Christmas observances that stresses the individuality of the family within the larger context of the rite. Stephanie says she hardly can believe the strong hold that the family's personal Christmas observances have on her 25-year-old daughter, for example.

"When the children were little, they insisted that we put food out for Santa's reindeer. At that time, we always seemed to have a little one teething, and since teething crackers were all over the house," begins Stephanie, "we'd just crumble them up and put them around the fireplace, in case some of the younger reindeer were teething, too.

"Would you believe," Stephanie goes on, "that even though my daughter has a college degree, a good job, and her own apartment—plus plenty of boyfriends—she still feels it's not Christmas if we don't put cracker crumbs around the fireplace for the reindeer? And she's not even sheepish or embarrassed about it!"

Stephanie's voice is full of awe as she says, "And the boys! Long ago we set it up so that everyone had to be at home and together before their father would go out to buy the Christmas tree. That family custom dates back to when the boys were too little to go and they cried all one night because only Kathy, the oldest, went with her father to get the tree. So later we made a rule that nobody goes until everybody goes."

Stephanie's voice wavers a little as she remembers: "One

Christmas Eve not too long ago, after they were all grown and gone and scattered all over the place, but all coming home for Christmas, our middle child's plane was delayed. My husband and the other kids just waited until nearly midnight for Jim to get home. Then they all went out in the middle of the night, just about, to look all over for a tree. They found one, a scrawny leftover one, but it looked beautiful to me because it meant they all felt still linked together.

"Perhaps," says Stephanie, "when they all are married, with their own homes and children, they'll do other things—start their own customs. I don't know how much they'll remember or want to share when that time comes . . ." her voice trails off.

Stephanie's family also turns outward at Christmas to the whole Christian world as she and her family participate in the sacred holiday music-making. They are a musical family and unabashedly seek out the best musical fare during Christmas week, whether it is offered at their own church or some other. Stephanie says that the communion between her family and other families through the medium of Christmas music is an especially significant part of the holiday to her. She describes it as making her feel that the world outside their own home is, for a short time at least, a peaceful and secure place for her family. Women of non-Christian faiths report the same feelings at the ingatherings of their religious or cultural groups.

Because contemporary mothers often are working—many more of them than in their own mothers' day—they are voting increasingly for summertime gatherings so that formal vacation periods can be planned to include family get-togethers. Long weekends over Memorial Day and Labor Day as occasions for reunions were reported as an increasing trend that serves to mesh school and work schedules. Unpressured time together remains the most difficult goal to achieve for busy modern families, but mothers pursue it with an impressive tenacity through all the complications of 1980s living.

Women also reported that commercially inspired holidays like Mother's Day and Father's Day count for much less with them than the big religious or national holidays, but a substantial majority of mothers (about 65 percent) confessed they felt hurt if Mother's Day passed with no contact whatever with any one of their children. Mothers said a lack of contact on Mother's Day always nicks them a little, even if it is a holiday they think was created specifically for florists, candy-makers, and greeting card manufacturers, rather than for mothers.

In spite of lapses on Mother's Day or forgetfulness on birthdays on the part of the adult children, mothers in the survey group actually were reporting a lot of contact, either on the major national or religious holidays or during individual family celebrations, and most of those gatherings, according to interviewees, are generally held on Mom's turf.

A group of 179 mothers answered questions on probable sites or traditional locales for family gatherings and 62 percent of those women said the get-together was most often at the mother's home.

Another 26 percent said they alternated with their children, dividing up the most important gatherings equally. Only eleven of the mothers—6 percent—said the key gatherings were always at the childrens' homes. Another slightly larger group—twenty women—said they often went elsewhere for the holidays, either out to a restaurant for dinner, taking a holiday trip together, or all as guests of another family.

These general customs about locale varied from year to year, mothers reported; sometimes strains between parents and one or another child or among the siblings dictated that the parents hold separate celebrations with each child apart from the others or, in some instances, the parents and children would simply duck out of the gathering, go on a trip somewhere, or have a postponed dinner at another time.

No matter how good a facade the mother may present on such occasions, I did not find one who truly welcomed that solution. Most saw avoidance of the whole event as sometimes grimly necessary, offering relief from anxiety and preferable to quarrels, but not really satisfying.

"The best of a bad bargain," muttered one fiftyish mother who had gone on a holiday cruise with her husband to avoid a Christmas gathering with their son and his live-in girlfriend, of whom the parents strongly disapproved. The parents managed a separate holiday observance with their other child before they left on the trip and a brief visit with the defiant son and his unwelcome partner when they returned.

With the family gathering taking place more often than one

might have guessed in the so-called era of the disappearing family, and with many of them taking place in the mother's home, are we back to the stereotype of the slave mother, a doormat for her children and husband?

Since this is a transitional generation of mothers, the answer is both no and yes.

A slight majority—a little more than half of the 169 mothers who answered the question "Who generally does the planning, organizing, and preparation for the family gathering?"—said they shared those jobs *equally* with the adult children. But a substantial minority—74 women—reported that the mother does almost all the work herself, sometimes with minor assistance from her husband or male companion.

This means that in 92 percent of the families surveyed, the mother does half, three-quarters, or all of the work necessary to float the celebration. In only 12 out of 169 instances do the grown kids do the major share of the work, and this includes families where the mother is ill or handicapped.

I tentatively suggested that women's liberation seems a little remote when it comes to family gatherings, and a good many women agreed. But weighing the work with the rewards brought some interesting insights, along with first signs of changing patterns on this topic, as on so many others in contemporary families.

Mother Rides the Roller Coaster of the Family Gathering

> We never have a reunion without a fight breaking out . . . but we keep having them anyway, because reunions bring out how much we care for each other. We patch our rifts, and in the end, the joys outbalance anything else that happens.
>
> ALEX HALEY, author of *Roots*, writing on family reunions in
> *Families* magazine

The cycle of events generated by a family gathering follows a three-step roller coaster series of emotional and logistical ups and downs for the women at the center.

First comes the anticipation phase. In the days or weeks before a family gathering, mothers say they feel a mixture of excited hope and worried anxiety. The staunch traditionalists say they love this first step the best; all still lies in the future while the mother's hands are busy at cleaning, cooking, and shopping chores in the present. This will be the time, she fantasizes, when old hurts will be healed and new parts of life explored . . . maybe!

"It's such a nice kind of 'bother,' " wrote one mother, "and I really love the bustle and the anticipation, even though it's tiring sometimes."

Stage two is the event itself. The moment unfolds with its share of mishaps, serendipity, reassuring repetitions of old times. It includes wonderful enlargements of the circle to take in new members, warm comforting of one another over the losses of those missing. Unresolved strains in the family structure also simmer and the mother moves rapidly between poles of laughter and delight and anxious watching that all should go smoothly and everyone's needs be met.

Stage three on the roller coaster is the postevent phase, in which most of the mothers shared explicit feelings of fatigue, even exhaustion, and sharp emotional letdown.

"Our house nowadays is normally calm and peaceful," says Selma N., the last of whose three children has been gone from home for three years, "and then the hurricane hits. All three kids and two spouses and two grandchildren are home at the same time. I love it—the house is really bouncing again. The phone never stops, the refrigerator door bangs constantly, I'm running all over to borrow cribs and playpens, it's great. Suddenly, the hurricane has passed on and all is eerily quiet once more . . . getting used to their return and their leaving again . . . I feel so funny. Breathlessly glad to have had the excitement, but a little empty for a while until I can start enjoying the peace again."

Another mother who says she always "overinvests" in the stage one anticipatory phase said wistfully about stage three: "When it's over, you find out that it was never quite as wonderful as you thought it was going to be."

But the sadness of having to say good-bye, which is the key part of the stage three letdown, is the element voted by most mothers as the hardest part of the whole gathering when their children live too far away for frequent visits.

I asked all 208 women in the core group to describe what they liked the best and disliked the most about this roller coaster ride that nearly all of them had experienced.

Their answers were succinct:

Liked the best: the warmth and love of being together.

Disliked the most: the work, noise, confusion, expense, and exhaustion, as well as the pervasive sense of failure if quarrels or hostility spoiled the time, and then the necessity of saying good-bye.

A small minority of mothers claimed vehemently there was absolutely nothing about the family gathering they disliked.

Peggy T., 57, mother of two sons, both married but as yet childless, living quite far away, wrote, "There's absolutely nothing about our visits or holiday celebrations that I dislike. Every moment is pure joy for me. My only dislike is that it always ends too soon and I am just miserable when we have to say good-bye."

Jeanne W. is the mother of two daughters, one of whom is married and has a child while her sister is single and sharing a glamorous city apartment with another young woman. Jeanne belongs to the "love it all" school, encourages her daughters to bring friends to the family gathering, sees it as an occasion to indulge her grandson shamelessly, and revels in every nuance of her family's rekindling itself after separations and absences.

Moreover, Jeanne is, as she readily admits, a tyrant in the kitchen, and the family gathering offers her gentle despotism its greatest opportunity. "The kids have given up trying to help," she says, laughing, "because I really love to do it all myself and I like to do it my way. I want to be the boss and I don't mind the hard work one bit."

Jeanne's sincerity was genuine, but raised the issue of the "queen bee" aspect of the family gathering, which may be typical of the more traditional and less contemporary mothers.

One woman who seemed to combine the old-fashioned "I love every minute of it" sturdiness of the traditional mother with more modern insights into herself was Louisa L., 50, mother of four, who was charmingly candid about why she answered "nothing" when asked what she *dis*liked the most about family gatherings.

"Let's face it," responded Louisa, "I'm the star of the production again! You lose that role when they leave, and you *should* lose it. I know that, I guess I accept it, but gee, it's fun to stage manage the whole thing again! I'm the one who knows everyone's favorite dishes and favorite TV shows and favorite friends and relatives, and I can bring it all together so that everybody has a wonderful time. I'm the leading lady, the orchestra conductor, and the gourmet chef, all rolled up into one!"

Louisa also points out, "I have a lot going on in my life now that the kids are gone." (She has been married to the children's father for twenty-eight years, is a remedial reading teacher, and is active in her union local.) "I don't think I want to play all those mother parts all the time again anymore, but once in a while, I just have a ball doing it up right."

Relinquishing this spotlight is hard, bitterly hard, for some mothers. Their feelings were best expressed by Beth T., a mother of two daughters and one son.

In response to a question about possibly sharing the work of the family gathering with the adult children or turning it over completely to the children, Beth showed sincere shock and disbelief. "Oh, no!" she exclaimed. "I can't even begin to imagine such a thing! *Of course* all family gatherings always will be at my home and I will always do them. Always have and always will."

Beth reports that never in her thirty-year marriage have any family festivities or wakes ever been held anywhere but in her home and fed out of her kitchen. From the children's earliest sticky-fingered birthday cakes to college graduations, wedding receptions, and three decades' worth of Thanksgiving turkeys and Easter hams—all are her exclusive province.

Beth proudly claims that she has never been too tired or too busy or too ill to stage these events ("Though the night before our younger daughter's engagement party, I was running a 103-degree temperature and no one knew it, not even my husband," she says). Beth believes she will go on doing these things "forever or until I'm a hundred, whichever comes first," she answers, smiling but earnest.

Mothers like Jeanne, Louisa, and Beth, who claimed there was nothing at all they disliked about the family gathering and viewed it all as an unalloyed blessing were, however, definitely in the minority of the respondent group. In fact, they constituted only 7 percent of all the mothers who were willing to talk about what they liked and disliked about holidays and family gatherings.

A clear majority of the women interviewed—55 percent—were frank and open about their dislike of the heavy physical work in all three stages of the event.

The unaccustomed business of once more cooking for a crowd, erratic eating and sleeping schedules, having three, four, or five extra beds going, lines outside the bathrooms, and shuttling back and forth to airports and train and bus stations in the holiday crowds left many women too tired and frazzled to enjoy their children and grandchildren or have much chance to be quietly alone with those who came long distances.

"I feel one thing in my stomach and another thing in my head" is the way Christine D., a hospital nurse, mother of three, and grandmother of three, expresses her dilemma.

"My gut tells me: Come, feed them, love them, enjoy them—do the whole thing and do it smashingly. But then my head says: What about the logistics?"

Christine returned to nursing after the last child left home for the service, and although all the children work, she feels that none of them, except possibly the navy son, "work as hard as I do." She believes that the children "keep remembering me as the mother at home—not as the woman who is on her feet many long hours with big and tiring responsibilities at work."

Christine is typical of the transitional mother who is caught somewhere between the stay-at-home traditionalist and the new mother, involved in a job or other interests and not wholly centered on her children.

Despite these inner conflicts between heart and head, Christine says most of the major holidays—particularly Christmas for this family of Czechoslovak immigrants—do end up at her home and she usually does "the whole bit and then some."

"You see," she explains, "we left the rest of our family—

aunts, uncles, cousins—back in Europe. We're immigrants and it is terribly important for our children and grandchildren to have at least this much closeness of family."

What Christine says she likes best about all the get-togethers is when everybody puts on hats and coats and goes outdoors after the feasting, either just to hike around or go to a movie or a church social. These outings bring back for her the many kinds of trips she and her husband used to arrange for the children when they were younger.

"We were a real go-go bunch," she says, nostalgia fluttering around her shoulders like a shawl, "and we were always off somewhere camping or sightseeing." For her, the holiday gathering and its attendant group outing represent a cherished memory of the best of family times. Reactivating it a few times a year with her adult children and grandchildren is her modest reward for the days and weeks of preholiday work she adds to her schedule.

Deanna R., 56, mother of two married daughters and two granddaughters, takes a more jaundiced view of the logistical problems.

"I think the holidays and most family gatherings are for men," she says flatly, "for men and for children." Then she adds, "No, not even for the children, because they're just rolling around like loose cannon. The men get off in some comfortable chairs somewhere and talk politics or sports or watch TV, nobody pays any attention to the kids until they get cranky and into some kind of mischief, and the women are just rushing around doing what has to be done."

Deanna is one of the lucky mothers who share the holiday preparations quite equally with an active, capable eldest daughter, but she still feels "it all goes by too fast and I'm never ready."

A handful of women out of the respondent group of 208 reported that they are trying innovative steps to minimize the work and expense and maximize the joy and pleasure.

One woman, Clara A., had to make a new life for herself after her apparently wealthy husband died suddenly, leaving a mountain of debt, two sons, and a wife untrained for any work.

Clara put her life back together as a skilled secretary, and while her two adult sons and their wives today are more important than ever to her, she decided that her real closeness to them should be pursued in more direct, less conventional ways, now that she no longer has a large home and household help.

Accordingly, she told her brood that at Christmas, Thanksgiving, and birthdays, she wants to enjoy them more and fuss less and she suggested they dismantle the traditional huge feasts and send out for pizza ("On Thanksgiving?" "Yes, on Thanksgiving") or have a casual pickup supper.

"Well!" she laughs. "The kids couldn't handle pizza for Thanksgiving—just couldn't handle it. But they did agree to a covered-dish supper. Now everyone brings whatever they want, we don't even work out a menu in advance, but everything gets eaten and enjoyed, and best of all, we can talk and laugh and reminisce without me jumping up every five minutes, and then we all clean up together and it's done."

Where the number of adult children is small—two or three as opposed to four or five—some mothers find that a modest celebration with each one, rather than a monster gathering with all, works out well, although that means forgoing the pleasure of seeing siblings together. "I miss that," admits Phyllis T., mother of two, "but the individual attention I'm able to give each person makes up for it."

Phyllis and her husband's decision to have separate holiday gatherings with their son and daughter highlights the gritty truth: Many women suffer real emotional fatigue, as well as physical exhaustion, at many family gatherings. About 30 percent—or roughly a third of all the women who wanted to talk about family get-togethers—said the ever-present threat of tension among family members hovers like an ill-visaged angel over the gathering.

"You make me feel I'm two years old again when I come home," complained one grown daughter to her mother, who, telling about the Thanksgiving incident, sadly added, "And I guess I get as bad as they do. I start telling them what to do for their cold or to be careful driving, forgetting they've been on their own and getting along fine for quite a while now."

Other mothers agree: The old patterns reassert themselves and unresolved issues are washed up on the shore of the family gathering, a strange island amidst everyday life, half a home-coming oasis, half a vacation retreat.

"Going home means you have to confront more than a mem-ory—someone from the past who is still right there, like a masto-don," points out Dr. Donald A. Bloch, executive director of the Ackerman Institute for Family Therapy.[6] "Unresolved family issues can be ignored or swept under the rug for most of the year, but people are forced to pretend [at holidays]—in a config-uration of joy and happiness—that everything is all right and it isn't all right."

The "mastodon" to whom Dr. Bloch was referring could be parents, grandparents, siblings—anyone with whom the return-ing adult child has not worked out some problems.

But if we assume the leftover relic from the past is a parent and look at the great return from the mother or father's view-point, it means that the adult child, someone who can cause guilt, worry, and problems, someone from whose difficulties you had temporary surcease, now is right back on your doorstep with the same package.

"I don't know whether I'm successful in smoothing out *all* the strains that can occur among all the different family members," recounts Eva N., mother of three daughters and two sons, "but I sure try like hell! Let me tell you what happened two Christ-mases ago. My youngest daughter really put me on the spot. We not only have all the children and their families at our house for Christmas, but we usually gather in all the stray aunts, uncles, and cousins who are around, too, so it's a big group. Most of the time I don't mind, but this one year was a killer. Our youngest, our 'baby,' had been married a few months before and this was the first time her new husband, a stage and TV actor, had met the whole family and joined in as an 'official' part of the group for his first Christmas with us."

Eva continues: "He must have been worried or nervous about taking on such a big group—though that would be strange for an actor, wouldn't it?—but anyway, pushed along by big help-ings of mulled wine and hot toddies, he hogged the whole spot-light . . . insisted on putting on lengthy entertainments, seeking stage center every minute. . . . It was so embarrassing.

"Well, naturally," Eva said, "my daughter called me anxiously the next day to find out whether her relatives had said anything about his performance, and of course I outright lied. I told her they thought he was amusing and entertaining—was I going to tell her they thought he was a jerk? And ruin her holidays? No, I didn't! And anyway, after he gets used to us and feels he's accepted, he won't have to carry on like that," she concluded with the flash of wisdom that comes to many women who've surveyed their crew over many a holiday table.

For the divorced mother, whether functioning as a single parent or as a stepparent in a new relationship, and trying to balance those requirements with the demands of earlier family constellations, the holidays and visits with her own and stepchildren carry an even bigger load of emotional challenge.

Similarly, women born into one religious background but who, by choice, convert to another often find the holidays an intensely difficult flashpoint, as old habits and new loyalties struggle together.

The Circle of Belonging

"Woman's world is kin-based, humanity-based," wrote Jesse Bernard in *The Female World*.

Since a good many of the mothers I interviewed were candid about the work, exhaustion, and expense—as well as emotional fatigue—that family gatherings caused them, I tried an experiment.

I asked the core group of mothers these questions: "Since these get-togethers apparently can exact quite a toll, how would you feel if you just scrapped the big gathering, especially at holidays, and let the telephone reign supreme? Should personal visits and big gatherings be less frequent, more casual? Should modern families streamline the holidays and have smaller events —not necessarily with every single person present—for individual family milestones?"

The reaction was loud, raucous, and instantaneous:

"No!"

"Never!"

"Absolutely not!" chorused the very women who said they

were exhausted and tense, as well as those who've always claimed to love every minute.

What is the source of this tidal pull that brings even sullen and rebellious adult children home, and stiffens the spines and energizes the hands of busy, often overworked, mothers?

Why, indeed, does everyone either want to be "home for the holidays" or feel they *should* go home for the holidays, even if the prospect does not fill them with undiluted joy?

For the mother, the joy and satisfaction of seeing everyone alive, well, and together far outweighs the work and pressure.

For the young adult children, the pull is to find their rightful place again in the small circle that protects them from the bigger, often harsher, outside world—the circle that, however ragged and emotionally fraught, still spells comfort and support. However fretful they may feel about parents and siblings, it is often with unobtrusive gratitude that they reclaim their roots and their place.

As a by-product, they often learn a good deal that's useful to them in solving their own problems about their past and the family heritage from which they spring. It is not an accident that, in an increasingly menacing world, the TV drama "Roots" had one of the biggest audiences ever.

For mothers, the mound of dirty dishes, the chaotic refrigerator, and the wet towels from one end of the house to the other are small prices to pay for three rewards that come to them in full measure, like the three wishes of childhood fables:

• A profound sense of connection, an understanding of how dear the circle is and how important that no one be cast out of it.

• The importance of continuity that parents and grandparents can hand on to succeeding generations.

• The satisfactions and pleasure of seeing their job well done as their adult children move into the mainstream of life, helping each other, reflecting well on their parents, and becoming interesting and worthwhile human beings.

In addition to these basic feelings, there is another aspect of the family gathering that mothers say they enjoy immensely, and that could be called the sheer entertainment value of the event. The news, the gossip, the catching up ("Doesn't Annie look great with that new haircut?" "Did you notice Jim quit smoking —I'm so proud!") that is part of the event is fun for most mothers.

Jacqueline L., mother of four children, reported on the last big summer family reunion two years earlier. At that time, two new in-law children were brought into the family and an announcement was made of an expected first grandchild. Jackie wrote the following thoughtful comment:

"It's gatherings like these make me realize that mothering is very rewarding. It doesn't last for just eighteen or twenty years. It's a lifetime job. It's great being with our grown children, sharing love, thoughts, memories, discussions, and . . . *mothering!*"

This sense of connectedness was echoed in words that were, in turn, touching, funny, sweet, and insightful as mothers in a group discussion gave full rein to their warm memories of past gatherings and wistful hopes for future ones.

"Welcoming into the family new members is so wonderful," said one mother of three grown sons. "There was one year when we had two new babies at Thanksgiving. I love that because it means the family is still growing and expanding, instead of shrinking and getting smaller, the way it first looks when the kids go away from home for good."

Amelia T., who has two children, said, "My husband's mother died last year and the breaks in the family circle only make you hold on all the harder to everyone you still have. To see all my children well and functioning gives me a deep feeling of satisfaction and contentment. It reminds me there are still people I'm connected to in spite of the losses."

In addition to connectedness, mothers (and usually fathers, too) value continuity. That element in the family gathering was brought to sad, bright life by the tale told by Melissa N., mother of two daughters and twin sons, who describes both the meaning of a chain of generations and the terror of loss when a link seems broken.

"Christmas is the holiday I care most about," says Melissa, "because, I suppose, my husband and I both come from big families [Melissa has four brothers, her husband has five siblings] and it's always been celebrated in the family I grew up in with just oodles and oodles of different rituals. My parents are English and we always had steak and kidney pie for supper Christmas Eve and then Dad would read Christmas stories to us before bed. A big part of our celebration was hanging the Christmas stockings— that was absolutely *it, the* most important rite. I remember as though it were yesterday how thrilled I was when my children were old enough to make stockings for their grandparents! The steak and kidney pie supper was only one of several 'set' meals we had at different times throughout the year when I was a child.

"At Easter," she goes on, "we always had 'drunken lamb' and 'drunken pie,' both called that because they were flavored with different liqueurs; birthdays, too, meant special favorite foods for each child, and Valentine's Day meant sweets. All these happened in my own family and are what I've handed down to my kids.

"But it's Christmas that's square in the middle of my heart, my year, and my family," says Melissa. "I prepare for it all year long. I put away gifts and I make gifts and I keep a huge stack of catalogs handy to look at all the time.

"The symbolism? Why is it so important to me?"

She looks thoughtfully out the window, then answers:

"It means we're not lost in the world.

"You see," continues Melissa, "for my children, it's their background—they belong somewhere, they're *attached.* It think that's vital for kids. The whole paraphernalia that goes with it —the special tablecloth for dinner, the special candles and candlesticks we only use at Christmas—it all adds up to things handed down from generation to generation and my sons and daughters know beyond a shadow of a doubt where they come from and who they are."

Because continuity with her own parents and grandparents is an important backdrop for her and her husband's creation of their own family, Melissa is also able to describe the "most joyless" Christmas she ever had.

"It was one year when one of my sons was away at college. Always, with all the kids, we sent them travel money to come home for Christmas because they were usually at school or work on a very tight budget. Well, this one year—I think Sam was a junior in college quite a way from home—he announced that he wasn't coming home for Christmas. He was open about it being a bid for independence, a way of not being too tightly bound to the family.

"I was devastated," remembers Melissa. "I just felt so terrible. To me it was rejection of the family, rejection of his past, rejection of all the things that have mattered to me all my life. I begged him to test his independence on something else besides this one thing that was so important to me. He was immovable —he wouldn't budge. He didn't come home. It was the most awful Christmas. I was miserable; nothing could comfort me. I went through all the steps, tried to make sure everything was okay for everybody else. Inside, I felt like lead. My husband was hurt, too, but nothing like me—he adjusted to it and didn't let it spoil the holiday for everyone else—but I just dragged myself through it.

"The funny part of it all is," she says, "that Sam is one of the children who later on, after college, decided to come back to our small town to live and work! I don't know—maybe he got it out of his system!"

After hearing about this jolt, I asked Melissa to try to recall the best Christmas she ever had. After searching her memory for some moments, she said slowly, "You know, I think it was one that was, superficially at least, totally uneventful! We were all together, everyone was well (my mom died two years ago and the times when she was with us are more and more important memories all the time), our children were not toddlers anymore —they were around nine or ten, big enough to play alone for a while but young enough to still get a thrill out of the doings. The mood was relaxed and nice—everybody helped, some cleared the table, others got dessert ready—it just felt so good, so right.

"Yes," she concluded, "I think that was the very best. We hadn't lost anyone yet, and all the new babies who were going to be born were here for that Christmas."

It used to be thought that Christmas—or indeed any of the major holidays—was a time of gloom and misery for everyone whose personal situation did not conform to the idealized family portrait of the Norman Rockwell Thanksgiving feast table.

But many of the women interviewed described a much more

resilient grouping. Where there have been divorces and remarriages, separations or deaths, or where family units are physically scattered but emotionally in touch, the ties often remain astoundingly strong, and many kinds of adaptations have been ingenious and loving, even if traditional patterns are in disarray.

Mental-health researchers found in a series of 1983 studies that the "holiday blues" are greatly overstated. Instead, they confirmed scientifically what mothers have known and demonstrated intuitively forever: The holidays just intensify whatever was there before.

In the words of the 1983 study, "Christmas is a time when lovers rejoice more than ever, while the lonely may sink into despair; when close-knit families bind together while warring households shatter; when most workers relax and enjoy themselves while workaholics fret and feel guilty."[7]

The possibility that holiday gloom has been overstated as a general malaise was also confirmed by a survey done a couple of years earlier at the University of Minnesota. In 1980, a representative sample of sixty middle-income midwestern families was asked for reports on visits back home and what they thought about them.

Despite complaints about lack of privacy, stressful reawakening of old dependence/independence battles, and unmanageable grandchildren overtired from too much excitement, both generations reported the visits "quite satisfying" and felt "generally very positive" about their family get-togethers, though "the parents probably felt sadder when they were over than the children did," the survey said.

But for their part, the adult children said they felt good about talking over important family matters, reminiscing, and strengthening family ties, and said, most importantly, that "their consciences were satisfied." Both the children and the parents said they felt "happy, useful, and valued" after their visits.

Affirming the themes of connectedness and continuity is a statement issued several holidays ago by Dr. Peter B. Dunn, director of the Division of Family Therapy at the Downstate Medical Center, New York. While Dr. Dunn was cognizant of all the strains and stresses that can cluster around the family gathering, he also pointed out its benefits: "It can be a deepening experience that affords the opportunity for coming to terms with a fuller sense of what life is all about."

Little Girl Lost: The Mother Self at the Feast

> I began to wonder how the shift comes about from the child's pure egocentric delight in a feast that seems to be planned almost wholly for her enjoyment to the adult's sense that this is a time when all obligations must somehow be met. . . .
>
> MARGARET MEAD and RHODE METRAUX,
> *Aspects of the Present*

It is during the major family gatherings that many women feel a dim stirring of some earlier, prematernal self. They described these yearnings in tentative, half-formed words and phrases, in tones of wistfulness and longing, sometimes close to a sense of haunting loss.

Before they were mothers, the women I interviewed were young wives, and before that, eager schoolgirls and wide-eyed children in their own families of origin. Holidays like Christmas and Thanksgiving or Easter bring a faint echo—in the midst of their current busyness—of times they spent with their own parents and friends, times that were joyful in quite another way.

Judith R. combines a busy job as an interior decorator with mothering four grown children, spouses, companions, and grandchildren. She suggested that most mature women are so busy trying to create an idealized setting for the nuclear family they have built with husbands and lovers that it is impossible to hear, over the din, those echoes of their own earlier and more carefree youthful selves who so enjoyed the holidays with such freedom from responsibilities and duties.

Even now, as a grandmother, Judith says she is not sure where her "real" self fits into the bustle of preparations for a family gathering.

Another mother felt the same stirrings when she wrote, "I'm never sure how much of my own life I should put aside when the children visit."

Her comment hinted at the subliminal sense of "Where am *I* in all of this? Where have I been and where have I come to?" that a number of women say they experience even while they are, on the whole, quite happily regarding the handiwork of their own established family.

Another woman wrote, "Of course, I love seeing how much my children seem to get a kick out of being together nowadays, but I do feel something odd and strange when they all club together and go out dancing or partying after the family dinner. When the door closes, I remember that I used to enjoy parties and dancing, too, and now—now my husband and I are the older generation! Can't believe it!"

Naomi W., mother of two, wrote, "When my son or daughter can't make it home for important family events, or for the holidays, I sometimes feel as though *I* am the abandoned child whose parents have gone off on some mysteriously wonderful jaunt without me."

This sense of a lost self is, of course, evoked strongly by the sensory memories of special times—the early darkness on the days of winter holidays, the bright sun and summer greenery of family reunions, the smell and taste of special foods, the family jokes bringing roars of laughter only to the initiated—and these memories are strong for both men and women at major holidays.

But for women, there is something special beyond the same youthful memories that flood back again for everyone at holiday time; there is what Margaret Mead, the noted anthropologist, called "the oughtness" of the holiday for women.

"And always," wrote Dr. Mead in her reminiscences about Christmas, "as on this afternoon of Christmas Eve, I wonder anxiously whether this will be one of the good years . . . when plans that were so long in the making go wrong, a holiday is not a passing disappointment, but a permanent loss. Each year the memory of it will return, a pricking pain—the time the presents didn't arrive, the time there was a blizzard and none of the guests could stay to enjoy the goose, the time all the children were sick in bed. . . ."

It is exactly this load of responsibilities, plus the need to keep all the generations from disappointments or loneliness or sorrow, to remember everyone, to be sure the feasting is joyful, the grieving comforted, that makes women pass most family gatherings firmly fixed on what "ought" to be done.

Meanwhile, some youthful party-goer or wide-eyed child inside themselves glimmers only faintly. Like a dream, that memory disappears in the rush of shopping and cooking, of meeting trains and planes to greet much loved children and their retinues, and in the positive pleasures of connectedness and continuity.

"Yes," wrote one mother on her questionnaire, "I *do* get tired, I *do* overdo it, I *am* terribly sad when they leave, but there are moments I wouldn't give up for anything. I love having all our [four] sons home, with their friends dropping in. My parents have been gone a long time, but my husband's parents are usually with us. I love the long, leisurely meals, everyone sitting by the fireplace, talking, singing, listening to music, and the wonderful interchange among the generations . . . that, too, is like a dream."

7

Dad and His Grown Kids, as Seen by Mothers

For him, indeed, it must seem sudden—one day infants, the next, they're grown and gone. There's nothing natural about the process. He hasn't watched it, hasn't shared in it. One can almost see him passing his hand over his eyes wearily, wondering, 'How did it all happen so fast?'

LILLIAN B. RUBIN, *Women of a Certain Age: The Mid-Life Search for Self*

Our discussion with mothers of adult children about this new orbital stage of their lives with their grown kids would not be complete without looking briefly at the father's role as well.

Actually, the father and his grown children deserve a book to themselves because the father's experience, as Dr. Rubin suggests in the above quotation, is quite different from the mother's throughout the whole family formation and launching period, as well as in the orbital stage.

But since we are agreed that the mother of today's young adult has been all along the primary care-giver and the psychological center of the family, and since we have said this book is devoted to her angle of vision as she contemplates her life in this new stage, we'll only examine Dad as he appears to the veteran Mom in three time frames: the present, as the couple moves well beyond the launching; the past, in which mothers describe how they and fathers reached the launch stage, and Dad's future with his grown children as both Mom and other observers see it.

Dad and His Staff: Mother as Chief Assistant

When the children are launched and beginning their satellitelike orbits out in space somewhere, women say they must intensify and deepen a role they have played before: they must become ever more certainly mission control in relation to the father. They have always been buffer, mediator, explainer, and interpreter between the children and their father, but now they must add several new dimensions to that role, women report.

First, they must help their husbands deal with the separation, which, to men, seems much sharper and more dramatic than it does to women. Mothers have all along been watching and supervising the natural growth stages; they've had a chance to get used to the baby turning into a toddler, then into a school child, then an adolescent. For Dad, away at work, all these evolutions have taken place dimly and mistily behind the curtain of his absence.

So while Mother may greet the launching with relief, Dad often shows bewilderment, confusion, distress. He feels loss more sharply in many instances, said some mothers.

"I thought my husband would be delighted when our only daughter out of four children brought home a lovely young man as a prospective fiancée," recounts Winona St. L., wife of a retired auto salesman.

"But to my surprise, he became moody, sort of churlish, and found all kinds of things wrong with Sue's boyfriend, most of them sheer fabrications. It caused a lot of tension between him and the daughter he loves so much. I finally just had to get alone with Sue and explain how hard it was for her dad, now that he has time to think about his family for the first time in his life, to face losing her. She's a sweet, understanding kid and she got the picture."

Winona's explanation to her daughter was almost a textbook illustration of what many experts have observed: that fathers experience the launching and separation period in a different way, partially because it often coincides with the first period in their whole mature lives when they are not totally preoccupied with working to support the family financially. Often, at the launch stage, fathers are either retired or at a point in their work where they are able to slow down a bit, to be less anxious about financial security, and to turn their attention more closely to other family members.

"And that," said Carrie M., the mother of a college-age daughter and two sons already launched into jobs, "is exactly when he wakes up and the kids are gone! Wives have to give their husbands a lot of understanding at that time, because he doesn't know how much parenting there still is to do and he thinks the children are lost in some sense."

In Dr. Rubin's book on mid-life women, one said of her husband's launchtime sorrow, "It turned out he felt like it was the end of our little family. He felt terrible because it would never be the same again."

Of course, the fathers who report the most distress, say their wives, are those with emotionally the most to lose. Perhaps they had fewer children, were older when the kids left, or both they and the mother feared stresses in the marriage that might surface when the children (also a buffer) were gone.

A good number of women in our sample (about a third of the 208) said their husbands felt relief, too, just like the mothers, but it was relief from *financial* pressures, rather than the relief from emotional responsibility that women noticed.

By contrast, a half-dozen women in our sample group said they felt their husbands had a good grip on what was "natural" in the life cycle. "My Bill has always been smart about when in life things were supposed to happen, maybe because he's a rancher and knows what every season brings," said Frances N., mother of five. "When the kids were ready to learn to ride, when they were ready to help with heavy equipment, when it was time for them to spend their first summer away with their grandparents in California, he took it all in good stride, and I really didn't have to help much. He was sad when the house finally got really empty, but he felt a lot of satisfaction, too, at how well we did with all of them. Now we are both looking forward to grandchildren, but I know I'll have to be the one to watch over that first pregnancy and report to him all along what's happening. He's lived around animals all his life, but when it's one of his own kids, I'll have to be the vet, I know!"

Frances's warm-hearted and loving appreciation of her husband does not dim her clear vision that mothers now must expand their role as chief contact between the father and the grown children, handling issues much thornier than whether Janie can have the car tonight or Tom has permission to go to a basketball game in another town.

It cannot be too surprising, given the emphasis that work and financial security have received in Dad's life, that mothers find themselves more often the buffer on money issues (see Chapter 4) than on any other single problem after the launch and separation, a majority of our mothers report.

"Men have such an investment in their children's financial independence and job security that they just can't help getting uptight about relations on that subject," explains Molly C., mother of a son and daughter. "The identification in that area is so strong," explains Molly, "and also the practical effect of a kid's *not* making it financially is to continue the burden on the parents, usually more on the father, even though more mothers are working now."

Women in our sample group hastened to say, however, that money is not the only thing that galvanizes the father's attention. Ordinary problems and pleasures of life such as the child's marriage, grandchildren, the stability of the young adult's own marital union, personality or developmental problems ("Keith can't seem to work for anyone else, seems like he does best without a boss," or "Sue has had four roommates to share her apartment in eighteen months; is she having trouble getting along with young women her own age?")—all these may be anxiously watched by fathers from the sidelines, but it is here that mothers are repeatedly called on as interpreters and translators of signals.

One confidence in particular is almost always given by adult children to their mothers, rather than their fathers, and it is a tense and fearful one for mothers to look at head on, they report.

This difficult assignment is primarily in families where the father has appeared to his children like the very incarnation of rocklike strength and firm guidance. In these situations, the children are scared this strength might wane as he ages and that, at some future time, they might have to think of him as a diminished and very old man.

Nearly 60 percent of our sample—a very large majority—said it was most often Mother (certainly not Dad and seldom even do siblings want to articulate these fears to each other) to whom this aching fear, with unfinished sentences and worried half-phrases, was whispered.

"Neither of our daughters expects their dad to be anything, ever, but strength and power, in control, healthy," says Kim H., whose two grown daughters are both married, one with a new baby. "They don't ever want to think of either of us as every any different from what we are now. They know this is an impossible fantasy, but how they cling to it!" (See Chapter 10.)

This particular repressed emotion is typical of the many unspoken feelings and attitudes that swirl within the family's view of father and work to keep Mother in that same "chief executive officer" role. Women said they are, at the launching time and beyond, still reporting back to Dad the quiet, buried, but deeply truthful facts about all sorts of things going on in young sons' and daughters' lives, including soundings on the job, money, and marriage situations.

There is a part of Dad's life in the new stage beyond the empty nest, however, that does not represent tasks for Mom, but instead, represents a large bonus for her as a result of all the successful mediating she has done so far.

Quite a number of our respondent mothers said they are now able to watch a kind of turn-around rapport developing between even somewhat emotionally distant fathers and their offspring. This rapport is based on two elements: The adult children now have jobs of their own to use as a focus of sharing with their dads, and also, adult children look at their fathers in a more mature way. No matter how many weary years the mother spent trying to explain Dad and the kids to each other and no matter how long that same road ahead looks to her, the weariness is considerably solaced by watching both sides find new help, wisdom, and affection by sharing work experiences.

"Our daughter decided to become a CPA, like her dad," says Leora D., mother of three sons and a daughter. "You can imagine how this pleased her father, since none of the boys were interested. She did well in school, graduated high in her class, and got a fine starting job with one of the very big accounting firms. She's only been there two years and just got a promotion that means a lot more responsibility. She calls her dad on her company's WATS line and they talk and talk!" Leora radiates joy: "He helps her so much! And she depends on his experience and his concern for her—after all, who else, besides me, wants her to succeed as much as he does? It's wonderful to watch it all happening now. We had a bad time when she was in her teens —she was a smart-aleck, rebellious kid, and she and her father fought all the time, with me trying to make peace constantly. But things are much better now. She has matured and he has mellowed, and he's so proud of her!"

Felicia V., mother of two sons, tells how the younger son, who has just begun a small automotive supply business (with help from his family), frequently calls his father, a purchasing agent for a large machine tool company, for lunch to get advice on dealing with competitors and suppliers.

"I just know how wonderful it makes his father feel, to be asked for information and suggestions, after all those years when kids make you feel you know nothing at all that they could ever care about," remembers Felicia.

This new channel of communication—shared work and career interests—is opening up especially widely for modern middle-aged dads because daughters, as well as sons, now bring work questions to their fathers as well as to their increasing numbers of working mothers.

"The old man is getting to be a regular guru for all four of our kids," laughs Shelley N., whose husband is a retired teacher. Two of their four children went into education, one son became a social worker, and one daughter is banquet manager for a small regional chain of hotels headquartered not far from the family home.

"When you get right down to it," says Shelley sagely, "all

kinds of work really depend on the personal factor—getting along with people, accomplishing things through other people —and their dad's got forty years' worth of all that to put out for their use. I'm just so happy they've got enough sense to see that." Shelley herself is a transitional mother, working outside the home for only the past four years, but enjoying her job as a receptionist for a busy local physician.

Interestingly enough, Dad's work and money concerns about the adult children come full circle and link up with each other as he now finds himself, the mothers report, the supervisor, advisor, and helper on money management, investments, and savings, as well as on major purchases like car, home, and business.

The other great plus, which seems to coexist along with the mother's continuous role as interpreter and translator, is that qualities of character and personality that children ignored or disliked when they were little now appear attractive or admirable to grown-up sons and daughters.

One mother reports that a bookish father now is seen by his children as a "heavyweight intellectual," and they are proud of and fascinated by him, though his interests were boring when the children were young.

Another tells with great satisfaction that while her salesman-husband's interest in sports was so intense when the children were little that it actually drove them *away* from sports, the whole situation is now reversed and the daughter who thought her dad a "sports nut" is now herself a physical fitness buff and goes jogging with her father when she's visiting at home and regularly attends sports events with him.

These wonderful signs that are so gratifying to women do not, however, relieve mothers of their roles as the main conduit for information and communications between and among all family members, particularly in the new stage of family relations that follows launching.

Besides their obvious training in interpersonal relations, there were also specific structures of daily family life that helped solidify these tasks for women, mothers said.

A review of how men did the fathering task in the past might help explain how families approach launch hour and what their past history indicates about the future.

The Past: How Dad Arrived at the Launching Pad

"Well, he had to work, didn't he? How else were we going to eat?" said Althea N., mother of three, who never worked outside her home.

"His contribution? He was the charming, loving prince from the outside world who could command the delight and attention of each and all when he was in the mood, or turn it all to ashes if he wasn't." Speaking is Georgia Y., 50, who had six children and managed them and a large house with no additional help. She excelled in housewifely skills and spread the family's moderately affluent income to cover special advantages for all the youngsters. She did not earn any money directly herself.

"Richard contributed to our life a sense of stability and security. His concern and interest in the well-being of our children was evident. He was a loving and affectionate father, although not with us as much as we would have liked, as the demands of his work were very great," reported Rebekah T., mother of two, who did not return to her teaching job after the children were born.

Among the hundreds of women interviewed by letter, by telephone, or in person, there was a surprising agreement (though not, of course, complete unanimity) about the father's role when the children were growing up and how the mother positioned herself as part of the team during those years.

The majority of women in my group painted the fathers as hard working, devoted to their families, but largely absent from the day-to-day concerns of the mothers and children, who almost constituted a separate "we" group with the father as "he" or "him"—alone, aloof, and separated from the nitty-gritty of hourly child care.

By far the largest number of women interviewed defended, explained, and apologized for this state of affairs. Less than a quarter objected vigorously, and of those, several said they had been resigned to, if unhappy about, the situation all along.

I must confess that the way women described themselves and their husbands in the years leading up to the launching stage contradicted my own expectations when I designed the original questionnaire to include queries about the father's role.

Given the work-related absences of most fathers throughout

all the stages of their children's growth, and the general delega-
tion to women of almost every single exhausting and demanding
daily task of child-raising and home management, I had expected more anger and resentment, some outraged sense (fed
by the dawning awareness of alternative lives) of injustice and
exploitation.

Instead, Dad's absence was explained on economic grounds
(which seemed valid to non-wage-earning women at that time)
and on cultural and social grounds, too, for many women now
in mid-life had bought the "separate spheres" theory of family
life lock, stock, and barrel—he to earn the livelihood, she to
manage home and children.

So looking ahead to the children's eventual schooling and
leave-taking, mothers rationalized their situations, at least on
the surface.

Some resentment and anger did appear like flashes of summer
lightning as our talks became more trusting and included more
women. When anger and resentment *did* show themselves, they
mostly had a tone of bitter stoicism, a kind of wry and rueful
cast, as though bowing to one's fate might be hard, but is the
only sensible course in the absence of perceived alternatives.

Of course there were several women whose families were not
typical, where the father's failure on every level led to divorce
or separation. Some women in the group removed their children
from homes where the father was abusive or seriously negligent,
if they could.

But for the conventional households, where the father was a
reasonable emotional support to his family, as well as its financial provider—but was constantly away at work—the mothers of
adult children said the fathers functioned moderately well under
familial pressures.

"From the obstetrician's bill for our first child's delivery to the
last payment on the used car we bought for our youngest so she
could go to a vocational school three towns over, my husband
never complained over twenty-four years and always tried to do
the best he could for us," says Minna R., whose husband is a
transit worker in the Boston subway system and the father of her
three children. Minna was a traditional mother, who never
worked and prided herself on managing her husband's modest
salary well, sewing for the children and cooking thriftily.

Minna's loyal defense was echoed over and over again by

women at every economic level and from every kind of educational, ethnic, religious, and social background.

Not only did the women in our core group show keen appreciation of how tightly their own and the children's well-being and status were linked to the father's income and way of making his living, but they also tried hard to amend the prevailing notion of fathers as people who have a hard time expressing their feelings. Women in the respondent group defended this paternal style as not nearly so impenetrable as it may appear, claiming repeatedly, in different words, "The children always knew he loved them."

The effect of all this defending, explaining, and interpreting, however, was twofold for the mother: It pinned her squarely to total child care and it began her role as intermediary between the father and the children, thus helping us to see how each of the parents could come up to launch time with such different histories with their soon-to-be-adult children.

I asked mothers to rate the father's performance on a scale of percentages (in increments of 10 percent) from zero to 100 percent in response to this question: "*Aside from finances,* how much did the children's father contribute to their upbringing?" The overall average for most fathers was 30 percent of the total needed to accomplish physical and emotional care of the children.

The key importance of this number, I believe, is not so much that fathers left about two-thirds of child care to the mothers, but that the young mothers of twenty to thirty years ago accepted this division of labor as inevitable and natural, even though nowadays it is identified as merely one kind of social arrangement among many possible ones.

The fact that 30 percent was usually tops in terms of father involvement also helps to explain quite completely why mothers reach the time when the young adults leave home with a sense of relief, while father are surprised that it's all gone so fast.

There were exceptions to the general attitude mothers described, however. If fatherly involvement fell much below 20 percent, it spelled trouble in our sample. Some women whose husbands' contributions were rated at 10 or 15 percent had been divorced or separated when the children were small, citing exactly this kind of father failure as one of the main causes.

Other mothers wrote bitter, angry letters even if they remained married to nonparticipating fathers. "His contribution was zero, except for money," wrote one mother, while another said, "He supported us all right, but he really gave us very little else. Our kids always envied other children whose fathers seemed so nice, such fun, who took them to sports events and camping, or even cared enough to scold them or punish them when they did something wrong. He ignored them most of the time and left all of that—both the fun and the discipline—to me. He used his work as an excuse not to give anything to any of us, except money—I will say he was a good provider while the children were growing up."

But where fatherly contributions beyond money were rated *above* 30 percent, mothers were enthusiastic, joyful, almost ecstatic.

"He was my partner in every way in bringing up the children," wrote Sally Ann N., a practical nurse and mother of four. "He was a more natural parent at first than I was," she continued. "He was really a better 'mother' because his personality is calmer, more relaxed, than mine. My husband handled the children with a lot of joy and confidence—I really envied it in those days. I grew into it later, but he was always good at it."

Sally Ann's reference to her husband's joy and confidence underscored an old slogan that says that from a child's point of view, Mom means work and Dad means fun.

This was mentioned repeatedly by many mothers, some of whom pointed out wistfully that since Father was spared the tiring and nerve-frazzling encounters of night-and-day child care, he appeared on the home horizon like a most welcome change, offering less judgmental, less harried, less uptight parenting in some cases.

Many mothers wrote of warm, rich memories of the earlier years with their husbands as chief reader of bedtime stories, player of games, sharer in team sports and outings, education in what were then seen as "masculine" skills of home and car maintenance for sons, and even, occasionally, for daughters.

The women who were able to report that their husbands shared more in the children's upbringing than the norm of 30 percent credited the more equal sharing with enabling them to be better mothers. They said it helped them to prepare for an adult friendship with their children in a much better way than those women who were so close to emotional exhaustion when their children finally left that it took a long time to build an adult relationship.

Nicole B., 52, is the mother of two daughters, three years apart in age, and a lucky wife whose husband tried to go halves with her in a contemporary egalitarian style way back in the early 1950s. She feels his contribution made her a much better mother then and a much better friend to her children now.

This is her eloquent description of how a fifty-fifty partnership worked for her: "My husband worked long hours at his main job and sometimes, while the kids were growing up, he even had to moonlight when there were some bad years," she says, "but even so, he managed to do so much on top of putting bread on the table. He put braces on the teeth, sneakers on the feet, and gas in the car when none of that was easy for our girls."

Nicole divides her husband's contribution to her and the children into four distinct parts, each of which she says she experienced with considerable gratitude. (There is a school of thought that holds gratitude to be an unseemly feeling between two adults who should be mutually appreciative partners; it connotes to some a subservient role, but it appears, nevertheless, very frequently in these maternal accounts.)

Nicole continues her story: "The first, and most important and strongest, contribution he made was that he loved me and supported me in every way, which, in turn, made me able to fulfill my responsibilities as a mother. This was important because I believe in the man as protector and provider—but I brought in some money, too." (Nicole returned to work as a nursery school teacher when her daughters were in their teens, still living at home.)

Nicole says she "reveled" in the sense of her husband as the symbol of the family's security and stability.

"Secondly," she says, "he did an excellent job of making the girls happy with themselves as females. He admired them in a fatherly way, not as a boyfriend or a pal, but as a dad delighted to have such attractive, nice daughters and so proud of them. He helped me in very critical ways that only a father can do to make them feel good about being women.

"Third, I'm an old softie, and his firmer discipline was very helpful. When I gave in too easily, he stayed consistently fair, but tough, and somewhat strict, at least compared with me. We balanced each other out okay, I think.

"And last but not least, he got across a sense of strong family love, even though not always in words, but somehow he did—they knew we'd always be part of each other. He didn't talk about it much, didn't spell it out hardly at all, but the girls knew —they just knew—how much they meant to him."

Not many mothers were able to report such a sharing and participatory experience, but they feel that the economic defense of their husbands holds up—that the kids could never have been launched into some kind of schooling or decent jobs without the financial foundation the father provided.

Given these reports of honest, hard-working fathers, who managed to communicate affection to their children despite a more laconic style than the mothers, we are forced to reevaluate the stereotype of the distant, emotionally frozen American male who is not a particularly good father beyond the breadwinning role.

Is the stereotype, then, a fabrication?

Have mothers prettied up the image a little? (One mother suggested the reason the children "just knew" their fathers cared for them deeply was because the mothers repeatedly told them so!)

Trying to track down the truth of the standard image of father as someone whose children don't really know him very well, we also run into the fact that paternal "failure" is an elastic term. Few Americans will brand as a failure the father who provides financially for his family, even though clergymen and social workers and school psychologists who see economically viable but emotionally very troubled families might differ with society's notions of success and failure.

Also confusing the picture is the small but vocal minority of mothers in the respondent group who *did* complain—loudly and frequently—about the father's absence during crucial child-rearing years, who did *not* feel that breadwinning was the total sum of fathering, and who are very far from gratitude, feeling quite overworked and unfairly treated in the parenting system.

These women said that in this postlaunch period they now face with their adult children, they are much more concerned about their own friendships with their grown kids and are not disposed to be especially helpful to their husbands if the men try hard to "catch up" and begin new adult friendships with the children. "However," grumbled Lillian L., who always felt that her husband loved his work much more than his family, "I suppose I'll get soft-headed as I get older and if it ever dawns on him what he missed with his kids, I'll try to help them get together . . . I guess. . . ."

Why are these youthful middle-aged women so adamant about calling "reasonably good" the fathering performances of men who left almost 100 percent of infant and toddler care to the mother, plus 70 percent of later care, and who have to be marked absent during most of the hour-to-hour milestones and crises of their children's lives?

For two reasons: They wanted the middle-class life that their husband's labor purchased and they had a gut-level awareness that the family could survive and progress in housing, education, and life-style only as the father's earnings and social status also progressed.

This complete reliance on the father's willingness to go into the "jungle" every day was, at that time, accompanied by a melancholy parallel belief: Few women who are now middle-aged believed years ago in their own ability to contribute anything substantial to the family's economic position.

This, many mothers reported, is the biggest change in their attitude toward the father's role as it existed when the children were small and as it exists now in the later stages of parenthood when women have proved to themselves they *can* make some financial contribution to the family.

Even the women who never returned to work described themselves as largely unperturbed by such complete reliance on their husband's income since this financial dependence appears to them to be neither servile nor lacking in self-respect; it appears, they said, much more like a respectably equal partnership. (Hidden behind this serenity, I also detected some fearful women whose marriages were rocky and who were terrified of being left on their own with no skills or training for the job market.)

Coming up to launch time, then, some mothers saw the fathers of their children as helping in all aspects of parenthood, while the great majority accepted the father's role as financial provider as sufficient reason for his absent, nonparticipating style of homelife.

The mothers' characterization of the fathers as contributing 30 percent to the total child care picture certainly raises a serious question for the future: Can such a father forge the same kinds of friendship with his adult children that a full-time, caretaking mother can achieve?

The Future: Old and New Styles of Fathering

Middle-aged men today face several difficult problems in attempting to do the later parenting that women are just now exploring in the new life stage that begins when the children leave home.

One is that contemporary images of fathers seem to be changing (at least on the surface and with lip service) and Dad's old style of working hard and leaving everything else to Mom is in a bit of disrepute at the moment.

Mothers are still acceptable to some degree as role models, women tell us, because although their daughters don't intend to be so home-centered as their mothers were, they still admire and respect their mother's practical knowledge about child-rearing.

Fathers who came of age in World War II, however, are viewed by both their sons and daughters as having been excessively preoccupied with their work and as having missed a great deal of family life.

So middle-aged fathers are looking down the second-stage parenting road and seeing that their value as role models is lower than they might have hoped or expected a generation or two ago.

Nina W., mother of three, whose husband will retire in another year, outlines the problem evocatively: "Look," she says, "what can my poor husband look forward to when our daughter is married to an ex-lawyer who is staying home now as a househusband to care for their two small children while she finishes up medical school, and our son keeps talking all the time about being 'into fatherhood' when and if he ever gets married? Jim just is bewildered. He loves his kids, he's crazy about his two little grandchildren, but he's . . . well, he's awkward with these new ideas. He doesn't feel comfortable when our son-in-law describes toilet training problems. . . ."

The contemporary old-style dad has the problem sharply focused for him every time he passes a bookstore. There, prominently displayed, are half a dozen new books with titles like *New Parenthood: The First Three Months for Fathers.* Also prominently displayed is another publishing phenomenon, author Bob Greene's book *Good Morning, Merry Sunshine,* in which a street-smart, urban-beat reporter writes a tender and observant journal of his baby daughter's first year. This book, virtually a bible for the new father (despite some old attitudes toward his wife), says explicitly: "I knew I would rather be here [in the room where his wife was giving birth] than in the waiting room of my father's generation. . . ."

Our sample group of mothers observe keenly that their husbands are seen by this generation of new fathers as having failed both wives and children in important ways, and that this generation gap on the issue of fathering once more draws in the mother to attempt to build bridges between the two.

"My husband really turned white when our son told him he eased the baby's head out and cut the umbilical cord at a home birth when our granddaughter was born," says Raefaela P., mother of four, "but I've had a good long talk with him, and I think he understands it all a little better now, even though he will never find it possible to think of himself in such a situation."

There are some factors that may eventually assist the mothers in trying to cross this gulf between old and new attitudes on fathering. One is that the change is far from complete. As some family historians have noted, the social fabric woven of old attitudes has taken generations to evolve—it will not be overturned in a decade or two.[1] There are still many, many young men to be found in the 1,500 adult children whose mothers speak to us in this book who want a traditional stay-at-home wife and who expect to father much as their own old-style dads did—earning the living, choosing the family car, going to football games without their wives, and never becoming terribly good at Pampers and Snugglis, while, perhaps being just as good as their fathers were at love, care, and concern.

A second factor that may boost old-style dads' standing is that the new young fathers haven't figured out yet how to combine much more time with their wives and children with the continuing demands that they be the primary wage earner. The perfectly equal marriage in which both wife and husband work the same number of hours and devote the same number of hours to home and child care is not with us yet to any appreciable degree outside of a few social strata in a very few large cities. Moreover, there's even a minitrend observable that has career-oriented young mothers deciding to temporarily forgo some steps up the ladder and stay home with their children for a year or two.

Mature mothers believe it is quite possible that when some of the dust settles from these role changes, their husbands' performance as primary wage earner will be reevaluated in the light of what young couples face as they aim for a brave new world of parenthood in the same old world of fierce economic pressures.

A research educator who recently wrote a book on day care for working parents said that when she spoke to young college women with strong career drives about how they intended to combine work with motherhood, "They didn't have a clue. They knew that there might be a problem, but they didn't know its magnitude. And they certainly didn't know the solutions. . . ."[2]

Middle-aged mothers in the respondent group are aware of these confusions among their young adult sons and daughters and are hoping they will lead to a more benign view of the old-style dad as one who perhaps "did the best he could with how he was brought up and what the times asked of him," as one mother put it.

But some of the changes are here to stay, most of our mothers agreed. Young new fathers do, by and large, want to share to at least a greater extent than their fathers did in family life, and there are bound to be some rocky times ahead for old-style dads if they don't shed fixed notions about what is appropriate masculine behavior.

"Our fathers may have taught us to fish, or play ball, or fix a car, or run a business, but *they did not tell us how to handle a baby who won't stop crying,*" wrote a young journalism professor in a recent issue of *New Age Journal,* a magazine aimed at the post-1960s generation.[3]

The mature partners of these old-style dads see an immense load of work ahead to smooth these paths for each other.

There is an overarching question in family management that plagues all generations and both sexes and has a bearing on how middle-aged fathers will handle both their sons and daughters in future adult relationships.

That question is: Do women really have a more "natural" involved response to infants than men can ever have?

Are women merely socially conditioned to coo at babies, with the implication that men could be conditioned that way too if society ever got as interested in father-bonding as it is in mother-bonding?

Or has evolution programmed something into females so that they are actually "better"—or at least more intuitively knowledgeable than men—about helping the human species to survive?

Wives who discussed their husbands' future with their adult sons and daughters had no scientific answer to the question, but they quickly saw how its interpretation would affect later relationships.

Said Betsy A., the mother of three married daughters, none of whom have children as yet, but all of whom say they have plans for families "eventually," mused out loud about the possible future.

"If it turns out that our sons-in-law really think they can't be any good at child care because our daughters were just born knowing it all, then I guess all the modern stuff about sharing will go down the drain and we'll see more of what we used to see: my husband and our sons-in-law going out back and fooling around with the cars and trucks," said Betsy. "But if our daughters insist they try or if just their own curiosity leads them, then I think they might get more involved with the grandkids and there would be a sort of gap for my husband . . . I'm just not sure where that's going to end up."

The prevailing belief among both old-style fathers and new young dads that women are endowed with a special built-in ability to deal with infants and small children, an ability that is forever foreclosed to men, was seen by one contemporary mother of two sons as "an awful lot of baloney." Angie F., neither of whose sons is yet married, said she would urge any prospective daughters-in-law to "nip that one in the bud—because men just use it as an excuse to duck their share of the work, the really hard work, I mean, of trying to understand what their kids are feeling as well as what they need in physical care."

Angie said she is convinced that throughout her own marriage of thirty-two years, her husband used that notion in what psychologists call "learned helplessness" to save the parts of child care for himself that he liked the best—taking the boys to ball games and sight-seeing, making music with them—and leaving the less enjoyable details to her since she "did them so much better."

She is convinced, too, that her husband will extend that to his grandchildren, if they ever arrive, and will seek to make an ally of his sons in the belief that women are just born knowing things about babies and children that men can never learn.

In fact, scientists haven't definitively answered the question of whether the way women respond to infants and children is indeed totally socially conditioned, learned behavior, or whether there is an innate something that came down through millennia of species development.

In the meantime, mothers see their role as helping their husbands share the parental support, sympathy, and understanding—in a word, the friendship—that their adult sons and daughters will need as they undertake new family styles.

Many students of human behavior and family patterns have noticed that men often do become more nurturing as they get older; there seems to be tendency for roles to reverse a little. As women get freer of day-to-day child care, they often move out into the world more strongly. As men get closer to letting go of well-established work patterns, they often are willing to take on more caring jobs.

Perhaps this is the tendency that will, in the end, make old-style dads adapt better to the possibilities their sons and daughters are exploring and mute some of the scorn heaped on the always working, never home dad of yore.

One mother told of receiving a letter one Christmas from an old college boyfriend who, she knew, had married and divorced and never remarried in the thirty years since they graduated together.

"In the letter," she recounts, "he spoke with great interest and pride of his grandchildren, since he had three children from his one failed marriage. He told me quite candidly that he had never been either a good husband or a good father, but now, listen to this"—she pulled the letter from her purse and read the following—" 'I have been to see my one grandson stationed in the Pacific in Hawaii with the navy, caught my granddaughter on a whirlwind sight-seeing trip to Washington, and expect to spend the Easter holiday with Jim's boy who is in college up in New England—it's been a little breathless, but I've enjoyed it right up to the hilt. Maybe it turns out that I'm a much better grandfather than I ever was a father. . . .' "

Maybe, said the other mothers in a discussion group, but don't bet on it—not without a lot of help from mothers.

8

Friendship and Familyship: The Role That Grown Children Play in Their Mothers' Lives Now

My darling: Be strong. Know that you are deeply loved by your mother and that it is even a strange thing to be a mother, seeing we are only just human beings who live together in our own ways. . . .

POET ANNE SEXTON, in a letter to her daughter

*I*n *Mid-Life: Developmental and Clinical Issues,* Malkah Topin Notman observes: "[Some women] do not perceive separation from children solely as a loss, but as an opportunity for adding something to their lives. . . ."

"How do I see my children now? They're delicious—delightful! They're fun and joyful . . . they're more like people now, like peers, they're easy to be with . . . and, of yes, of course, I worry about them constantly!" says Jill N., mother of twin daughters and a son, all in their twenties.

"We're friends now!" This is the surprisingly frequent answer from middle-aged women to this question: "Though your children are grown and gone, we assume some sort of continuing connection; what role do they play in your life now?" More than half the core group of 108, and about 45 percent of the larger group of nearly 500 women, gave some version of Jill's answer.

But there were a good many who consciously considered, and then rejected, the friendship description. These women answered, with a slightly startled air, "Why, they're my *family!*" One mother explained: "Family are people you don't have to stay in touch with all the time to know you're connected—and very importantly connected, at that. With friends, you do have to stay pretty much in touch; otherwise the friendship just kind of withers or melts away."

Still other mothers said: "Yes, they are more like friends my own age now, but yet . . . there's something else there, too." A small group of women said they were struggling toward friendship with their adult children but didn't think they had arrived there yet.

The smallest group, about 12 percent of the core sample, said their own or their children's lives were so full of disappointment and sorrow (from the mother's viewpoint) that a real adult friendship was unlikely in the foreseeable future. This latter group said their battles were, instead, to preserve some sense of a family, at almost any level, no matter how minimal, and they would have to hope for progress toward friendship later.

But there was no question that the largest group of women, in describing the changing roles the children played in their lives from birth to young adulthood, saw the current stage as being that of enjoyable friends.

"At birth," explained one mother, "they're sort of an achievement, a success. From then on until they leave home, it's responsibility—big and heavy, probably the heaviest I'll ever know. But now, it's much more carefree, much more like the pure pleasure you have with friends for whose lives you are not so responsible."

As interviews and group discussions progressed, as history unfolded, and as research into generational relations produced new information, the frequency with which women described this friendship within familyship became pleasantly surprising. It seemed to me that the odds might be weighted against such a workable friendship for three major reasons:

One is that these same women were sadly unanimous about *not* having been friends, as daughters, with their own mothers.

Loving, dutiful, responsible, yes; friends, no. Only a handful said they admired or approved of the way their mothers mothered them; only 12 out of 208 said they tried to model their own maternal styles closely after their mothers', though most admitted they included at least a few elements of their mothers' methods (and not always the best ones) in their own family-raising patterns. So they had virtually no "friend" model with their own mothers.

Second, true friendship between the generations is problematical for many reasons, but surely primary is the difficulty of resolving the dependence/independence conflict that lies at the heart of maturation for the young generation and graceful letting go for the older one, and no one I interviewed felt this had been perfectly resolved with each child.

Even though friendships with one's own age peers may have aspects of competitiveness and power struggles, seldom do same-age friends take the responsibility or blame for the lives their adult friends led before they met; that particular albatross can only be around the necks of parents and children, mothers point out.

The historic quality of this responsibility was insightfully put by Mary Kay Blakely, a writer and essayist, describing the sometimes thorny path she and her mother had traveled toward friendship as the daughter matured: "She has mother hankerings for a Good Daughter, I have daughter yearnings for Mother Approval. . . . We tried to withhold our ideas from each other, avoiding conflict . . . but it was always a temporary truce because, for all the right and complicated reasons, we required more than a peaceful coexistence with each other. . . ."[1]

The third reason I found the "friend" role surprising as described so frequently by mothers is that friendship between such unequal partners as an always-adult parent and an only-lately-adult child depends peculiarly upon the child's memory of the family situation when he or she was small and growing up.

Memory is faulty at best, and few human relationships can be more distorted (as many psychotherapists know) than what children think they remember about their parents. Inaccurate memories, hazy judgments based on error, imaginary barriers of all sorts, including idealization and canonization of parents up to sainthood, have blasted many a potentially fruitful and mature mother-child friendship. When this happens, I observed, the mother is often bewildered and hurt; ultimately, there is a pathetic resignation and acceptance of a chilly relationship. Mothers said that, obviously, their experience of the past just doesn't jibe with how the children saw the picture.

Simultaneously, women also reported that they believed the growing-up children caught, with incredible precision, highly significant feeling states within the family, but they said this could go on at the same time that the same children might have been misinterpreting all sorts of events in the family's life.

With the potential for confusion so great, and with certain intergenerational strains built into the relationship, how have so many of today's contemporary American mothers found it possible, at least intermittently, to reach a brand new level of active friendship with their now grown kids, to achieve a modern "tone" unknown between them and their own mothers?

And how have so many more found their way, if not to what they wish to call friendship, then to a kind of "familyship" that includes a component of conventional friendship?

Experts have said that the goal of the relationship of parents and adult children should be "intimacy at a distance"[2] or "dependent independence."[3] These definitions of how adult children could be comfortably located within their parents' lives, to the satisfaction of both generations, reflect some of the feelings women have been describing under the rubric "we're friends now."

To understand how this has been achieved against strong odds—including the staggering social discontinuity, the break in established standards and values caused by the watershed 1960s—we have to turn to the past, to these women as daughters, and then later, as mothers of adolescents.

In addition, to define this friendship realistically, we'll look at the contemporary world of this moment that both mothers and young adults are inhabiting, and see what strengthens and what threatens that friendship under the pressures of our times. Finally, we'll look briefly at the unhappy families where friendship is elusive, and the possibilities of new hope there.

First, the more distant past in which today's middle-aged mothers were themselves daughters.

Scenes From Home Movies

> "I know one *thing*," she said hoarsely. "I know that if there is
> an afterlife, I'm going to have a very different kind of family. I'm
> going to have nothing but fabulously rich, witty, and enchant-
> ing children."
>
> JOHN CHEEVER, "Goodbye, My Brother"

Lisa R., 50, mother of three, had devastating words for her own
mother: "My mother was a negative force in our lives; she was
a nagging perfectionist, insecure, a harsh woman, unable to
show affection. I've tried to be the exact opposite with our
children."

There they stand—the woman who is a mother, and her
grown sons and daughters—facing each other across a gulf of
time and place, a chasm of history, memory, vastly differing life
experiences. Our modern mothers believe they have somewhat
bridged that gulf and are on the shore of friendship, but did they
also reach back in the other direction? Were they friends with
their own mothers? Was that where they saw a model of familyships that contained friendships?

Not only is the answer negative, but in discussing the question, the mothers interviewed drew such shockingly rejecting
portraits of their mothers that one can only wonder how they did
the reasonably good job they did with their own children; the
friendship they currently describe seems even more remarkable
in the light of this past.

For nearly a third of the core group of 208 mothers, the whole
subject was even too painful to discuss. More than 80 of them
preferred not to talk about their own relationship with their
mothers or how their own maternal guide had influenced them
for better or worse.

Of the 121 women who agreed to discuss in depth their view
of their own mothers' mothering performance, only 8—or a bit
more than 6 percent—saw their mothers as admirable models to
be emulated, wonderful mentors who could inspire their own
maternal behavior.

In this small number of instances, these women saw and described mothers in whom two fortunate events had come to-

gether: The women themselves were clearly sensitive, intelligent, and attentive to their children's needs, and the external circumstances of their lives (enough money, good health, support from the father) permitted them to give generously of these qualities to their children, now the middle-aged mothers of this book.

But for nearly 95 percent of the respondent group, their view of their own mothers ranged from, at best, pitying sympathy for a life so different from their own, to, at worst, a resentment, anger, and hostility still palpable in ordinary conversation.

In the middle of the spectrum was the largest group of women, whose attitude toward their own mothers—the women who came of age half a century or more ago—was affectionate, even loving, but not at all comradely or peerlike.

Representative of this middle group is Paulette M., a slim, pretty woman whose youthful blond haircut and designer jeans belie her fifty-three years of hard struggle as the daughter of working-class parents and the mother of now middle-class grown sons and daughters, two of each.

Paulette is the first-generation American child of Ukrainian immigrants who labored hard with their hands at bottom-of-the-ladder jobs all of their lives, but she and her husband, an equally hard-working, white-collar bank employee, together (Paulette has always worked) have achieved these signs of material success: a home of their own and recently, a second vacation home, modest community college degrees for three of their four children, and enough affluence that travel, dining out, and quality clothes, cars, and household goods are not unknown in this close-knit family.

Paulette and her husband not only accomplished all this with little formal education and only the smallest help in nonmonetary forms from their own parents, but they have managed to build enviable friendships with their grown children along the way.

Here is Paulette discussing her own mothering task as differentiated from her mother's: "My mom was great in many ways and I respect the job she did—but there's no question, also, that there were many things that stood in the way of her being what I would consider a good mother. Being foreign-born and old-fashioned was just part of it; people in her day just didn't know as much as we know today about kids. There were several ways in which I did the same things my mom did, but also there were some big, important things I did very differently. For instance, my mom was very strict, a real tough disciplinarian, who demanded and got respect from her children. . . . I have not been that tough, but I have always demanded and easily received respect from my children, and on that point, I agree [with her own mother] that respect is very important. My children know it and have always granted it to me. Another thing: My mother impressed me mightily with her ideas about how important it was always to be a 'lady.' That meant you were never loud or rude, you were careful about your reputation, you always tried to look as nice, as clean and neat as you could, even if you couldn't afford fancy or expensive things. There were certain things she felt were the refined ways a lady acted and looked, and I think, deep down, I sort of agree. I've tried to be that way myself and to raise my daughters as ladies, too, and they are, but I don't think that's ever been a burden—for my mom or me, or for my girls, it was just the way my mother was, and I must have absorbed it without question.

"But on big important things, I hate to say it, but my mother was nowhere. I am much more modern, much closer in touch with my children about everything. And there is one big, *big* thing that I go in a diametrically opposite way from my mother, and that is, anything to do with the body—menstruation, sex, all those things were strictly taboo with my mother. She did not prepare me at all for menstruation and my girl friends at school had to explain to me what was happening. She always used the strangest kind of words and indirect names for bodily processes and sexual matters. I try never to do that with my kids; I'm really a bear about always using the correct words to describe the body, sex, and things like that. I think those phony words were seriously bad, I really do. I feel that the way I discuss sex with my children—both my sons and daughters—is much more the natural way I talk about so many other things with them, too. That open way of talking, of including the children in what you're thinking and doing, is something my mother never could do with any of her kids. Our chidren are just so much more in touch, we communicate so much more than I ever could with my mother."

Paulette continues: "As a result, Franny and Donna are just so much closer to me than I ever was with my mother—and my sons and their wives, too. I've always been much more aware of where my kids were at any given moment in their lives [Paulette meant emotionally, not geographically] than my mother ever was about me. We had to live with my parents for a while after we were married, and even after our first baby was born, and I was working, I felt there were so many things about my life as a young wife and mother that I really could not discuss with my mother. She made me feel too shy or she didn't seem to under-stand—or something—you don't really share things with her. No, I didn't have any real companionship or friendship, or shar-ing, as an adult with my mother after I grew up, and maybe that's why I enjoy it so much with my daughters and daughters-in-law now—because I never did have it as a young married woman with my own mother."

Paulette's portrait of her mother, sad as it is in some ways, is positively benign compared to these comments from other women:

• "My mother raised us as if we lived in the Dark Ages; she wouldn't let us do anything at all. I hated that life, and made sure it would be completely different for my kids—they are open, fun-loving, adventurous—they're wonderful kids."

• "My mother demanded complete, unquestioning obedi-ence; our church was strict and narrow; a good switching was not unknown if you asked about anything, and there was very little love expressed, though it may have been there. My husband and I have made it completely different for our kids—we hug and kiss and joke and they have much freedom to be active, par-ticipating members of the family."

• "My mother never respected my individuality or my privacy; I felt I was like a possession, an object among others, that needed constant cleaning and repair, but I never felt she knew who I was as a person, just as an obligation of hers. I am much, much more aware of the individual needs of my children."

• "My mother was very possessive; she clung like a leech. I try to give my sons much more freedom to be themselves and to grow toward their own independence; I think what parents are about is to raise their kids to be totally self-sufficient, to do without the parent, in other words."

• "My mother threatened us all the time in order to make us behave; I grew up being punished constantly and was fearful of God, the policeman, bogeymen, and other vague threats. I was never allowed, as a girl, to think of sports or games or outdoor fun, because it was seen as too dangerous. Naturally, I've tried to do things very differently and both our sons and our daughter are encouraged to try anything they're interested in."

• "I never told my mother anything—nothing that was important—never! I loved her and she loved me, I know, but we could never really talk about anything; talk about fears and worries or about love and sex—with my *mother?* There just was no way she could ever understand my life. She lived only for the church and the house, not even so much for my dad or us kids. She never understood why I wanted to go somewhere, do something, have some different kind of life . . . but she loved me deeply, of that I'm certain, and I was heartbroken when she died, but she never had the faintest idea what my life was about after I grew up."

This litany could continue for more than a hundred reports, but they bear a depressing similarity to each other.

What seems to be emerging here is the outline of a maternal generation that perhaps has to be viewed with a more dispassionate eye than its own daughters can summon.

The women who appear in these memory portraits to be so unloving and strict, or, if affectionate, hobbled by all kinds of constraints of convention, history, and economics, are women whose lives were limited by circumstances their contemporary daughters have never known. Therefore, their ability to be good models has been sharply compromised.

The mothers of our middle-aged group of respondent women were born in the late nineteenth or early twentieth century and came of age around the turn of that century or a bit later on into the World War I era. Many were either immigrants themselves or first-generation American-born children of immigrants, often living in genteel poverty or economic struggles difficult for their own children to remember.

Moreover, they bore their children, many of them, either in the "old country" or in an American culture so strange to them —fast-paced, transient, socially mobile—that it seems quite possible they would hold their children close, cling to the old ways, and make the youngsters fearful of the huge, dangerous world outside, trying to enforce a strict discipline as a way of coping with the shifting, unstable tides of immigrant life.

Not all the women in our sample suffered from the hardships of "The Uprooted"[4] or from harsh financial struggle; six of those in the core group came from quite wealthy families and five from families they described as "much better off than most in those days." All eleven of these women, however, recalled with bitterness and resentment that they had received little mothering from either parent (and what they got came more often from fathers than mothers in this upper-class context) and that they had been raised by nurses, governesses, and other servants. Of the eleven in this group, eight said they rebelled strongly aginst that pattern and while they themselves freely employed all kinds of household help, they never permitted nurses or other servants to care for their own children, except for very brief periods.

"Circumstances have a great deal to do with child-rearing," observed a 73-year-old grandmother who accompanied her 51-year-old daughter to a group discussion.

This was certainly confirmed by accounts of many of the mother interviewees, who described how shifting breadwinner fortunes, premature deaths of mothers from childbirth complications and other medical problems now largely conquered, and ironclad social conventions of that era altered the ebb and flow of their relationships with their own mothers.

They describe an abyss of "modernity" and affluence between themselves and their mothers that is not so starkly present between middle-aged women of today and their adult children.

Moira T., a vivacious middle-aged cosmetics saleswoman, who says she is good friends with her 27-year-old businessman son and her 23-year-old librarian daughter, describes this abyss as a "knowledge gap."

Here is Moira's description of the problem: "Between me and my mother, an Irish woman who had four of her kids in the old country and three more, including me, here in America, there's this knowledge gap. I mean, my mother was a wonderful, brave woman—I probably couldn't have done what she did, leave her home and family to come here—but between my dad's small wages and the hard work of bringing up seven kids, what could you expect of her? To get us all brought up alive and well—one of my brothers was killed in World War II—was enough for her and she deserves all the love and respect and praise in the world, which we kids tried to give her.

"But," Moira points out, "between me and my kids, it's just such a whole different thing. We really have a lot more in common; we have the same kind of entertainment and recreation, we all love TV and the movies, we take trips together. And I've worked steadily since the children were in junior high. I understand their working life and they understand mine and their father's. Besides, I just know a lot more about children. I read Spock and other books when I was pregnant, I had a great pediatrician to help me, I had two years of college. Being a mother is a completely different thing in my day . . . and don't forget, I have two kids, she had seven."

An ability to close that knowledge gap does, indeed, seem to be one of the major propelling forces that bring today's mothers together with their adult children in patterns these same women never had with their own mothers. That, plus a determination to behave in a different way than their own mothers, helps push the generations together. Another vivid description of the knowledge gap is provided by Lillian T., mother of two sons.

"The difference, really," says Lillian, "is that we now know about child psychology and our mothers just plain didn't. I'm sure there were smart, observant women who figured out very well what was going on with their kids, without needing to read it in books, but I think a lot of them really did not know what children need to grow in a healthy way. My mother, the children's grandmother, is now eighty-three, and to this day she does not believe there is such a thing in this world as sibling rivalry, she is horrified about our ideas about sex education, and she is appalled at how we used to take our kids to restaurants and on trips when they were small; she still thinks small children should always be at home."

In discussing the differences between themselves and their own mothers, many women touched on these aspects of their own lives: better education (most of their mothers were barely able to manage a high-school diploma and many did not go beyond eighth grade), better health as a group, more income, and a larger world of expert knowledge at their disposal.

In addition, today's middle-aged women had many more labor-saving devices than their mothers, although feminists and family historians are split over the benefits of that domestic convenience, some claiming that it simply introduced higher standards of performance and cleanliness into the household and resulted in women working about the same number of hours at gourmet cooking as their mothers did carrying water from the well to heat on a wood stove.

But there seemed little doubt that contemporary women feel they have, to a very great degree, escaped the limitations that fate placed upon the earlier generation.

In addition, a number of social trends have accentuated the feeling of today's mothers that they share more, have more in common, with their adult children. One is the "youth cult," combined with greater longevity and better health, which makes the physical and emotional difference between a 30-year-old and a 50-year-old somewhat less dramatic than it was seventy-five years ago.

The homogenization of fashion (today's grandma wears boots, jeans, sweat pants for exercise, and the same perfumes as her granddaughter) and the pervasiveness of the media and all forms of instant communication mean each generation is receiving the same messages at the same time about what is going on in recreation, leisure, money management, home decoration, and style on all levels.

Over and over again, women described the closing of the age gap and the newer way of staying in touch. These were among the most popular images:

• "We [parents and grown kids] talk about everything, really very little is taboo, except what we think might cause tension."

• "We have conversations with our kids on subjects we never dared talk to our mothers about—money, love, politics, religion, social values. Those were seldom discussed and always indirectly in our house."

• "We *do* so many things together as adults. You never heard about that in my mother's day; parents did things with the kids when they were little, maybe, but when we got too big for family picnics or church socials, we never were much with our parents —they seemed so *old* by then. But today, why, we go skiing and golfing with our kids, we go out to dinner with them at the drop of a hat, we watch TV and we go on trips together—it's just a whole different world."

• "We raised our kids to be part of the family, to present their own opinions and thoughts on things . . . as *our* kids were growing up, the old-fashioned idea that children should be seen and not heard was passé (maybe too passé!) but I do think it makes for a friendly, more comfortable exchange now that they're adults."

What does this friendly exchange consist of? Is there truly a new sort of contemporary tone in the friendship mothers describe, or are they guilty of wishful thinking about dutiful, but emotionally quite distant, young adult children? Let's take a look at what women report about friendship within the family.

The dictionary defines "friend" as "one attached to another by affection or esteem."

The likelihood of what is conventionally thought of as friendship between mothers and their adult children depends on a number of possible definitions of both friendship and family-ship.

There is a point of view that defines mothering as caring for small, dependent children. According to this school, perhaps best exemplified by Elinor Lenz's book *Once My Child, Now My Friend,* one becomes an "ex-parent" by successfully bringing the child to independent, self-sufficient, well-functioning adulthood. Mothering then ceases, and friendship begins, according to this thesis.[5]

But others disagree with the notion that one can outgrow or abandon one's motherhood, and become just friends, as one might become friends with an ex-spouse after an amicable divorce.

"You can never take your parenthood back . . . but you can redefine it," wrote child psychiatrist Dr. Stella Chess in her book *Daughters.* [6]

We submitted this conundrum to our respondent mothers: When are you a mother and when are you a friend?

The majority of women (110 out of 174) did not believe it was either possible or desirable to become an "ex-mother." They thought it very possible to stop treating grown children as though they were small kids, but they saw no path toward denying or abrogating the basic fact that they were mothers to their children.

The friendship they said they sought with their children—and that many felt they were achieving to one degree or another— was a friendship that was based on (1) the long history of the road they already had traveled with their children; (2) the reality that the grown son or daughter no longer needed the same kind of ever-present care and attention they needed as young children, but now needed other kinds of attention, love, and support; and (3) the recognition that the mother's world has changed through the changes of the past twenty years and that she is now more aware of "where the children are coming from."

Obviously, this friendship has a great many family-colored strands of affection or esteem and this intertwining of past history with present comradely concerns is called by one articulate mother "friendship extra strength."

Dolores R. is the mother of five grown children, three of them the natural children of Dolores and her husband, Bob, and two of them Asian children adopted in the aftermath of the Korean War in the 1950s.

"On one hand," says Dolores, "there's no question that we do things with and for our grown kids that our mothers never were involved with. We have serious, mature discussions about every important topic under the sun; we've talked about racism and sexism with our grown children, about nuclear war, and when they were teenagers we talked and thought a lot together about drugs, about too much TV, about too-early sex—subjects our own parents would have never dreamed of talking about with immature children. And besides all that, we do a lot of fun things together. We do gardening and we can and freeze our produce together, we go to street fairs in the city and hiking trips in the country with our kids—we share many, many things with them, and I admit that these are pretty much the sorts of things we also do with friends our own age—so it looks like our kids are just like all our other friends.

"But," explains Dolores, "the difference comes in times of trouble or times of happiness—in good times and bad crises. Of course, we all feel bad for our friends if they have trouble and we try to help them as much as we can, but oh, it's so different when it's one of your own children! So, so different! And the way the kids care about us is different, too, in some way I can't quite put my finger on—different from even the way our closest friends of our own age care about us. There's something special there and I call it 'friendship extra strength' because I can get it over the telephone from my sons and daughters whenever I need it, like aspirin out of a bottle!"

Another mother snorted indignantly at the notion of "ex-parents" or "just friends" as the texture of the relationship she wants with her adult children. She leaned forward earnestly in her seat at a discussion group, pointed a finger vehemently at the six women gathered together, and asked urgently, "Do you want to be down somewhere in the middle of the list, along with college roommates or friends at work, when it comes time for your son or son-in-law to call you and tell you your daughter or daughter-in-law just gave birth to your first grandchild? You bet your sweet tootsies you don't! You want to be at the very top of that list—or least Number Two right behind the other grandparents—and you know it!"

Besides the long and special history that creates a bridge, there's also another fresh route toward peer-style friendships that many mothers described.

It is the fact that many transition mothers (those who stayed home when the children were young, but have returned to school and/or work over the past decade and a half) now share a common world of work with their adult sons and daughters just entering that world. They share common concerns ("We talk about office politics") and a common language ("We all know what 'reorganizing the staff' means") that is more peerlike in its outward lineaments.

An amusing, yet telling, example of this new, fresh way of

bonding was provided by one mother who brought with her to a group discussion the Mother's Day card that her eldest son, recently graduated from an expensive training school and launched on a career in real-estate development, sent her from a business trip thousands of miles away. The card was delivered to the mother's own office, where she handles customer complaints for a large furniture manufacturer.

The cover showed dialogue emanating from an invisible voice (meant to be the son's) that shouted, "Where's dinner?" and the mother's hands were shown serving dinner; the son shouted, "Where's clean laundry?" and the mother's hands were shown on a pile of folded shirts; then, "Where's the cash?" and the mother's hands delivered a stack of bills. Inside, the card said: "We have an excellent working relationship; you're promoted, Mom, and Happy Mother's Day."

The women who passed the card around the group said it was a good, if unsubtle, microcosm of the transitional mother's life: There were certainly many years when the steady delivery of services was the main coin of exchange between these women and their now-adult children. But as of today, both generations understand that a "working relationship" can provide a colleaguelike friendship that is enjoyable for both.

Terry B., the mother of two sons and a daughter, wrote on the back of her questionnaire: "I believe that my working for some years now and my youngest daughter's just beginning work after finishing secretarial school is one of the very big major things—almost *the* main thing—right now in our relationship. We tell each other about our bosses, we talk about clothes for work, we specialize in giving each other quick recipes, because she just got married recently and her husband works a different shift than her ordinary office day. She has to give him a fast dinner after she gets home and before he goes off to work. I don't know whether she would believe that I understand how pressured and busy her life is now if I wasn't working."

Another mother tells how her oldest son, who is in his last year of engineering school, already has been recruited for his first job by a large company. He is clearly beginning to think of himself as a worker and thus looking at his mother's life differently, since Carla N. is one of the mothers who always held temporary or part-time jobs when her children were in school all day. She believes that although her children never saw her as a career woman, they did form some idea of her as a competent person outside the home, as well as in it.

"Now," she says of her engineer son, "he is beginning to realize that he will be working a nine-to-five job soon, just as I and his father have all these years. The other night, when we were talking to him on the phone, I mentioned that my office had been going through a reorganization. He asked, 'Is that going to be a problem for you, Mom?' The silence in the air was different. It was a grown-up question—like a colleague might ask."

There is no doubt that the working mother and the working adult child have a world in common that acts as cement for their present relationship, but what of the mother who never did return to either school or work and continues her more traditional role of worker solely within the home?

About 75 women out of the 208 in our core sample continue to be traditional homemakers, and they were split right down the middle, almost evenly divided on the pros and cons of how that traditional role affects their friendship with their working children.

Some stay-at-home mothers admitted to nervousness on the subject and one woman said she felt her daughter had a well-disguised but genuine "contempt" for the way the mother spends her days. Another said that her grown son "worries about me—he's afraid that if I'm ever widowed, I won't be able to cope." But many more women said they felt perfectly comfortable in the respect their children showed for all that they had done for the family, and they felt their friendship with their adult children was not at all adversely affected by their having different kinds of life-styles and a different sort of marriage than the patterns their children are pursuing.

"We all just live in different times," said Louisa T., mother of two, cheerfully adding, "I don't want to live their lives for anything, and they needn't ever feel sorry for mine—I'm having a great time!"

"It does make a difference, though," mused Ada N., mother of three daughters. "When I was growing up, I wanted to marry Audie Murphy or John Wayne and have a hope chest, a diamond engagement ring, and a colonial house with an early-American kitchen. My daughter wants to be the head of her own business, own a sailboat, and take vacations in Tibet or somewhere; she says marriage and kids will come along whenever. Yes, she *does* see my life as sort of terribly narrow and somewhat dull—but," Ada grins, "we're moving toward friendship and it will get better as she gets older and finds out that steering a big sailboat by yourself isn't that easy. I've got patience—we'll get together eventually."

Almost all the women, whether traditional or transitional, felt there was a maternal component of relief in the new friendship —relief that since the kids were now moving into major adult areas of life on their own two feet, they thus became much more likely candidates for the role of friend.

"To sense that they're so strong and sturdy—they have good judgment and are maturing—it just makes me giddy with relief and happiness," exclaimed Patty W., mother of four. "It works to loosen me up and let me talk to them in ways I never thought I would. I confide some 'heavy' stuff in them, now—I tell them about my own hopes and dreams, what's become of my life, both the goods and the bads, because they're really able to be grown-up friends now.

"Of course," adds Patty, "you never stop worrying about them—now you worry whether they're happy in their marriages and whether they'll ever have kids and—well, no, it isn't *exactly* like a friendship you have with people your own age."

Gina F., the mother of three adult sons, summed up the question of the role the children play in her life now this way: "I think, among other things, we're good friends. We can do things together as adults. They are somewhere between being children of mine and being peers."

These friendships now in the making also hold the seeds of all the ordinary kinds of difficulties and strains that arise between age-peer friends, too. Mothers described the same sorts of misunderstandings, annoyances, and frustrations common to any long-running friendship. Three women were particularly outspoken about the feelings of envy and competitiveness they have with their grown children. One mother who is a gifted musician, although she never pursued a concert career of her own, recounted with embarrassment how conflicted she was when she saw many facets of artistic talent, including a strong musicianship, arise in her youngest child, a daughter. Bonnie P. admitted that while she enjoyed seeing the young woman "so creative and so full of artistic energy," she was sheepishly glad when the daughter decided on dance as her vocation. "I've got to admit," says Bonnie, "that it did flash through my mind—how would I feel if she turned out to be a better pianist than I am? Would we be such good friends then as I think we are now? Not sure!"

"The amount of tact it takes to be friends with your grown kids is just mind-boggling," contributed Marge N., mother of a son and a daughter. "Even though they're out and on their own, you still can't tell them you don't like the new couch or that they're making a mistake spending so much time in a relationship that isn't going anywhere. Of course, you would be diplomatic about those things with friends your own age, too, but the difference is this: Your friends don't need your approval the way your kids do. No matter how old your children are, they want an okay from Mom; even if they act in the opposite way, that's what they really want—we all do, forever—for as long as our mothers live, I think. So you have to watch what you're saying a lot more, but on the other hand, the friendship you get back probably means more than most of your other friendships, anyway."

Marge, like Gina and a number of the other mothers mentioned earlier, was describing a middle ground somewhere between friends and family that offers a resting place for both generations. On that middle ground, the special caring of the early years is not discarded, but is structured, instead, around the attachment by affection or esteem that the dictionary defines as friendship.

I asked the many women who felt they had gained that middle ground to try to trace how that bridge had been constructed across the generation gap and how it works in the normal ups and downs of daily life.

Postadolescent Rapprochement: The Roots of Friendship

> But you couldn't control which, out of a day's events, would lodge themselves in your child's memory, to apply to his life and maybe alter the course of it. That was one of the most frightening aspects of being a parent: you never knew *what* a child was going to remember or how he was going to remember it.
>
> GAIL GODWIN, *A Mother and Two Daughters*

"At fifteen, he started to curdle; by twenty, he had smoothed out and was almost a human being, and now that he's twenty-six, we're friends," said Harriet L., mother of an only son.

From the accounts of the respondent group of mothers, the bridges they've been building to their grown children had a specific starting point in time: They began during a period that could be called the "postadolescent rapprochement" phase of the mother-child history.

This is the often-remarked-upon period when children who've been hostile, distant, rebellious, and who have displayed a whole range of other not very charming moods, begin to leave the storms of adolescence behind and try to reintegrate themselves on a more grown-up level. If this reintegration is reasonably successful, mothers say the new growth begins to become noticeable at around eighteen and continues for a decade or even longer, as some late bloomers finally reach stable ground in their thirties. ("When your kid becomes fit to live with, he or she is usually living with someone else," wryly observed one veteran mother of four children.)

To the question "Was there a noticeable time when the uproar of the teen years began to subside and you felt less tension and more communication with your growing-up children?" a group of 86 women out of 132 answered, "Yes, I could see a definite time period when our relationship improved." (Interestingly, a substantial minority of women—40 of them—said they experienced no, or very little, adolescent uproar and thought of those years as very happy and enjoyable for both generations.)

The sense that the period beginning in the children's early twenties was a "coming back together" on new, higher ground was very important to the women who experienced it because, they said, it often followed ten or more years, including, but not limited to, adolescence, when they felt that they and their children were not really in touch and were missing each other often on the road to better understanding of one another. "I stopped talking when she stopped listening," said one mother of her daughter's behavior in this period.

"Loving," explained one wise mother, "is not always the same as understanding. And though I know my kids were perfectly sure of my love for them and I felt theirs for me, we just weren't really able to figure each other out very well from about the age of twelve until they were gone from home for a couple of years. Then things got much, much better; some of the confusion cleared up."

This murky period for mothers—the years between late childhood and the beginning of an adult friendship—arises at least partially from the distance between the mother's actual life as she is living it and what the child remembers of it.

Hazel B., the 54-year-old mother of three grown sons, recollects how hard she and her husband worked to give their boys cultural and material advantages the parents had never had and how proud they were when they could afford a summer camp for their youngsters.

"How good we felt," she recalls, "when they came home so brown and healthy, full of new things they'd learned and new friends. We missed them, but we knew this was the life that privileged children led, and we were so glad they could have some of it."

Imagine her dismay years later when her children said they resented being "sent away" and reproached her with "trying to get rid of us" so the parents could be alone together.

"Of course we enjoyed a little vacation from the kids, too," says Hazel with shocked candor, "but my God, there was no way that the prime factor in our slaving away like dogs to afford good camps for them was determined by wanting to get rid of them —no, no—they have it all wrong!"

Hazel's indignant and hurt response to the differing memories and interpretations of the past is typical of the reports from many mothers, who not only showed shock and surprise at the blind-man-and-the-elephant versions of the past that differed so much between them and their grown kids, but also feared the two memories could never be reconciled.

"Isn't it too late?" asks Ramona K., 61-year-old mother of five, who only recently learned that two of her five grown children cherished deep resentments and angers over what they claim was her failure to come quickly to their bedsides when summoned in the night to deal with nightmares and childish night fears.

"They say now that I didn't really tend to them quickly enough," she reports, "but *my* memory of the time they are talking about is of an exhausted woman, home alone with five small children while my husband worked nights to make ends meet, stumbling around in a constant fog of overwork and tiredness. I can't even remember," she says with a mixture of indignation and guilt, "ever even getting a whole night's sleep during those years, much less remember specific incidents they seem to recall so clearly."

Ramona's blurred image of a period her children claim to see clearly was echoed by Margaret T.'s description of a similar phenomenon as the turbulent years of adolescence approached. Margaret, 51, mother of two, feels that the "memory gap" and the "understanding gap" begin to be serious as the children reach their teens.

Here's her explanation of what is happening: "As a parent, you're usually reaching a new level of work and struggle and responsibility—trying to buy or pay off a house and car, you have debts, you're trying to move forward in your work or help your husband move in his, and you still have a lot of other demands, too. You're still a daughter to your own parents, usually, and then you have your friends and some kind of part in the community where you live—it's a lot.

"And," she goes on, "what are the kids doing while you're struggling to keep the whole thing afloat and put away money for their education? Well, you have to understand that ever since the day you brought them home from the hospital—twelve or thirteen or fourteen years ago—they've been studying you.

While you've been going crazy trying to pay for the dungarees and the dentist and the piano lessons, they've been single-mindedly learning about you."

Says Margaret, "When they reach adolescence, they make their move! The first of many. They have your number and they proceed to get you over a barrel. They know you like your most intimate friend or lover. Are you a sports fan? They will refuse all offers of baseball mitts or hockey sticks. Are you an intellectual? They'll stop going to school in any meaningful way. Are you devoutly religious? That's the end of church."

Margaret actually understands this adolescent rebellion very well and knows that it is an important developmental phase, but it is here, she believes, that the way of looking at the world from different points of view first emerges as a pattern that will make understanding between adults difficult until the kids are in their early twenties.

Margaret's wry and witty view gets serious backing from the Center for Youth Development and Research at the University of Minnesota, where several studies done in the late Seventies and early Eighties show that teenagers and their middle-aged parents *are* having simultaneous crises.[7]

While youngsters are "discovering sex in Technicolor, their parents are feeling a little gray," says the Minnesota report, and while young people are looking at a whole range of possible jobs and careers, their parents are facing up to possibly permanent career plateaus and even peeking ahead at retirement.

These collisions of the generations are very real, according to the researchers, who confirm what mother interviewees put in achingly personal terms.

Betty N., 49-year-old mother of one daughter, reveals bitterly how she helped and supported her 16-year-old through a frightening abortion and then acceded to her daughter's request that her father not be told.

Later, says Betty, her daughter claimed she did not remember ever making such a request and blames her mother for coolness between herself and her father years later, after the father inadvertently discovered the event!

Even where memory may roughly coincide, interpretation of events can be so widely different as to make the outsider wonder whether the mother and the adult child are looking back on the same situation.

Mildred K., 58, mother of four daughters, confesses now, when her oldest child is 35, that she incorrectly saw sibling rivalry as much less important in her children's lives than her kids now tell her it really was.

"Things that happened because they were jealous or envious of each other went right over my head," she admits now. "When one or another would refuse to go along on some family outing where one of them was going to be the star—like a school play or Girl Scout trip—I always put it down to boredom or immaturity and never recognized that it was envy and jealousy."

When the children now tell their mother how intense their rivalry was, she is shocked and still a bit disbelieving—partly, she discloses, because she had been raised in a home where sibling rivalry was not allowed to be shown.

However, it continues to be true, throughout their differing memories of the past, that both generations seem to have an almost instinctive urge to climb over these barriers and reach toward one another, like wildflowers climbing a rugged wall of stone toward the sun.

The flexibility of maternal spirit required to move from the turmoil of adolescence to the hope of a new, more mature relationship as the kids strike out on their own was eloquently narrated by Glenda F., mother of four, grandmother of seven: "You have to trust kids as adults while still being Mother. You must guide them, be a role model, adviser, nurturer, Mrs. Wonderful, and at the same time, help them to see your feet of clay, so when they get old enough to see it for themselves, it won't be a trauma."

But is it possible to avoid that trauma?

Paul Goldberger, the architecture critic of *The New York Times,* in reviewing a book in which he discussed a father-son relationship, asked: "Who has not felt distressed upon discovering that a parent is not precisely what one thought in childhood, or has changed since then?"

This distress that mothers so keenly feel flowing toward them from their children sometimes continues throughout the mother's life span, especially if both mother and grown children are mired in the social conventions, historical attitudes, and spirit of the times reflected in differing generations.

But the majority of women in our sample were able to seize fairly quickly on any signs that the postadolescent rapprochement was beginning, and tried in many ingenious and warmhearted ways to start the bridge-building process toward their adult children.

When asked whether they and their adult children had, for example, later talked about the things that caused tension during the adolescent period, a group of 120 mothers out of 166 women said they had, indeed, held such conversations. Two more said, "Rarely," one said, "Sometimes," and one said she never initiated such talks, but sometimes her children did.

Did these later talks help?

Some 106 mothers said they did help clear the air of misunderstandings, increase confidences, and promote sharing of memories and feelings. Sixteen mothers said they found such talks counterproductive, sparking old angers and leading to new arguments about old problems. Another group of 44 women said they were glad they had such talks, but didn't think they really made a difference in reconciling different points of view. The remainder said they had not participated in such backward-looking talks.

Of the large group of mothers who reported these conversations as the beginning of reaching across the generational gulf to one another, a great many reported funny, nostalgic reminiscences, as well as serious ones, that emerged in retrospective talks with their kids.

For some women, it recaptured the childhood years in ways that were bittersweet, moving, or humorous. Family pets long since gone were revived in memory ("They confessed when they were in their twenties that they'd always fed table scraps to the dog when they had been expressly forbidden to do that"); teenage escapades the mother had never known about brought mutual gales of laughter (when the pranks were mischievous, not when they were dangerous or harmful).

Positive childhood memories retold by the young adult children brought many smiles to the mother, but the later-told tales the mothers took most to heart were the ones in which children confessed adolescent miseries they had kept hidden from their mothers at the time.

Fear of failure in school, shame or embarassment at not being as pretty or popular or athletic as a sibling or a friend, unhappy or frightening early sexual experiences (including sexual abuse by relatives, neighbors, or strangers), and the first experiments with drugs, notably marijuana—all tumbled out in later conversations with young adult kids in ways that often tore at the mother's heart.

These later confessions had the effect, mothers said, of opening up floodgates of feeling that poured out between mothers and children. Mothers were remorseful at not having known of the child's unhappiness, while adult children—if they were feeling reasonably good about themselves at that point—tended to be forgiving and comforting since, in many cases, they felt they had triumphed over these adolescent disasters and had become more self-confident, self-assured young adults.

These we-just-talked-about-it-recently conversations seem to reflect a number of positive trends that start operating about this time to make the friendships more possible.

Here are additional elements the mothers mentioned that buttress the possibilities of comradely relations:

First, the child's struggle for autonomy is being won. The mother is not perceived as such a threat to independence. Often the child is well launched into work, education, or self-involved personal relationships and is truly living his own life, experiencing himself as really outside the mother's control, if not influence. Mothers report with much pleasure and relief a diminution of "enemy" status.

Second, as the adult son or daughter encounters the harsh reality of an uncaring world outside the family, the traditional support functions of parents and other kin, including siblings, begin to take on a halo they never had when fights over the family car or allowances were the chief features of the parent-child drama. "Best thing that ever happened," says Gail T., mother of three, "is when our kids went off to the navy and to college. There they met young people whose parents had, for all practical purposes, abandoned them years before, where kids literally had no homes to go to on vacations or leaves, and where men and women had just been such inadequate parents—for whatever reasons—that the damage they inflicted was painfully obvious to our more sheltered kids."

Gail describes what happened: "After about six months of exposure to those sad cases, *our* parental stock rose about 25,000 points! Our children found out that their horrible parents weren't so horrible after all."

Third, children themselves now begin to experience the great milestones of life: first job, marriage, their own children, perhaps the first deaths in the family circle. With an almost automatic or instinctive gesture, they turn to look back at how their own parents dealt with these turning points, and often a new respect and understanding are born. This accounts for well-known phenomena of daughters becoming much closer to their mothers when their own children are born, sons becoming more distant from their families of origin when they marry (their wives customarily take on the "kinkeeper role" the mother used to play), and similar well-documented familial processes.

Fourth, the child begins to play another role in the mother's life in addition to that of friend: The young adult becomes reward, satisfaction, prize. A small cycle of success is set up in some families. The young people begin to show that they can get along out on their own, and this makes the mother feel that she's helped to create a well-functioning, attractive adult. Her approval, in turns, helps spur the child to even stronger self-confidence and more achievement in different spheres—work, money, personal relations.

Now, new emotional currents begin to flow back and forth. The middle-aged mother is not quite so child-centered as her life passes its halfway mark; she is frequently out and about on her own concerns, whether paid or volunteer work, whether hobbies or educational projects. The young adult, sharply focused on the interests appropriate to his or her life stage, feels a lessening of the overheated growing-up period. Both can touch each other gently as they pass on their way to exploring that looming world outside the familiar walls of home.

But, however much the mother and the adult sons and daughters may appear to be living out absolutely conventional friendships, there almost always comes a time when the glaring spotlight of trouble or crisis reveals just how different mother–

adult child friendships are from ordinary ones among unrelated people.

At turning points in their children's lives—the young person
moving far away to take a new job or having her or his first child
—or in times of serious trouble—illness, accident, disaster—a
whole different set of responses is visible.

In fact, just recently, there has been a good deal of public
attention paid to the strange fact that adult friends all too often
turn away from each other (when they are not related by blood),
as though afraid of "catching" the unhappiness and despair of
ill fortune.[8]

But the reactions of parents at such times are exactly the
opposite; they tend to pull tight the emotional bonds that have
become slack with good luck and easy living, and usually rush
to offer help.

Looking at the "friendship extra strength" that mothers and
adult children are trying to put together, we can see that, under
pressure, this friendship glows with a special light showing
clearly the outlines of a bond that must change with time, and,
changing, illumines both generations.

9

Friendship Under Pressure

Part I: Crisis Mothering

Can it be that parents are sentenced to a lifetime of worry? Is concern for one another handed down like a torch to blaze the trail of human frailties and the fears of the unknown? Is concern a curse? Or is it a virtue that elevates us to the highest form of life?

ERMA BOMBECK, "Endless Worries of Parenthood"

But she had no power anymore—had never had the power, although at one time she thought she did—to stave off ruin, to guard her son against his share of pain. . . .

SUE MILLER, "Leaving Home"

"*I* was prepared to go down on my knees to the Ayatollah and plead with him for the release of Kevin," Barbara Timm, 41, mother of a United States serviceman held hostage in Iran in 1980, has said. Women whose adult children are in trouble have entered the land of paradox.

On one hand, they care deeply about their children at every

stage of life, they keenly observe their sons' and daughters' sorrows and disappointments, and usually want very much to help when hard times strike.

On the other hand, the rules of the adult friendship decree that they must wait until asked for help, and then often can help only modestly and indirectly—and most difficult of all, sometimes they cannot help at all.

All the guidelines for handling trouble have shifted, mothers point out, since those days when youngsters lived at home under parental supervision; now adult friendships have to call forth much different behavior than in the old days when parents could storm a city council meeting to get a traffic light at a dangerous intersection or kiss it and make it better with childhood scrapes and bruises.

A small number of mothers (between 2 and 3 percent of the sample group) were quite open about being almost glad about crises and turning points which force sons and daughters back into some degree of dependency, and said that they don't mind at all reassuming the old role of omniscient parents.

But many more women—by far the majority—say that although they have an instant "helping" reflex, they know that they must try not to infringe on the independence the young person has won, often after a considerable struggle. Mothers say they want to help as grown friends might help each other, but admit it's hard to keep that intimacy at a distance when the child is truly under grave threat.

Nearly two-thirds of the 208 women in the core group said their first impulse in a crisis is to try to take fate or circumstance into their own hands and wrestle it down to the ground on behalf of their kids.

A number of factors generally act to slow that impulse, however, mothers reported. Fathers often act as a brake; the nature of the problem sometimes prohibits such action; and then, too, the son or daughter is often enough in command of the situation to make instantaneous intervention less necessary than when they were much younger.

Nonetheless, mothers say, the old habits are there at the first sign of threat, flaring into life quickly and making their good intentions to handle the problem as they would with any close friend more difficult to achieve.

Shy, soft-spoken women become loud and angry in defense of grown sons and daughters, even if one of those adults is head of an office and has thirty people reporting to him or her. Women who are ordinarily fearful of those in authority can be found arguing aggressively with godlike doctors or college deans; retiring homebodies who like to sew and put up strawberry jam attack government officials and heads of state in front of television cameras if their children's lives or safety are at issue.

These actions are usually conducted in a maternal spirit made up of equal parts of affection, adrenaline, guilt, and stern notions about a mother's duty and responsibility. A number of women expressed in different words this idea: "There's no use kidding yourself; if the crisis is scary enough, the tone of a just-friend-to-friend relationship wavers or disappears completely."

In addition, several mothers confessed they saw crises where the adult child did not. A college dropout may think quite positively of himself or herself for taking time out, while an education-oriented mother may see dropping out as a crisis of life-shattering intensity. A young person breaking up a three-year-relationship with a live-in partner may be hurting badly, but doesn't see that the situation calls for much maternal action. However, Mom may be heating up the chicken soup, turning down the guest-room bed, and calling the psychiatrist for an appointment for her 30-year-old daughter, all the while muttering about fear of commitment.

Analogies with the animal world—the female tiger protecting her cubs, the mother bird dive-bombing predators who come near the nest—or stereotypical images of human mothers sacrificing their own lives to save their children from flood, fire, and earthquake are simply too sweeping to apply to all mothers everywhere all the time.

In fact, some mothers say they wait quite a while and look for a lot of smoke before investigating any metaphorical fire.

Despite such attempts to keep a grown-up friendship as the tone of the relationship with adult children, the large majority of women interviewed also admitted that nothing rings clearer in their ears (as far as the grown kids are concerned) than the bell that softly signals "Maybe trouble?" or loudly clangs

"Alarm!" Divorce, among the most frequently encountered crises mothers face with their grown-up kids, calls out an especially complex response from middle-aged women, a reaction we'll examine more closely later in this chapter. The maternal response to crises includes all the obvious elements we mentioned earlier—guilt, fear, love, close identification with the adult child—but also a less obvious one reported frequently by many mothers in our sample group. That motivating force is an inarticulate but deeply felt set of beliefs about what mothers are supposed to do in a crisis, what the proper role is for a mother.

For example, in 1982, the Reverend Sun Myung Moon, head of the Unification Church and spiritual leader of a generation of "Moonies," officiated at the marriage of 4,150 young people in a mass wedding ceremony in New York's Madison Square Garden.

For many parents, this unusual ceremony—in many cases joining a young man and young woman who did not know each other at all or had been acquaintances for only a week—was a tidal wave of disaster crashing against their hopes and dreams for their children.

Nevertheless, parents, mostly mothers, showed up at the Garden by the hundreds. Several were interviewed by a thoughtful reporter from the *Washington Post,* Joyce Wadler.

"Why are you here?" she asked a number of mothers. "Do you approve of what your son or daughter is doing?"

"My only daughter, so I'm here," answered a woman from Queens, New York.

"He's our son," said a British woman who came from London for the ceremony. "We're not believers, but he's twenty-four and grown. He's our son."

One woman said her husband had refused to come.

Why had *she* come and brought along her own mother, the bride's grandmother?

The grandmother answered. "She's the mama," explained the older woman; "Mama's different from a father. Mama's got to come."

"Mama's got to come" wrung a cry of acquiescence from mothers whenever that story was told. Many mothers said that for a crisis like a "Moonie" mass wedding, they might have to force themselves to attend, but admitted they'd probably wind up not only

at Madison Square Garden, but at any other place their children's troubles drew them.

Barbara Timm, the Wisconsin mother of a marine sergeant who was one of the fifty American hostages imprisoned in Iran for more than a year, defied a government ban against hostage families traveling to Teheran on their own, and persuaded her son's captors that, indeed, "Mama's got to come." They let her have an hour's reunion with her 20-year-old son, the youngest captive, after a tearful confrontation between Mrs. Timm and the Iranian militants guarding the United States embassy.

Most of the crises and turning points that elicit an urgent call for help—or sometimes an indirect or silent appeal—are not as dramatic as a mass wedding or an Iranian hostage crisis. But for the mothers who witness their children's divorces, who worry through their accidents and illnesses, who learn in horror and sorrow of rapes and abortions, who listen to the misery of unemployment, of career and job losses—for these women, an old aphorism is engraved on their minds and hearts: "To have a child is to be a hostage to fortune."

And, as in all facets of the mother–adult child relationship, it isn't always clear who is responding to whom, and who seeks what out of the crisis time. Sometimes certain kinds of help are not appropriate; sometimes young adults are so conflicted about how much help they want or will accept that their signals are completely garbled and the mother misses the message. And often, the pressure and urgency of a crisis so mix up communications that it's hard for each to know what they seek and what they can give.*

Susan M., a 58-year-old mother of three, described hearing over the telephone that her middle child, a 29-year-old son, newly married and with a new job, was threatened with blindness from the sudden onset of a serious eye disease.

Fighting down a rising wave of fright and near panic, Susan struggled to keep her voice steady and her response direct, warm, and calm. She inquired about doctors, treatment, imme-

---

*In this chapter we will not examine the lifelong difficulties presented to parents of chronically ill children or permanently handicapped youngsters because those require not emergency mobilization, the subject of this chapter, but rather a reordering of long-term family patterns not investigated here. "Crises" or "emergencies" as used here means problems usually resolved in shorter time frames.

diate plans, and gave constant reassurance that love, money, time, and careful attention to the illness were going to be mobilized by his parents at once. "We're right behind you, son," she reassured him and his young wife. "We're going to fight this, all of us together, and it's going to be all right.

"But all the time I was saying these words," Susan said, "I felt inside myself the craziest wish: I wanted to just take him on my lap in my big old rocker and rock him as I had when he was little and was up all night with a fever. I just couldn't believe how much I wanted to do the most basic mother things," she said, "and it took me a while to realize—hey, wait a minute, I'm talking to a grown-up man with a wife of his own, with responsibilities to an employer, all of that."

She added, "Of course, somewhere in my head I knew all along that we'd be showing love and support in a more mature way and that his father and I were perfectly competent to do that, but honestly, *I just wanted to hold him on my lap.*" The story had a happy ending for Susan, as her son was successfully treated and did not lose his sight, but she says she learned something she hadn't quite known about what she calls the "gut" bond as opposed to the ordinary friendship she thought she was pursuing.

Susan further reports that the moment she hung up the phone after hearing the initial terrifying news, she immediately called her own 83-year-old mother and sobbed out all her anguish and fear—feelings she had kept well hidden from her own son, trying to sound calm and reassuring while on the telephone with him.

The friendship with her son was certainly still there, but clearly, other feelings were operating in a crisis.

This reversion to the closest ties and the most physical part of the mother-child link was described by several mothers, including Rhoda M., whose 32-year-old daughter suffered three miscarriages before successfully completing a fourth pregnancy and joyfully delivering a healthy, though premature, boy.

"The night of her third miscarriage, I cried all night," remembers Rhoda. "I sat by the window in the darkness, with tears running down my cheeks. I felt so awful for her, so terrible. And you wonder, you can't help but wonder, Is this something inherited? I had never had that kind of problem, but somewhere in the family did we pass on something to her that was causing this? Actually, the doctor could find very little physical explanation for it; still you can't help wondering when something so basic goes wrong.

"I felt so miserable for her," Rhoda continued, "partly because I felt that this was not like other things that go wrong in their lives, you know, like . . . well, like money. Now with money, you can always work something out; money isn't that hard to deal with. But this! This is life—life itself. And she and Tom want children so badly. It was so terrible—the loss, the sorrow —it's something that goes so deep.

"What I really wanted to do," the worried and irrationally guilty mother confessed, "was bring her back here to the room where I'd nursed her through the two earlier miscarriages, to the house she'd grown up in, and just nurse her the way I used to when she had the flu or chicken pox. I just wanted to hold her," Rhoda made a cradling motion with her arms, "and make sure that nothing more that was bad could happen to her."

Rhoda was greatly comforted that at the most difficult moment, her son-in-law was tenderly caring for his wife, but that made Rhoda ache for his sorrow and loss, too.

In the days that followed, she suddenly began to notice all the photographs of babies in magazines and pictures of babies in pervasive television commercials, and she felt tortured all over again in her daughter's behalf.

"I began imagining Ellen seeing all those pictures of babies everywhere she turned; do you *know* how many pictures of infants you can run across in a perfectly ordinary day without at all trying to?" Rhoda demanded vehemently. "I thought of every newspaper and every magazine and every TV show flashing pictures of adorable, cuddly, healthy babies at her and I just didn't see how she could bear it. I never brought it up and she never mentioned it to me, so maybe I was just worrying about nothing. When we talked, I always tried to sound optimistic and straightforward, felt that was the best I could do for her, but inside, I wanted to throw out every magazine in the house and turn off the TV set forever."

Her daughter's fourth and successful pregnancy was eight months of intense anxiety for Rhoda, who nevertheless felt her role was to appear reasonably sure of success in a low key, unruffled way. "My husband says I should get an Oscar for hiding my anxiety as well as I did," says Rhoda, now ecstatic with her healthy little grandson, "but I don't think I hid it so well. I'm sure Ellen knew all about it!"

It would seem from both Susan's and Rhoda's stories that when the threat to the child is physical, a strong, almost primitive physical response reasserts itself, and the mother sometimes wishes to refold even an adult child into her own body as a means of protection and safeguard from further injury.

Even when the mother learns of physical harm to the adult child well after the fact, she may still respond in physical terms that are light years away from even the most sympathetic of conventional friendships.

Patricia H., 61, mother of four children, illustrates this physicalness by telling of her reaction when she learned that her 23-year-old daughter, arriving in a strange town to begin a new job, had been raped in her own apartment building by a knife-wielding attacker.

Pat describes her feelings: "First was sheer terror—was she all right, was she *alive*? Then, the intense fear of whether she had been badly hurt in some way additional to the rape—beaten, perhaps, or, my God, mutilated in some way. You go crazy, imagining every horror possible. When the hospital explained that she had escaped additional injury, I had a funny, mixed sensation. First I was grateful to the rapist for not beating her to death, as some have, and then, a murderous rage. I wanted to kill him, I wanted to shoot him full of hundreds of bullets. Then disbelief—this just couldn't be happening, a sort of denial, I guess. Then the haste to try to be with her as soon as possible . . . it was an explosion of adrenaline I'd never felt before in my life."

Patricia immediately flew to the western city where her daughter had begun her new job and it was only some time later that she experienced a deeply physical tie with her daughter. Emotionally, she explains, they had been able to be close from the first moment she received the news, and there were no serious barriers to a comforting exchange of thoughts and feelings, but Pat never expected to have to intervene in a different way.

Some time after the rape, her daughter, Jessica, said she wanted to have a curettage, not because there was fear of a pregnancy (tests had shown there was none), but because she felt unclean and wanted to be rid of any trace within her body of the stranger's invasion.

Pat was sympathetic and believed, she said, that this was an understandable response to rape. She agreed that it should be done as soon as possible to relieve her daughter's feelings. To her surprise, she and Jessica had to battle the entire staff of the local hospital and a local female obstetrician/gynecologist as well. All the medical personnel they initially consulted felt that in the absence of a pregnancy, there was no need for a surgical procedure that always carries its own risks, however minimal.

"Basically, they were not interested in Jessie's feelings—but *I* felt them, right in my own body, in my uterus, and in all the surrounding organs, very specifically—and I also knew in a less literal way, sort of in my blood and bones, that if I had been in her place, I would feel the same way." While her daughter was at work each day, Patricia grimly and persistently went through the telephone book until she found a doctor and hospital more willing to listen to the psychological components of the problem. The curettage was done safely, Pat reports.

Other mothers, listening to Pat's story, said that sometimes it is a relief to know the nature and dimensions of a physical crisis (not in cases of rape, but in accidents or illnesses) because many find a health emergency more manageable than emotional traumas that are complex and often obscure, in both their causes and cures.

"An illness from which a son or a daughter can recover, one which is, in some way, reversible—or even a bad accident that doesn't kill or permanently maim—you can hope it will fade into the past at some point in the young person's life," said one vital, active mother of five, "but with broken hearts, broken families, broken careers," she sighed, "we seem to go on with those for a long, long, *long* time."

Typical of such a crisis are the contemporary phenomena of both divorce and the split-up of long, if unmarried, living-together relationships.

Much has been written and discussed about the mother's divorce, and quite properly, much attention has been paid to the impact of the dissolution of the parental team on the children.

But little regard has been given to the mother when she must bear witness to the pain and sorrow of her adult children's divorces and to the loss, failure, and misery *she* feels in that situation.

An adult child's divorce is a painful event that reverberates both backward into the past and forward into the future, one that the women now in their middle age are peculiarly ill equipped by their own upbringing to understand or deal with.

With divorce now so common among the baby boomers, many mature mothers and older women are called on to patch together the family life left in shreds. Today, one out of three marriages in the United States ends in divorce, and in some parts of the country, the ratio is one out of two.

Not only have lifetimes of social change driven a wedge between the generations on this issue and strained the fabric of friendship, but every such stress situation amplifies the problems inherent in each family's own unique history and pattern of communication or, in many cases, *non*communication.

For many reasons, then, one of the most frequent crises contemporary mothers have to face is the challenge of their children's divorces.

Modern Divorce: Who Keeps the Wedding Pictures?

Only a few short years ago, it seems, the fashionably graying mother stood in her wedding finery, crying a little, smiling a lot, lifting her wine glass in a toast to both her own child and the new in-law child as the ancient marriage rite launched the new couple.

Now that mother sits staring at the happy wedding pictures and wonders in pain and bewilderment what happened. She has just learned that her child has separated from his or her spouse and there will be a divorce.

If grandchildren are present (though in most cases of young people under 30, they are not), her thoughts fly immediately to them, and here too, she encounters a mountain of worry, fear, and hurt.

If there are no children, she finds herself feeling guiltily relieved and the words "Well, thank God for *that*, at least" form themselves in her somewhat numbed head, even though grandchildren might have been her dearest wish until a few minutes ago.

How has the bright promise of that day come to this? Who is to blame? Should she and the child's father bear a share of the guilt and responsibility for this? What about their old, cozy, comforting belief that children who come from a stable, happy home will tend not to be vulnerable to divorce? Gone, blasted, no answers in sight.

Is this a bitter failure for her child, or just a painful but bearable detour on the way to a better life for the adult son or daughter? And what will happen now to the home, the grandchildren, the partners—how will they manage, how *can* they manage—financially, emotionally, logistically?

In the weeks to come, as all these bruising questions batter her waking moments, the mother will begin to remember things. Perhaps she and the child's father, or maybe just one of them, had misgivings about the marriage from the start, but tried to hide them, sweep them under the rug.

"We did that," says Pamela N., 59-year-old mother of three, whose eldest daughter remarried two years ago, some five years after a painful youthful divorce. "We knew Richard was an unstable charmer from the beginning; we *didn't* know he was promiscuous and a compulsive gambler, but we always knew Penny would have her hands full with him. But you live in hopes, don't you? He was such a handsome, appealing boy—he could always wind people around his little finger. We just hoped for the best.

"But," she goes on, still reliving the problem and thinking it through again and again, "we often ask ourselves whether our philosophy about our kids' marriages was the right one. You see, we had a creed; it applied not only to our kids, but to the marriages of all our friends and relatives, too. And it was this: No matter how you felt about the partners, or how much you may have advised against the match originally, once the two people decided to go ahead and marry, then you were honor bound not to sabotage any chance for success they might have. If you could support the union wholeheartedly, with no mental reservations, terrific. But even if you couldn't, we still felt you had a sacred duty to do everything reasonable to help them make a go of it!"

She nodded vehemently. "And we particularly believed this

when it came to our kids' marriages. After all, *all* marriage is a gamble; you mustn't weight the odds in any way. If you have some worries about the mate your son or daughter has chosen, we thought we should just gulp, swallow hard, and try to be welcoming—or at least don't present the young couple with another problem . . . but I don't know."

Pam still broods about whether some all-out opposition— even to the brink of estrangement—wasn't the right approach to Penny's marriage at 19 to a husband she left when she was 24.

"About the only comfort we have," she says, "is that she told us at the time of the breakup—and even that rake, Richard, confirmed it—that of all their divorcing friends, they were the only ones who didn't have any kind of in-law problem, the only ones who broke up for other reasons entirely."

Vivien P., 57, mother of four, had almost exactly the opposite reaction when her youngest son of three was divorced. Vivien felt her own son to be almost entirely at fault; he was too "macho," she says, for a sensible, independent, sturdy young woman like her daughter-in-law, whom she loves, admires, and tries to stay close to.

Vivien believes that, indeed, she *is* somehow to blame for raising a son who would make outrageously old-fashioned masculine demands of his wife, insisting on a level of personal service and housekeeping that "went out fifty years ago," she gloomily explains. "It's all the more amazing," says Vivien, "because I've both had a career and been a homemaking mother all my life and he certainly never saw any of that macho nonsense while he was growing up. His dad always helped when he could and paid for extra help when he couldn't. I simply cannot understand in the slightest how Johnny could have grown up wanting almost a servant for a wife, or how he was able to hide those demands from Sarah until after they were married. She tried to work out compromises . . . but just couldn't, I guess."

Vivien hopes to be able to stay in touch with her cherished ex–daughter-in-law, but is realistic about the fact that if and when Sarah remarries, their tie probably will be harder to maintain.

Vivien's affectionate tie with her ex–in-law child illuminates one of the saddest parts of the modern mother's divorce dilemma, the virtual loss of a child.

"We hear all the time about the effect of a mother's divorce on a child, but very little about what the child's divorce may do to the mother," points out Vivien, "but in my case, it was like a death in the family. I mourned for my own child that his world had broken apart, and I mourned because I lost Sarah, even though I do see her occasionally. But she's not my child anymore, just a woman friend with whom I now share a sort of strange history."

Of course the mother's first concern is her own child, and often here, too, the mothers can feel a devastating separation and loss, because the consuming difficulties and pain of an angry divorce often drive their own child deeper into himself or into closer relationships with peers or to seek help from counselors or therapists. This pain can wipe out, at least temporarily, all the gains made by both mother and child toward an adult-to-adult friendship.

Leah R., mother of a son and a daughter, suffered through this when her daughter, 31, with two small children, told her mother of the impending divorce.

"Our daughter felt such a sense of failure and disappointment," said Leah, "that she really didn't really want to let us come into her pain very far. We didn't stop speaking, or anything, but she just felt it was easier to talk to her friends about it than to us. I'm sure there was the natural sense that she had failed not only herself and the children, but us as well, and she didn't need that extra failure right at the moment." It was a long time, says Leah, "before she could come right out and in plain English tell her parents that her marriage had been a big mistake and that divorce hurt, rather than pretending that a divorce is some kind of chic, sophisticated adventure."

Many adult children, like Leah's daughter, also know clearly that divorce still looms as a tragedy to many people of their parents' generation and they find it wretchedly difficult to cross that Rubicon of telling the folks. Among mothers of adult children, stories are legion about how long it took some young adults to break the news (months, even years) and what charades of seeming indifference and feigned casualness the young person felt it necessary to stage.

Many mothers in our respondent group admitted they could not easily adopt the modern view that divorce is just one fairly value-free option among many in contemporary relationships.

And in addition to the difficulty middle-aged women have with that idea, there is the end of the chain reaction of divorce/loss for them: the possible loss of grandchildren.

Recently, support groups have been formed around the country for grandparents whose grandchildren are being torn away from them as a result of a possibly embittered divorce in which an angry ex-spouse forbids grandparental involvement.

Judges have occasionally overruled such vengeful mandates and in some cases have insisted on the rights of both children and grandparents to have contact with each other, but much more litigation is in the offing, with the outcome uncertain. The only sure thing, say family law experts, is that as families become more complex, such issues will become more numerous and complex, too.

Sometimes, though, divorce brings surprising gains to mothers, usually in the form of new grandchildren whom they attempt to mold into the family in brave, sweet, and often quite successful, patterns.

Katherine G., a 74-year-old great-grandmother, was pleased when her only daughter married a divorced man who had won custody of his only child, an 8-year-old girl. Katherine took the youngster to her heart at once and in time established a relationship with the little girl that she says is almost exactly the same as her warm ties with her natural grandchildren.

"My daughter married late," she explains, "and may never have kids of her own; I'm not sure. But in any case," says Grandma Katherine with considerable satisfaction, "she won't miss out on the mothering experience and I enjoy little Debby very much. I'm delighted with my new son-in-law, too—he's a fine man and he and my daughter are very compatible, get along very well."

Part of Katherine's contentment with the new family is not only the addition of a pleasant son-in-law and a charming new grandchild to the family circle, but also a sense of newly restored "rightness" to her daughter's life: Her daughter now has a husband, a home, a family. Before that, as far as traditionally reared Grandma Kay was concerned, Marjorie was only a lonely jobholder with a barren life. (It should be noted that Grandma Kay was married in 1927 at the age of 19, and her daughter married in 1980 at the age of 39—worlds apart.)

"I have an 'instant' grandchild," proudly reports another grandmother, a 58-year-old Michigan mother of two grown sons. Her younger son was divorced at 23 and remarried a few years later, this time to a woman with a 5-year-old boy from a first marriage. "You know how you get an instant grandson? You take one adorable little boy with freckles, mix well with hugs, kisses, bike rides, pizza, and love; stir thoroughly, and there you are—an instant grandchild." She laughs delightedly, then shrugs and says, "Much better than no grandchild at all—right?"

Whether the mother is coping with the complexities of modern marriage and divorce, dealing with stepchildren, ex-spouses, and half-brothers and sisters, or whether she is simply nursing her own child through a broken family life, she is finding a painful truth that most adult children would rather not face: Divorce is a family affair.

A young adult, sunk deep in the unhappiness of a dissolving marriage, would like to say mutinously, "It's my life, my problem, my solutions—leave me alone, this has nothing to do with you," but the facts are otherwise.

The pain, mothers report, ricochets around the circle of all who are connected to the divorcing pair, and even the most independent of young adults frequently must seek some kind of emotional, financial, or logistical support from parents, particularly if there are children to be considered.

Our sample group of mothers, more than a third of whom had children who had been divorced, demonstrated clearly that often picking up the pieces falls to Grandma.

One 71-year-old grandmother, living in New Jersey, finds that her newly divorced 42-year-old son has fallen into the habit of stopping by for breakfast two or three mornings a week on his way to work so that he can talk over with his sympathetic parents the problems he is encountering with his own two teenage youngsters as a result of the dissolution of the younger family.

His aging mother says she feels during these morning times together that she and her middle son are the closest friends they have ever been. She is glad, too, that he finds his old home a refuge in a troubled time, but, she says wistfully, "I think when a woman begins to get really old, as I am beginning to, she ought to be allowed to have a little rest, don't you think?" Amanda P., it became clear from several conversations with her, really wasn't talking about the physical task of preparing a more abundant breakfast than usual, but the emotional demands of worrying about her son and grandchildren, as well as the ex-wife who had, after all, been her daughter-in-law for nearly twenty years.

Divorce or wrong choices of mates are hard on mothers because the emotional stakes are high and the bad effects shadow everyone's life for such a long time. It might be thought that crises that appear to be only one-time emergencies would be easier to handle, but more than a quarter (27 to 30 percent) of women in our respondent group said that even a brief crisis that seems to be quickly resolved can send haunting echoes over their years with their grown-up children for a long time and make an uncluttered friendship harder to achieve.

Beatrice R., 54, mother of one child at college and two away at boarding school, remembers when the college-age daughter had a serious accident on the hockey team of which she was a member.

"They called me at work from the college when it was all over," says Bea, a serious, hard-working store manager for a national retail clothing chain. "They assured me Alice was okay, and then she got on the phone and said she really thought it was all right, although she admitted that for a while she was scared the right arm might have a touch of paralysis. But when I spoke to the doctor and the coach, it seemed absolutely clear that no serious damage had been done. Probably the real danger *was* past. She did not ask me to come up to school and I was very busy in the store at that time and I didn't volunteer—I just didn't go. She really was all right, but I still wonder . . ." Bea stares deep into her coffee cup. "I still wonder whether I shouldn't have just up and gone, no matter what everybody, including her dad, kept telling me it wasn't necessary. *She* didn't give me any clues one way or the other; I guess I should have asked her directly. It was a crisis she's probably forgotten a long time ago, but I haven't. I think I'll always remember it as a time I failed her."

Beatrice's sense of failure is directly related to the thorny problem, reported by many mothers, that the help that is sought and the way in which the adult child seeks it are so unclear, compared to those long-ago days when the child came running to be comforted after each of life's hard knocks, that the mother is equally tentative in her response. Many mothers said they learned to their sorrow that this tentativeness is often misinterpreted by the adult child as rejection, disinterest, or withdrawal.

"When my son was thinking about dropping out of college in his junior year, I was deeply upset," confides Michelle R., 57-year-old mother of an only child. "I come from one of those families where education is like religion—and my husband does, too. I was so upset, I can't tell you. This was such a crisis to me. I saw David's whole life going down the drain; I saw him drifting from one menial job to another all his life—lost, purposeless—awful!

"But the critical thing," remembers Michelle, "was really: what to do? My husband counseled patience, but I was too upset. Yet I knew that treating this as though he were dying was wrong, too. I wanted to do all kinds of things, like fly down there and have long talks with him, or bring him home and make him *stay* home for a couple of evenings and talk this thing out with us, or *something!*" She waves her hands in looping dives through the air to express confusion and frustration.

"I lay awake nights," Michelle says, "worrying and I thought about it all day long at work. We had sacrificed so much to send him to a good school and now he wanted to throw it all overboard. I went from fury to fear to self-pity to . . . I don't know what. I kept twisting and turning trying to figure out how to handle this crisis, trying to figure out what we did wrong.

"And while I was stewing around, his dad was doing much better. They were having long telephone conversations that I didn't take part in —I was too tense and upset—and it finally dawned on me what my husband was trying to accomplish: He was trying to help Dave leave school comfortably and not feel he'd failed, if that was the thing that was best for him to do at that time."

As Michelle tells the end of the story, her son did drop out for a year, but transferred to another school and finished his studies in good order.

"I'm not proud of myself during that whole thing," admits

Michelle, "because during the year he was out of school I nearly drove all three of us crazy with fear he would never return. But he did. Still, I wonder sometimes whether I might not have performed a *little* bit better if Dave had been willing to simply say, 'Mom, Pop, I think I'm in a spot and I need your help,' instead of trying to tough it out and act so brazen and self-confident about what seemed to me to be the worst mistake of his life."

Michelle is not helped much in her retroactive confusion by the fact that her son much later confided to his parents that during that difficult year, her uncertainty had translated itself to him as disinterest! Her inability to be straightforward and calm with him was frustrating to him, too, he explained.

"As a crisis manager or even as just a good, concerned friend, I was a flop," admits Michelle, but she smiles disarmingly. "I lived to see him graduate and it was wonderful!" Her son had got back on course and his mother's joy was a sight to behold.

Part II: The Crowded Empty Nest

Will you still need me,
Will you still feed me,
When I'm 64?
THE BEATLES

A greeting card sent by a 25-year-old son to his mother half a continent away reads: "Mom, you asked me in kindergarten, you asked me in grade school, you asked me in junior high, you asked me in high school, you asked me in college, you asked me after college, and I finally know what I want to be: A KID!"

Of all the many crises that throw into stark relief the precise outlines of the friendship between mothers and their adult children, perhaps the most difficult of all, because of its deceptively unthreatening surface of normalcy, is the crisis that develops when adult children move back home after a period of being on their own.

That this is a crisis can't be doubted. It's been the focus of enormous attention by specialists ranging from social workers to anthropologists, and the subject of extensive coverage in the media, commented on in every tone of voice by social pundits who go from humorous to psychoanalytic as the nation examines this contemporary development.

There seems little question that the weaning of America is taking a long time.

The empty nest, on occasion, gets crowded, as the adult children, now in their twenties and thirties, stream back in their frayed dungarees, with their unemployment checks, their broken marriages and romances, back to the old homestead. Even if the childhood home has been sold and Mom and Dad are now headquartered in an apartment, it still looks strangely just like home—and more of a refuge than the trap they once called it.

From one end of the country to the other, middle-aged parents are opening guest rooms, buying sleeper couches, digging into their savings, surrendering time and privacy they thought they'd have at this point in their lives. They're also hanging on the telephone and using up a lot of stationery, contacting friends and business acquaintances far and near who might give a hand to their adult children in finding jobs or an affordable place to live.

Parents are confused, bewildered, surprised, and not a little guilty about this, according to reports from mothers. Of the several hundred young adults whose mothers were surveyed, well over 10 percent of them have come home again for stays of from three months to two years and longer.

In some ways, the whole operation looks quite innocent. Is it really so strange for the children in a family to be in their own rooms? And aren't parents doing just what they'd do for any close friends who needed, for whatever reasons, a temporary refuge, a place to regroup their forces?

But *is* it just like that conventional friendship extended to a peer who has had, say, a difficult divorce or separation and needs a place to crash?

Not really; the mother feels very differently as a parent, for one thing. Several mothers admitted they were sneakily glad that the house wasn't so quiet anymore and the phone and the stereo were as noisy as in the old days when the kids were at home.

But these aren't the old teenage or even visiting college student days anymore. Whether the young adults return because they are out of money, out of work, or out of love, they tend to evoke two anxious questions in the majority of parents: "How did I fail as a mother if my kid can't make it in the real world?" and "What is this going to cost me—in money, in worry, in vanishing peace, in time and energy, in privacy?"

None of the answers come easily; guilt about the young person's difficulties nearly wipes out or at least postpones the peer friendship that mothers and their grown kids were just on the point of developing, and the costs often don't become clear until the fabric of the budding friendship is strained beyond all bounds.

The causes of the return aren't easy to discern either, though some of them are fairly clearly economic. The early 1980s recession was deep and frightening; for some, the fear of sliding downward out of the shrinking middle class became a threat that united both generations and gave parents and adult kids a common goal of survival.

To a generation raised in relative affluence, the sinister term "downward mobility" became a real-life situation, and like true comrades, the generations joined forces under the family roof to defeat it.

Other economic factors in the early 1980s included the incredibly high cost of housing (many mothers in our sample could remember the $8,000 Levittown house on Long Island that was the prototype for postwar housing developments, the house that made their own dreams come true), the twin hurdles of high inflation and high unemployment, and the continuing rise in the cost of education.

In terms of whether parents and adult kids can maintain some friendship within the familyship under the pressure of once more living together, there are really two different groups of returnees who bear on the problem.

One is a group of young people who actually are able to get along in the world pretty well and who have solved at least some of the dependence/independence struggles that each generation must work out anew. These are the sons and daughters who are functioning reasonably well, but have run into temporary roadblocks, often not of their own making.

Few parents mind offering a shoulder to cry on or a couch to flop on temporarily when a divorce has been painful, a job has been lost, or illness or accident make living alone unwise for the younger person. In fact, as we have seen earlier, most parents rush to find life preservers at the first sign the ship is encountering heavy weather.

It is the second group of young adults who are causing anguish and record consumption of late-night coffee up and down the land, however. These are the grown children whose returns are caused by an uneasy blend of the kids' immaturity and inability to cope (often subtly abetted by parents unwilling to give up control or tight involvement), mixed well with ever-ready parental guilt, and all of it seasoned with a roller-coaster economy and intense competition in every arena because of the huge numbers of the baby boom age group.

It is the young adults in this second group who seem to arrive with an indefinite visa to the land of comfort and support, and they are the ones who rack up extremely lengthy stays stretching on into years.

This blend of elements is illustrated in the story of the Taylors.

Kathleen and Doug Taylor are 59- and 61-year-old parents of four children who have handed them just about everything the turbulent sixties could manufacture to destroy family ties.

In their pleasant four-bedroom home in a suburb of Tulsa, Oklahoma, they have lived through drugs, abortions, divorce, and dropping out of school, not to mention motorcycle, car, bike, and sports accidents by the half-dozen. There have been tears and fights and confrontations, reconciliations and hugs, letters and phone calls, and enough laughter and sorrow to provide at least twenty scripts for family soap operas. The oldest child is now 36, the youngest 25.

Kate and Doug, replete with their own marital and financial problems throughout their thirty-nine-year marriage, have slogged through it all with their eye on the main goal: not to lose their children, not to get so badly out of touch that communication was completely severed.

In the past few years, they started to get some fruits from their anxious harvest. Rewards came as first one child and then another would—however late, however haltingly—find their vocations, choose mates, and begin to shape lives that seemed to have some direction or to hold some promise of useful work and stability. Adult friendship became a distinct and pleasurable possibility with all the children but one—the eldest, a daughter. She was always the most difficult, Kate reports, and the one ripest for the many revolutions of the past two decades. Now, in the 1980s, Tina is a leftover flower child, still clinging to the counterculture and drifting through menial jobs with a long-time unemployed boyfriend to keep her company.

Kate and Doug don't object to the boyfriend as a person— "He's sweet and gentle and kind to Tina," explains Doug help-lessly—but the young people's floating existence drove Tina's middle-class parents wild with concern.

Three years ago, Tina and her boyfriend, who usually roamed the country in a van, asked if they could come back home for a brief while as they were temporarily out of money.

At first, they bartered services with Doug and Kate in exchange for getting Tina's old room with bath back again. They painted the house, produced an extensive garden, and pulled their weight with exemplary attention to the parents' needs.

But their job-hunting efforts began to be spaced further and further apart in time without anyone quite realizing it. And their participation in household chores—getting the car serviced or picking up Grandma at the airport—gradually lessened.

"Suddenly we saw," reports Kate, "that they had regressed almost completely to early adolescence. Here they were, in their thirties, living at home and being supported by us. We had regressed too; we were behaving like young parents with their first teenagers on their hands. But we were so guilty! Why was Tina so immature? Why was she hooked up with such a loser? Why had she dropped out of art school, dance classes, and finally, auto mechanics school? It *must* be our fault."

Doug picks up the narrative: "They just became nonpaying guests and we were horrified when we realized we were going to have to get them out of the house some way. Throw out your own child? We couldn't—we just couldn't—or at least I couldn't."

Doug was speaking truthfully; he couldn't bring himself to do the job that both he and Kate agreed had to be done. He was so distressed that he had to turn the job over to his wife and made it his business to be out of the house the night Kate was going to tell Tina and Robert they would have to find their own place.

Kate describes her feelings: "It was absolutely the worst day of my life. I've lived through a lot with my children, but this was the worst. I agonized over it for weeks beforehand and when the moment came, I saw Tina turn white as a sheet and Robert gasped. 'You're turning your own child out of her home?' he asked me, really shocked, in a way that made me more miserable than any number of Tina's reproaches might have done.

"But," she said, "I somehow stuck to my guns. I was firm. I explained it just had to be; this living with us was bad for them and bad for us. I gave them three weeks to find another place but I made it clear—I expected them out by the end of the next month."

The result?

"They were furious at first and there certainly was a definite period of coldness; not really a complete estrangement, but cool, cool. It broke our hearts—their evident dislike—but we just had to stick to our decision. They moved out on schedule, found a place, and later, each got a regular job," says Kate.

"That was about ten months ago," reports Doug with obvious satisfaction, "and just lately, the coldness has begun to thaw. I think eventually we'll get back some of the old affection with each other, but," he sighs, "it'll take time—it was a terrible experience for all of us."

While there are many lessons to be learned from the Taylor saga, it must also be noted that such rampant immaturity on the part of the children is often matched by individual problems within each of the parents and with the parents' own marriage.

One nonworking mother, for example, admits that she still does her 26-year-old live-at-home daughter's washing and ironing, even though she and her husband permit the young woman a totally free life, coming and going like a hotel guest, oblivious to the operations of the household.

"There's so little I can still do for her—I don't mind it at all," claims the 54-year-old mother, who also has another daughter who is married, with a child of her own, living some distance away. The mother, Jane R., admits she wishes she still had young children at home and says wistfully that life won't be half as interesting as it is now if the younger single daughter finds her own apartment and moves out as she periodically announces she will do.

In a recent Broadway play, *Alone Together,* author Larry Roman chronicles the story of three returning young adult children and their impact on their parents in a fashion that is both witty and deeply touching.

In the end, say the leading characters—the parents—it's really a question of "What do *we* want to do with our lives?"

The mother in the play always claimed that child-rearing interfered with her desire to become a painter, and when the children return, she effectively postpones that project yet again. After some insightful but confrontational scenes between the parents, the mother realizes she must get on with her life and the children with theirs—outside the home.

Although laughter abounds (the father suggests planting a For Sale sign on the front lawn as a way to get the kids out), the play pivots on what the mother and father want to work out in reenergizing their marriage, pursuing new careers, cutting back on parental duties, and remaking their own lives without the children as shield, buffer, and excuse.

From research and studies on this 1980s version of the United States extended family (which is still common in many European countries), a few observations emerge:

• The key to successful intergenerational living seems to be a short time span with defined limits. As long as everyone knows there is going to be a reasonable limit to the children's stay, tension is much more controllable, according to workers at family service agencies who have dealt with the returnees and their parents. In this respect, parents more nearly replicate the conditions of a living arrangement with peers their own age.

• A second requirement is setting firm ground rules on practical matters of everyday living. For example, arranging enough privacy for each person, even in crowded quarters, can be done if everyone will recognize the need and be willing to make adjustments to allow "alone time" for all family members.

• Money is hard for parents to talk about with their grown kids when the children may have been forced home in the first place by money or job troubles (see Chapter 4). The method that experts suggest here is that parents show sympathy and understanding of the problem, but also make it clear that as soon as possible, they do expect financial contributions to the household if the son or daughter is still there when a job is finally obtained.

• Parents have to stick firmly to their own way of life, say family therapists and social workers. If a parade of their children's live-in partners bothers them, or if pot-smoking still is not comfortable for them, they have to assert their rights to ban these things from under their own roofs. And this respect for the parents' values must be exacted from the young people no matter how impatient with or contemptuous of these values the children may appear to be.

• Parents whose kids show marked immaturity are urged to guide and help in ways that will help the children grow up, not encourage their dependency. Kat and Doug Taylor finally stopped subsidizing their grown children and gave them a chance to learn their own strengths in job-hunting and money management.

Sometimes there are points in the parents' lives when having the children around again is a delight, a solace, or a help, and not the problem it is in the above situations.

In one family, a widower father said that his son's return home to recuperate after an auto accident coincided with the sudden death of the mother. The two men were able to help each other through a difficult period of bereavement. The father saw the son finally depart to pick up the threads of his own life with a good deal of loneliness, but with pride that his son was sturdy enough to make his own way after a number of blows. Their friendship now is all the sweeter, if more poignant, because of what they shared during the son's return home.

A 52-year-old divorcée whose son was unhappy with the first college he attended was glad for the help around the big house that the young man gave when he dropped out of school for a year to save money to transfer to a more expensive college. But this savvy mother admits there are two tendencies she must monitor carefully before they cause trouble. She herself could find it too nice to "have a man around the house again" and subtly discourage her son from leaving, and he, in turn, could be come too comfortable puttering about a home that is not really his and for which he does not have the ultimate responsibility. So far, reports his mother, his plans for a new school next fall look firm.

Many women openly feel a joyous pleasure in the youth, humor, vitality, and stimulation the kids bring home—but for visits or vacations, not as permanent residents.

That the generations are thus evolving toward a continuing importance, combined with considerable distance, in and from each other's lives is becoming a newly recognized reality on both ends of the equation.

When Friendships Falter: The Weight of the Past

"When they come home, it's nice, but I don't feel we really are much in touch, any more than we were when they were actually living at home as teenagers; I'm afraid we never had much communication. My husband and I didn't talk much 'kid stuff' at the table. In some ways, their role in my life now is even less satisfying than when they were home. Maybe we're even further apart, or maybe that just has to do with their going out toward their own goals. That would be healthy, and good, of course, if that were the reason for my feeling we didn't have all that much contact . . . but their needs make them ever present in your life, don't they? When the phone rings, you're there and the connection requires that you act. . . . As far as roles go, I wouldn't mind relinquishing the title mother for that of friend—but with the blood ties, I don't think you are ever really *just* a friend—maybe mother and friend if you're lucky, but I'm not there yet and maybe I'll never be one of the lucky ones." So says Deirdre N., a biologist working for the government in Washington, mother of two daughters and a son.

In conventional friendships among people of the same generation, friendships drift apart, end, or sometimes explode in a shower of hurt and anger. Most adult friendships that fall away do so primarily, however, because one or both of the friends have changed and now looks for different things in their lives.

What one seeks in a friend at the age of 45, for example, may be very different from what one wanted at 25, points out Dr. Michael R. Milano, a psychiatrist who discussed adult friendships with a reporter recently.

"Such changes in the self occur over the years and it's basically a healthy phenomenon," said Dr. Milano, assistant professor of psychiatry at the Columbia-Presbyterian Medical Center. "But if a friendship validates our sense only of what we *were* and does not validate our sense of what we are now, then it can become untenable."[1]

This changing sense of self that suggests we are becoming different people at different times in our lives is one of the biggest obstacles mothers reported in the way of achieving friendships with their adult children.

Ruby T., a 54-year-old divorcée, believes that a dramatic midlife crisis of her own that featured a shockingly sudden divorce and a bout with alcoholism (now controlled) changed her from a sheltered, children-centered, small-town North Carolina wife and mother into a grimly determined survivor, living a fast-paced life in a new job in a large city. Ruby believes that these changes in the very essence of her picture of herself have permanently foreclosed a close friendship with the eldest of her three children.

"This daughter," she recounts sadly and grimly, "took the brunt of my troubles and has never been able to handle the fact that I couldn't deal with her life problems at the same time I was enduring severe turmoil in my life with her father. We're close to estrangement now. We do have some contact, but it's tense, hostile, strained. . . . I don't know"—Ruby stares at the ceiling —"maybe if I just quit trying for a while; maybe there just has to be a period when I let it go and see what happens . . . a period when she might try to understand who I've become now."

Adult children, too, feel that their mothers and fathers don't understand "the person I've become now," and the tragedy of this misunderstanding was carried to its ultimate conclusion in Marsha Norman's Pulitzer Prize–winning play *'Night Mother,* the story of a young woman who feels her life is futile and informs her mother exactly when she plans to commit suicide. In a desperate attempt to change her mind, the mother pleads, "But you're my child." "No," answers the young woman, "I am what became of your child."

If conventional families face these burdens in trying to repair the wounds of the past, the struggle is compounded for stepparents and single-parent families, those units in which, increasingly, the family drama is played out.

K. C. Cole, a writer on family relations and the author of *What Only a Mother Can Tell You About Having a Baby*, married a man who had two daughters by a previous marriage and learned that everything in the stepparent's life is only part time.[2]

"Having the children only half the time poses twice as many problems," she writes; "it's hard to be an instant family . . . everything is makeshift, compromise." Cole sees that the difficulty in making friendships out of this collage of experiences comes from this fact: "My stepdaughters don't really know me much better than I know them. That's because I'm not myself when they're around." She recounts a conversation with a stepfather in another family; he tells her: "You get duped into violating your own sense of self because you want so badly to be liked . . . the temptation is to change everything you normally do and everybody feels the fakeness of the situation."

This fakeness of the situation, says Cole, could be diminished by giving up the role as mother of a "pseudofamily" and taking up, instead, a role as a full-time potential friend. "They are his responsibility. Everything you provide should be icing on the cake," another stepmother told her. "The icing," observed Cole, "is of course the best part."

Both natural parents and stepparents would like to be the icing on the cake for their children, but the inherited relationships of the past are complicating that friendship task between the generations in ways far weightier than they do in same-age friendships.

Jill Johnston, a feminist writer, commenting on the fact that she and her mother had been estranged, wrote, "Our estrangement in no way affected or diminished our importance to each other, it simply altered the structure of our involvement."

Working through the structural problems of an unhappy involvement concerned a number of women.

"Face it: the problem may look as though it comes from things happening now, but it probably goes back a long way. . . . Try to unravel it somewhere—by yourself, with the child's father, with the adult son or daughter, or, if you have to, with some outside help."

This common-sense comment at a mothers' discussion group came from Hope P., who is an assistant in a clinical psychology research center and is thus—perhaps atypically—oriented toward accepting the possibility that people outside the family could help mothers understand how and why they're losing out on friendship with their grown children.

But in our core group of 208 women, there was a very substantial number, albeit a minority, who felt so uncomfortable with or unused to the idea of outside help that Hope's advice is not really workable for them.

For many women, confiding in a stranger is difficult, if not impossible, even if that stranger is a well-trained, credentialed professional. Often they don't believe "mere" talk can change anything deep-rooted in personality or life patterns.

There were a small number of women who had already abandoned the effort, given up hope of improving their relationship with their grown children. They wrote in letters and talked in interviews about being resigned to a limited, dutiful but barren interchange between themselves and their adult kids. The rewards of mothering adult children and of also being friends with them do not seem available to these women, at least not in the near term.

But there were a handful of mothers who said they had changed their minds about unsatisfactory relationships with their grown children; they determined to make things better and they shared a few of their strategies with the other mothers.

Here were some of the suggestions they offered:

1. Put some emotional space between yourself and the "problem" child. Maybe you've been trying too hard. Several women said the best thing they did toward building a friendship with their children was to become deeply absorbed in some other project—a job, a hobby, or perhaps travel to new places. "This does two things," reported Joy L., the mother of a daughter she describes as pleasant and dutiful, but uncommunicative. "It loosens up the tension a little and it also makes the adult son or daughter look at you in a different light, respect you a little more perhaps as a separate person, instead of regarding you as a piece of furniture they've lived with too long to really see."

2. "Get off the guilt trip!" loudly exclaimed Sophia N., mother of five, at a coffee hour for mothers. "Yes, you made mistakes; yes, the fact that you're not friends is partly your fault—but it's also partly the grown kids' fault. Start expecting them to contribute something to the party, and things might get better. It's just like always," said Sophia, "what you expect from them, you usually get. If you expect them to grow up enough to understand and maybe even forgive your mistakes, they just might." ("When you come to accept yourself, you will stop picking on your mother," said a 35-year-old daughter who was participating in another family relations meeting elsewhere and was unaware of Sophia's lecture.[3])

A way to get off the guilt trip has been advanced by Arthur Maslow, a family therapist and author of a book on parenting adult children. Maslow suggests that if parents can just get their heads around the idea that they don't have to continue leading, guiding, and instructing their children, but that they can shift to just "being there" and lending love and comfort, rather than the correct advice, the possibilities for better connections are improved. "People should not expect it to come easy," said Maslow, "because it does not come easy. But it is certainly possible."[4]

Whether middle-aged women are now including friendship in their familial relations with their grown kids or whether they've arrived at some other modus vivendi, a whole series of additional phases in the relationship are appearing over the next hill —the hill of years that brings mothers to old age and adult children to middle age.

In the next chapter, we'll take a look at what mothers think, hope, fear, dream, and want as they contemplate getting older —and perhaps wiser about those special friends, their grown children.

10

Mothers and Grown Children Move Through Time: Close Encounters of a Future Kind

It would be terribly convenient, of course, if our parents would really retire, would lead their lives according to the original life plan . . . without being touched by death, divorce, disaster, vulnerability, insecurity, or certainly, sexuality . . . there are those of us who seem to insist that it is inconsiderate of our parents still to be in a state of change after fifty-five or sixty at the latest. Especially when we want them to be our parents, for heaven's sake, and they keep turning out to be people. . . . I simply do not know what is happening to the older generation these days.

ELLEN GOODMAN

*A*uthor Goodman's gentle irony, seen from an adult daughter's angle of vision, reveals a genuine problem for young people: They often do not notice or cannot quite grasp what is happening in their mothers' development through new life stages.

The middle-aged women who've been sharing their family lives with us are, as mentioned earlier, pioneers moving into a fast-changing future.

The extra number of years predicted for their life span, constantly accelerating new knowledge about human relations, the turbulent modern political and economic history these women share with their offspring—all make their march onward with their children different from earlier patterns of generational interaction.

And not the least important of the agents of change is the broad social movement that is today's feminism. This movement, among other things, has meant the emergence of the transitional mother we've seen in close-up throughout this book.

This is the woman—you, your neighbor, your friend—who has gone back to school or to work or both when her children left and who has moved the focus of her hour-by-hour concerns away from the child-centered home. Yet, at the same time, this woman has at least one foot and all of her heart firmly planted wherever her husband and children are operating.

The transitional mother is no longer so child-centered as she was brought up to be, but she remains always child-concerned.

And the more traditional mother has had her horizons changed, too, even though she may have chosen not to work outside the home. Both the women's movement and the normal growth toward perspective and wisdom have influenced her as well.

"It's amazing how I've changed in my reactions to the kids," says Eileen L, a traditional mother of four. "I can just turn off so much now that I didn't used to; I don't get so exasperated anymore. I found out that the exasperation took more energy than cooking and cleaning the house."

Stella F. is a veteran of divorce, and discovered new ways of coping that neither she nor her children knew she had. After twenty-six years of marriage and three children, Stella was left with no home and little money after a bitter, angry divorce that dragged on for years. Stella describes how upset and disbelieving her children were when they sensed she was trying to change and grow so that she could handle what fortune had presented to her.

"They [two daughters and a son] were so used to being the most important thing in my life that they couldn't believe I had other priorities after the divorce was finally over. I needed to be a *survivor,*" stresses Stella, "and that meant taking care of myself first in a way I never had done before.

"Of course I cared about my children and of course I worried if anything went wrong with them. But after twenty-six years of being a rather sheltered housewife, I had to go back to school, get a job, support myself and the children to some extent (their father was no good on support payments), plus build a new social life. Well, Mommy just wasn't there anymore, and believe me, they didn't like it one bit! They understood in their heads that I had to do these things, but in actually living it out, it was terrible. They felt abandoned, thrown out of my life, deserted, even though they were living with me part of that time. It took them a long while to understand where I am now, where I have to be, and that in the long run, it's best for them that I don't become a problem for them."

Stella reports that very slowly her children are beginning to see and know the human being underneath the title of mother and to know a little of what her needs, her joys, her future might be.

"They are beginning to respect me now a little bit more," she says with considerable satisfaction, "as a separate woman, with some strengths and abilities, not just 'Where's Mommy?' when they look at my life now. It's been eight years since the divorce and they spent a lot of that time hunting for Mommy, I can tell you."

Hunting for Mommy is a complex phenomenon among young people and is not at all limited to the understandable confusion that may attend divorce. For many young people it bespeaks immaturity and dependency, but for others it is more simply the ordinary human wish for the unconditional affection and security that no one of any age wants to give up.

"Once a child, always a child. Knowing that someone loves and understands you 'as is' is a durable and unique sense of comfort. Children, whatever their age, always want it, always miss it when it's gone," observed Dr. Stella Chess, child psychiatrist and author of *Daughters.*

The plaintive hope that mothers will remain exactly as they've always been, so that children will, in some elemental way, have to give up as little as possible of what *they* have always been, is especially widespread today precisely because modern parents are so much more youthful, mobile, and active—and thus offer the threat of change more sharply—than earlier generations tended to be.

Robin Fleisig, a Staten Island, New York, writer, highlighted this vague sense of betrayal and abandonment as parents move into a changing future when she wrote a column a couple of years ago for *The New York Times.* It was called "When *Parents* Leave the Nest" (italics added).

Writing about her parents' decision to move to Florida after her father's retirement and to leave the home where Ms. Fleisig grew up, she wistfully describes her losses: no more easy grand-parenting love for her own children, no more of the helpful offers to babysit, no chicken soup when somebody in the younger family was ill—in short, no general sense that the nest was always warm for her and her husband and children.

"Yes, we think you should move, Mom and Dad. We just don't know how you can" was the way she ended what was essentially an homage to the past.

For key in this loving daughter's recognition that her parents shouldn't have to be burdened with the old house anymore was a keen understanding that when the "term papers from junior high and the Barbie dolls" were thrown away, it would be her own girlhood that was gone.

It is this farewell to the young adult's own growing-up years that is symbolized by the parents changing careers, changing homes, changing life-styles, even changing spouses and lovers. To the young adult it means erasing the swing under the tree, forgetting the favorite music teacher Mom drove you to so patiently for so long, and never again tripping over that worn spot on the path up to the front door.

"But you're my bucket of earth," remonstrated one 24-year-old son to his widowed mother when she suggested she might sell the small frame house with the beloved and bedraggled backyard where her son had grown from sandbox to baseball to chef of family cookouts.

Another articulate son, given the task of showing the old family home to prospective buyers one evening when his parents were out, was asked by a possible purchaser what the older couple was going to leave in the house (meaning furniture, drapes, appliances, and so on).

"Only my childhood," responded the son.

When the parents returned and heard about this exchange, they were so moved and so dreadfully guilt-stricken they almost (but not quite) took the house off the market! In that instance, cooler heads prevailed, but the incident highlighted a certain slice of reality: The task of adult children to watch and understand how their parent's lives are changing is a task fraught with subtle wariness. That emotional tiptoeing reflects their own progress through life, too, facing all the problems attendant on maturity.

Mothers interviewed described a reluctance on the part of their adult sons and daughters to notice that there are some real, live people with new hopes, dreams, and challenges before them under the familiar facades of Mom and Dad.

This reluctance was reported by so many mothers and turned up in so many versions that I labeled it "the freeze-frame syndrome."

In its clearest manifestations, this seems to be a process similar to taking a stop-action photograph, said mothers. The young person wants to see in his or her mind's eye a snapshot of the mother perpetually standing in the doorway of the place where the young adult grew up. It could be a leafy suburban street, or an urban apartment building, or a farm, or a small town with a square, or a ranch, or an army post.

The physical place that spells home may vary, but remarkably consistent is the mental image—frozen in a frame like the one created by the click of a camera shutter—of mother in the same place, both literally and figuratively, she occupied when the child was growing up.

Maureen F., the mother of four sons, laughs ruefully describing how this freeze-frame image works with her young adults, who range in age from 21 to 31, and of whom only one is married.

"First of all, they want our home to stay exactly as it is, and of course, for my husband and me never to leave it or even to change it very much. Most especially, they've let me know in a dozen ways they have a particular idea of who *I* am; they think of me as sort of bright and kind of bouncy and outgoing, if not downright sassy. They do not want that to change! They're not interested in a more thoughtful, less shoot-from-the-hip sort of mother, because that is not the woman they remember as Mother when they were growing up.

"But," explains Maureen, "that is truly not me anymore. I've learned some things myself, I should hope! Life has taught me a lot, and one of the things I've learned the hard way is to think more before I shoot off my mouth. But they aren't interested in change for *me,* though of course they want change for *them.* They want to move on from school to work and to bigger and better adventures—but I should stay the same!"

"My daughter explained it to me very clearly," said Sara J., mother of a daughter and a son. "She said that the child is always supposed to be leaving the mother and the mother is supposed to *stay there,* be the safe base she was when the child was two or three, I suppose."

A substantial minority (about 38 percent) of the 208 in the sample group affirmed Maureen's report that the grown children remain attached for a long time—some forever—to the physical setting they called home and, by extension, attached to home and Mother.

One mother, Pamela K., continues to respond to this attachment and, indeed, to nurture it by doing all she can to satisfy the mental snapshot of the modest two-family house and small yard where the children grew up.

Pam has two daughters and one son, the latter in the army stationed overseas. "I sent Jim a little piece of the new vinyl tile we had put down in the kitchen a year or two after he was sent to England," says Pam, "and my married daughter, who sews very well, asked for a sample of the paint color we used in doing her old room over and she offered to make some curtains and a spread for it."

Pam describes her own reaction to the offer: "I was really very startled that she wanted to do that—pleased, of course, but surprised. She works—has a very demanding job, as a matter of fact. She does a lot of things around her own house and is a kindergarten homeroom mom for our little grandson, so I never dreamed she'd have time to do all that, but she offered. . . . Funny . . . I guess that staying connected to home, even though she loves her own home she has now with her own family, has some meanings to her that I just don't think about very much."

Almost all the mothers in the group said the children eventually give up this tie to their childhood home, of course, but not before they've activated enough maternal guilt and general parental ambivalence to practically scuttle the real estate industry.

And it isn't just changes in the old homestead that young adults resist, but other kinds of changes in their parents' lives as well.

"I think my children would describe me as pretty self-centered these days," said Mona S., 47, mother of a married son and a college-age daughter. "I've decided to go back to school in a serious way and even though the kids say they are proud of me and approve of what I'm doing, they get sulky when I'm not available for the big holiday dinner and when I try to control their visits if I have a term paper or an exam. Sometimes it seems to me they're so annoyed that they're not the absolute fixed stars around which my life revolves that they try to make me feel silly about going back to school at my age.

"I'll be past fifty—way past—when and if I ever do get my degree," explains Mona, "and to tell you the truth, I'm not that sure about the whole project myself . . . so sometimes they do shake me up. But most of the time, it works out—they're okay, they come around."

Mona reveals how hard change is for both generations when she adds resolutely, "They surely know by now how important they are in my life, but it's time for me now, my turn."

Mona's remark—it's "my turn" now—found a lyrical and intense repetition in the voices of many women in the mothers' group. They said, in a variety of styles and languages, that even now the adult children cannot imagine how much of their mothers' selfhood was suspended or put on hold during the child-rearing years and how much now is open to change and exploration.

The forces driving mid-life women and their children toward a changing future they must map together are both universal—normal developmental phases of all human beings—and specific to the era that both generations inhabit, an era characterized by rapid social change, by exploding technology, by the threat of a nuclear doomsday, and by a large number of economic, social, and political pressures.

Young adults, by and large, don't resist the time-specific pressures creating change (technology, instant communications, and so on) as much as they resist the timeless and ancient phases of human growth and development.

Corwinna D., mother of three adult sons, tells of an amusing but anxious resistance to her own changes on the part of her youngest son: "Brian just got his first job out of college last year; he's getting settled in Minneapolis, where his new company is located." The children grew up and the parents still live in Vermont, while the other two sons also live in the New England region. "Naturally, we're all excited whenever he gets a chance to get home—like for a holiday or on a quick business trip. Last year, he saved up all his vacation time so he could spend about a week with the family over Christmas and it was great . . . worked out great."

Corwinna continues: "We had a fine time, he met a new girl-friend—it was really fun. We went to the movies and had after-ski suppers here and did a lot of things together. His dad had to leave a little early on a business trip of his own and the other boys left a day early, too, and just at the end of the holiday week, Brian and I were left at home together.

"On the last night of his visit," said Brian's mother, "it was as though he was trying to cram everything into one more day. We went out for dinner and then to a show and then to another place for a nightcap and it must have been past one o'clock in the morning when we finally got home. I was really out on my feet, I was *so* tired, and to my surprise, he wanted to settle down by the fireplace and have a good-night game of checkers or chess like we used to when he was twelve years old! I looked at him —I was amazed—and I said, kind of weakly, 'But Brian, I'm exhausted. I've been up since six o'clock this morning to drive Dad to the airport; it's been a long day, Son, aren't you tired?'

"As a matter of fact," said shrewd Corwinna, "he *was* tired himself—he'd been skiing in the afternoon, too—but he wanted to repeat that long-ago pattern as though things were exactly the way they had been when he was a youngster at home."

What Corwinna did not say, but what hung in the air as other mothers murmured and listened, was that her son did not want to know that his mother was not a very young woman anymore, and though her supply of energy and stamina was quite abundant enough for an active life of her own, she was getting to the stage in her life where she didn't want to replicate all that she had done as the mother of three energetic, tireless, and robust little boys.

This resistance to the mother moving through yet another doorway just ahead of him has a number of elements.

First and most frightening, it suggests the parent's aging and eventual death. Second, it brings into view a possible period for the parent in which some ominous demands might be made on the child—a period when some heavy responsibilities and obligations might face the young adult.

And third, it brings the requirement that the young son or daughter become mature, reach a new level of what experts call "filial dependability," and, as a corollary, face his or her own mortality.

None of these, the mothers pointed out, are issues the young adult feels particularly cheery about, and in addition, the younger person hasn't yet had the concrete opportunity to discharge possible obligations, so has only fantasy worries without even knowing how fantasy satisfactions and contentment might come from having done the right and loving thing for parents.

When the parents are youthfully middle-aged, it's a kind of limbo period for the young adult, who has neither the mother of his childhood nor the parent who may require much assistance from him, and most of the mothers in the core group were sympathetic with both Brian and Corwinna in their respective roles.

But the genuine opportunities for getting reacquainted with the person each has become are also tempting for mothers in this mid-life period. A deeper feeling of empathy as the children reach for their own maturation is one of the great possible rewards for parents, along with some of the strain and tension of changing needs in both generations.

Let's take a close look at what happens to this group of mothers and their adult children as the mothers move toward the new challenges and possibilities, as well as problems, that come with getting older.

From the PTA to Golden Pond: Myth, Fear, and Hope

> Do not yearn after immortality.
> But exhaust the limits of the possible.
>
> PINDAR

As today's young adults grow toward middle age, they find themselves in a lockstep with their mothers, a lockstep decreed by time to bring yet a new phase of the mother-child history.

With women living so long, going on so many new journeys with their grown children and grown grandchildren, what will travel through time be like for those millions of women who bore so many babies in the 1940s, 1950s, and early 1960s?

What will they want, expect, owe, fear, hope, and dream about their lives with their children as they move into new private eras?

Most of the women whose voices you hear in this book didn't want to talk about getting older at all, and though they are full of worries and anxieties, as well as hopes and wishes for the later parts of their lives with their grown children, they'd really rather not discuss that chapter in the family saga.

I found that most of the vigorous, middle-aged mothers I interviewed were quite willing to talk about some of the most intimate and painful problems of their lives with their children *now,* but retreated from our discussions like frightened animals when I raised the question "What about when you are older?"

Pursuing this obvious fear as far as I could, with as much gentle persistence as the situation allowed, I found that the question of generational obligations and responsibilities, each to the other, was inextricably tied up with feelings about aging in general and aging in contemporary American society specifically.

Before we can hear what these women think they will want from their adult children, how they think those children will deal with the changing future, and what the mothers, in their turn, may feel they will owe their children to their last breath, we must allow the women to speak first of how they view the whole process of getting older in our culture.

Old age is not a disaster; it's a triumph!
MAGGIE KUHN, leader of the Gray Panthers, an organization of
elderly social activists

As Lives Are Extended, Some People Wonder If It's Really a
Blessing.
Wall Street Journal headline

Whether the individual man or woman sees getting older as
triumph, disaster, or something in between, the fact all too clear
to middle-aged people now in their prime is that old age is
largely scorned in this country; the elderly do not enjoy much
status in restless, success-driven America.

"In America," wrote Dr. Robert N. Butler, one of the nation's
most humane gerontologists and author of the Pulitzer Prize–
winning study *Why Survive? Being Old in America,* "childhood is
romanticized, youth is idolized, middle age does the work,
wields the power and pays the bills, and old age, its days empty
of purpose, gets little or nothing for what it has already done.

"American attitudes toward the old are contradictory," says
Dr. Butler. "We pay lip service to the idealized images of beloved and tranquil grandparents, wise elders, white-haired pa-
triarchs and matriarchs. But the opposite image disparages the
elderly, *seeing age as decay, decrepitude, a disgusting and undignified
dependency.*" (Italics added.)

It is this last description of prevailing attitudes toward old age
that I found to be typical of the nightmares haunting the dreams
of the mature mothers I interviewed.

"From where I sit," said Brenda M., 54, the attractive, youth-
ful-looking divorced mother of three adult children, "I can't tell
you how terrified I am of getting old. I think it's going to be
awful—awful! I honestly don't want to think about it."

At the time of our interview, Brenda had just returned from
a painful visit to her 84-year-old mother, who was stricken with
a sudden heart attack that brought Brenda hastily flying down
to Florida from her Connecticut home and from her hospital job
as a laboratory technician.

This close personal brush with death obviously shook Brenda
badly, even though the outlook for her mother was pronounced

good at the moment. Brenda was coping with a number of stresses at once and they piled up toweringly in her mind as we talked. First, of course, was the fear of losing her mother, with whom she enjoyed a warm, close affection. Second was the confrontation with her own mortality that her mother's illness brought to the forefront of her consciousness. And third—a most reluctant third—was the scary, barely endurable question "How will *my* kids behave toward me when I'm in that hospital bed?"

Faced with the inescapable fact that older people are meanly devalued in a youth-worshiping culture, and faced with many negative stereotypes of old age, it is little wonder that more than three-quarters (78 percent) of the women in the core group of 208 betrayed a shocking, almost pathological, fear of getting older.

Except for a small, pensive amount of gallows humor ("The only thing worse is the alternative . . ."), most of the responses drew a portrait of getting older as unrelieved decline, loss, and misery, with virtually no compensations, rewards, or benefits.

"I can barely stand to talk about it," said Karen B., the mother of a grown son and daughter. "I think of it as little as I can, hide my head in the sand. . . . Talk about ostriches, I think I'm the champion."

Actually, Karen was not the champion at all; dozens of women who responded in letters, telephone calls, and face-to-face interviews and discussion groups vied with each other in telling stories of pathetic disabilities, lengthy illnesses, and progressive disintegration of families under the blows of fate.

In the catalogue of sorrows these women detailed, most of the central figures either were within their own immediate families or were the parents of friends; they were case histories that these modern women saw up close, and they shuddered at the sight.

Only a handful—six or eight—had stories to tell of parents or friends or former colleagues or teachers who provided a model of older people who had met the challenges of aging with some success and dignity. Practically no one spoke of the freedom to move to one's own rhythm that finally comes, especially to women, when the heavy burdens of the middle years are resolved.

Virtually none of the interview subjects wanted to try to fantasize about what a "good" old age might be like, seeing it as a complete contradiction in terms. None of the women had ever heard the late anthropologist Dr. Margaret Mead describe the later years for women as full of "PMZ"—postmenopausal zest!

Probing the depth of this unrelieved gloom over the inevitable, I tried introducing some notes of optimism about recent scientific advances that suggested that more Americans than ever before are reaching later years in better health than their parents did. I pointed out, too, that researchers have now found that learning can continue throughout life and that senility is by no means inevitable in every older person.[1]

Nothing worked; every hint of a more positive outlook was turned away. Examples of powerful, productive, interesting old people like actress Helen Hayes in her mid-eighties, and Picasso painting away when he was 90, were put down as too special and too exceptional to provide useful role models.

Even though gerontologists have now divided the aged into three categories—those from 65 to 75 are called the "young old," those from 75 to 85 are called the "middle old," and those over 85 are called the "old old"—the women in my group would have none of such distinctions. They saw old age as beginning whenever they could no longer operate at top speed and full capacity. It seemed an either/or proposition in their minds and little could dissuade them from distress over any sign or signal from time, no matter how gradually the effects might come.

In truth, the "young old" (the next step for the middle-aged mothers who are our subjects) are really much more like the middle-aged of an earlier era; it has been generally accepted now that the entire first decade following formal retirement (usually at 65 or earlier) is a continuation of some of the best features of middle age: in many cases intact partnerships as yet unbroken by a companion's death, reasonable health, some degree of economic stability, and freedom from pressures of child care and educating and launching young adults.

Yet the mothers of grown children could not bring themselves even to look at the relatively optimistic near term, the oncoming period in which they would be the "young old," because it spelled an advance into alien territory, into a new country: that of the aged.

Moreover, the fact that women are sexually devalued at a

younger age than men (who can almost always associate with women fifteen or twenty years younger than themselves without serious social disapproval) was only one more worry about change and by no means the primary one.

The core group of mothers felt quite keenly that though they have suffered, even in their youthful forties and fifties, from "ageism" in the sexual marketplace, the later years were bitter for men, too. Many of the mothers saw men as often pathetically disoriented after many working years, lost without their work identities, while women may keep a homemaker role forever if they wish.

Against this bleak backdrop of fear and a willful desire to ignore the calendar, I attempted to examine the impact of the oncoming years on the relationship between these contemporary women and their now-young adult children.

What would they want from their children (especially given the dark existence they posited as old women) in their later years; what could they reasonably expect?

What did they think their children owed them, if anything? And what would they owe their children if they reached their eighties or beyond?

I asked them to imagine, to speculate, on what the texture of the relationship might be. Sweet, full of shared memories and what one affectionate daughter called "the same mental geography"? Bitter, with a lifetime of unresolved pain and conflict? Might their children be supportive, indifferent, coldly dutiful? What would the strains of old age impose upon the average tangled loves and hates of the ordinary family?

Their fears were poignant, their anxieties intense, but their hopes for the relationship remained warm, and their confidence in their children to behave decently in crisis times was moving beyond words.

Let's listen as women muse about their later lives with their adult children.

Becoming a Burden . . . or Completing the Bargain?

"I would take pills before I'd become a burden to my
children. . . ."

BERNADETTE N., mother of three sons

"I just hope I'll be in enough control at the end of my life to
be able to decide to quit if I'm destroying my children's lives
—sometimes people don't have that control, you know, if
they're unlucky. . . ."

ALTHEA T., mother of four, a practicing nurse-midwife

"I do feel that the giving and taking of everything—money,
care, interest—should not flow just one way between the generations; that they should go back and forth, with each taking and
giving different things. . . ."

AMY R., mother of a son and two daughters

"My kids don't owe me a thing—nothing. It doesn't work that
way. I had 'em because I wanted 'em; they didn't ask to be born
and they shouldn't be burdened in their lives because of my
needs later on. . . ."

JUNE MAE T., mother of two sons and two daughters, a beautician

"My children were raised to cope with whatever life brings
them, and if I get to be a problem to them—well, they'll cope
with that, too. At least, I feel pretty sure they will. . . ."

CHRISSY S., mother of three, a schoolteacher for twenty years

These are just a few of the issues that began to surface as I
coaxed women to try to think themselves into a changing life.

Out of the welter of anxiety, two major responses emerged
that were overwhelming in their force and consistency among
women of varied backgrounds.

One was a dark, foreboding terror of becoming a burden to
their children, imposing real sacrifices on the lives and families
of their sons and daughters.

The second was a perhaps peculiarly American belief: A majority of women said their children owed them nothing—especially not financial or other kinds of day-to-day help, such as

health care on a steady basis, or living together in case of illness and economic need.

A substantial minority, about 25 percent, disagreed with the majority on this issue and reflected more typically the obligations to elders that characterize some other family-centered cultures such as the Chinese and other Oriental societies and the Greek and Italian among Mediterranean cultures.

But fully three-quarters of the 208 respondents *denied* any notion of reciprocity, of a mutual "owing" between mothers and their adult children.

Surprisingly, many of the women who denied their children owed them anything at all for a lifetime of maternal care did believe that a mother's obligation continued for all of her life, even if the children returned nothing.

This seems to be saying that the middle-aged mothers of our sample group could not really envision much change in the old pattern of maternal giving and children taking, except for a few who said thoughtfully that perhaps the giving on their side would slow down in real old age through limitation of energy, money, and other resources.

The heaviest anxiety—around the possibility of becoming a burden to their children—set off reverberating waves of anguish among dozens of mothers.

"I'd jump out a window before I'd bring the kind of grief to my children that my father brought to me," said Alice E., 52, mother of a grown daughter and son. "We cared for my father during a very long illness, right in our home, right while the children were growing up. It put a terrible strain on my marriage and I know it caused me to fail my own kids in lots of ways that will always bother me."

It was jolting to hear healthy, active, involved women, many of them at one of the most productive periods of their lives, talk so seriously of suicide when the specter of becoming a burden to their children shadows the future. This kind of discussion is, however, finding its way into public discourse more and more often as the graying of America proceeds. A rising suicide rate among the elderly, the growth of "right to die" movements, and a renewed interest in euthanasia—all contribute to a growing willingness to think the unthinkable for many people, including mothers staring at a life that might, through no one's fault, become a heavy cross to bear for children and grandchildren.

While this fear of harming their children's lives was consistent in almost all responses, the majority of mothers did not see suicide as the solution to crises, should health or money woes strike hard in the "old old" stage.

Instead they saw alternative paths that reflected different timbres of temperament, different histories, different ways of approaching life in all its seasons.

One popular point of view called for the mother to struggle with every fiber of her being to remain independent and to live separately from her children if at all possible. A breathtaking majority, 97.4 percent of 208 mothers, said that their notion of an absolutely ideal old age was to be independent of their children in every possible way.

A series of "what if" questions highlighted this intensely held hope. "What if you were widowed?" they were asked. "Would you expect to move in with one of your children?" The women were virtually unanimous in preferring to carry on alone. Only 1 percent said they would expect to move in with with their children. My private suspicion here, although I gathered no evidence to sustain it, is that this number is far lower than it might have been one or two generations ago, when it was assumed there would always be a female relative—wife, daughter, granddaughter, niece—available at home to give consistent care to the elderly. The case of the unmarried daughter who did not work outside the home and gave up her life to nurse an ailing father is not that far behind us (Mary Gordon's wonderful novel *Final Payments* was published in 1978) but that scene changes as women change their view of themselves and the purpose of their lives.

And although women are increasingly out of the home and thus unavailable for day-to-day care-giving to the elderly, we have not yet reached the nirvana where this responsibility is seen as a task to be shared equally by sons and sons-in-law, although with the current emphasis on encouraging the nurturant parts of male personalities, such care-giving might be done by males at some time in the future. However, I believe that the tiny fraction of women who saw themselves as willing to move in with their children reflects women's awareness that it would still be on the shoulders of their daughters or daughters-in-law to provide care if they lived together.

Particularly interesting within the large majority who would not see the answer to widowhood as moving in with their children was the subgroup of divorcées. A dozen or more women in the core sample were divorced, most after lengthy marriages. They had thus already dealt with the loss of a spouse and the end of a marriage, and they had, in some cases, achieved a hard-won independence that they cherished fiercely and protectively. For this group in particular, the notion of moving in with their adult children was especially negative, they said.

Another "what if" question was: "What if you were old and ill, had little money, and needed care—would you rather go to a nursing home or move in with one of your children?"

The dilemma posed by this question was agonizing; more than a quarter of the whole group refused to answer, but of those who did, 70 percent said they'd rather go to a nursing home if things were that unmanageable on their own.

This answer is especially piercing because the majority of women thought of all nursing homes as sheer hell! There were two exceptions: a few wealthy women whose relatives had always been able to purchase the best of institutional care, plus a small group of women whose relatives had been lucky enough to be cared for in model philanthropic or religious public homes for the aged. But most women were unaware of any acceptable nursing homes. Even so, they said they preferred bad ones to moving in with their children.

More than half the women who chose nursing homes did, however, cite some special circumstances in which they might consider living with their children. In almost all such instances, mothers said the move would be conditional on the adult children having plenty of space, more than adequate income, and a general family structure and life-style that would permit the older woman and the young family a great deal of privacy and separation in day-to-day living.

Although all of this in retrospect sounds like calm and orderly thinking, choosing, and deciding, the fact is that during discussions of these issues, women showed a jumble of anxiety, fear, and apprehension. The uncertainty of what the gods will deliver for the second half of life, combined with the uncertainty about the course of the adult children's lives—"Will they be able to help, even if they want to?" and "What if they had bad luck of their own, like health problems or a handicapped child?"— made most mothers prayerful about being able to continue indefinitely in an independent mode.

But the deepest concerns, as well as the most hopeful optimism in a melancholy emotional landscape, were revealed around this question: "How do you think your children would respond if a real catastrophe struck when you were in your eighties or older—some dire crisis of health or money or emotional problems?"

From the torrent of feeling this question released, a number of heartening answers developed:

First and most importantly, the large majority of mothers *did not fear that their children would abandon them in times of trouble.* This was a most important finding, I believe, because it flies in the face of some myths that adult children almost uniformly abandon, dump, and otherwise turn their backs on their parents when bad times strike.

There certainly are families, perhaps quite a number on a national scale, where abandonment does take place, but I question whether that is the norm. In the nearly 500 women of the major ethnic, religious, and socioeconomic groups I surveyed, only one mother said she would turn to strangers before her own children if she were in extreme need.

This sole disbeliever, who had a somewhat rocky relationship with both her grown children, stated flatly, "Women who count on their grown kids to help them out in their old age are kidding themselves. It just isn't going to happen."

Said Joycelen T., "The young people today just haven't got the kind of character that does for others or cares about others. I think the 'me' generation is here to stay and we'd better realize it."

Joycelen added to this no-confidence vote by recounting this story:

"When my own mother was very ill and possibly dying, we took her into our home to care for her. Even though we have a big house and could afford plenty of help, it was still hard on all of us. The kids were adolescent at this time, and as her illness progressed, things got very bad and the whole family was put through the wringer. At one point, my son said to me: 'I don't know why you are doing this when you know we could afford to have Grandma properly cared for somewhere else. If you are doing this to set an example for us kids, *forget it.* "

Joycelen was cut to the bone by this speech, has never forgotten a syllable of it (although it took place more than fifteen years ago), and believes it to be the rule among young people.

But most of the mothers in the respondent group did not at all believe the children would walk away from them in a crisis. They displayed a warm confidence in their children's sense of honor, decency, and empathy. (A cautionary note: It is impossible to guess how many women verbalized such confidence without being really sure of it, out of either wishful hoping or a disinclination to face any other possibility.)

The problem, most women said, was not abandonment by their children, but realistic external difficulties such as hard times in the adult son's or daughter's own life, a bad national economy, a housing shortage, a changing view of women that recognizes the unfairness of expecting women alone to provide all care, and a host of other real-life problems that, say the mothers, don't reflect badly on any individual young adult.

In fact, mothers defended their children in advance against critical accusations before any questionable behavior even occurred.

"Abandon me?" asked Phoebe T., 56, mother of three. "Abandon me? No! Never would my children leave me to suffer. Why," she said tenderly, "how could anyone ever think such a thing about them? My children are good people. They are not hard-hearted men and women. No, indeed, they are not hard-hearted."

Another woman, Rachel L., mother of two sons and a daughter, had an even more spirited defense of her children against some phantom future accusations.

"Not only do I know they never would abandon me," said Rachel, "but I think they would be quite up to the job of having to make serious sacrifices for me if it was necessary."

How would she feel about a situation like that?

"I wouldn't like it, I'd feel bad about it, but if it were a realistic survival situation—not a frivolous or just a convenience need—I wouldn't be devastated by it. I have no patience with these women who say they would jump out windows or take pills before asking for heavy-duty help from their children," answered Rachel heatedly. "I don't feel that way at all. The reason I don't is because we raised our children to handle life's problems, not run away from them. They learned caring inside the family and common sense outside. If doing something hard to help me stay alive would cause a temporary setback in their lives, I think they would go on later and catch up, get back on track."

Interestingly enough, while so many women kept insisting their children owed them nothing in the way of tangible help with money or health problems, they seemed to have more abstract expectations in the realm of feelings.

"Love if possible, but respect for sure" is the summary of what more than 180 of the 208-mother group said they would expect in later years.

"Also, they owe me a good-faith effort to make something of their lives—that's all they owe me. They should pass on to their own kids the love and care we gave them and they should amount to something. Beyond that, they owe me nothing" was the firm statement of Dina M., mother of five and stepmother to three children.

One of the clearest explanations of the worried but hopeful stance of many women was given by Dulcie N., the recently widowed mother of two grown sons.

"If I need help and they don't give it to me, they'll feel guilty. If I need it at a time when it's hard for them to give, they'll feel resentful and then *I'll* feel terrible. So it seems to me the best thing to do is for the three of us to talk about it openly, long before there is a problem, and then continue to share what's possible and doable when the time comes—make it a joint decision, in other words; all of us working together for the best outcome. I'm not saying that's some kind of magic panacea, but it might be a way to get a handle on it" was Dulcie's thoughtful contribution to a group discussion.

Roberta T., mother of three unmarried adult children, agreed with Dulcie very strongly and said she felt it was especially important that mothers communicate their expectations to their children.

"There are two ways you can let them know what you expect —if you expect anything—when you reach real old age,"

Roberta said. "You can show 'em by example—and I think that's the very best way—but I think it's okay to talk it over with them before you get there, too. Lots of times they just don't think about it or really understand what is happening in this country between parents and their grown kids."

Roberta feels strongly that families are under heavy stress in the United States from two cultural forces that tend to disrupt the natural links between the generations.

She claims that one such pressure is the still-strong frontier spirit, particularly in regions outside the biggest cities, in small towns and rural areas. Rugged independence is still a highly valued trait in such areas, says Roberta, and while this is admirable in many ways, such an "every man for himself" spirit can be hard on the helpless and infirm, she believes. (It should be noted, however, that many such regions have an equally strong tradition of looking out for the old folks right along with the frontier ethos.)

In addition, this mother is angry over the way the American emphasis on work and monetary success builds walls between the generations. "To become what we call successful," Roberta claimed, "we're expected to pull up roots, tear up families, travel anywhere, and do almost anything in the name of the job."

Although Roberta and her family did not personally suffer from the ills of the work-seeking, mobile family (Roberta's husband is a civil engineer and has his own office not far from his home, and she is a traditional homemaker), many of her friends did suffer from the work hunt and she is appalled at the emotional costs.

"The bigger companies talk a lot about how important it is for a man to have a family, but they expect them, and women, too, of course, to put the company before their own wives or husbands and children, and *certainly* to put it before their aged parents.

"Can you imagine," Roberta asked, "what would happen if a male corporate executive refused a promotion and a transfer because he didn't want to leave his eighty-three-year-old mother who was in a nursing home nearby?" She added indignantly, "That would be the end of his career at that company! And if it was a woman executive who gave that reason, she'd be crucified and used to prove that women are just not fit for the business world. No, it's a very, very tough problem, I think."

Asked how she intended to handle this with her own children, Roberta said brusquely, "I've always let my kids know all along that there is such a thing as character; there *are* such things as loyalty and responsibility . . . and one just doesn't walk away from duties and obligations of all kinds, including those we have to older people."

On the question of what mothers will expect from their grown children, Bettina P., mother of two married daughters, had another angle of vision to report. Bettina said she didn't expect to live with her children ("Desperation Gulch," she called that arrangement) or to take money from them; what she expects, she says, is to share significant information about the lives of both parents and kids.

"When they talk to me," she explained, "I expect them to be interested in what their dad and I are doing and thinking and how we're feeling . . . and I want to hear those important things from them, too. Not only about their physical well-being, but . . . you know . . . how they are *really* feeling, in emotional matters as well as work and the house and the car and the grandkids when they get around to having them."

However, Bettina is one of many, many mothers who do not encourage their married children to confide marital problems to them, and on the whole, Bettina's daughters do not.

"I would listen, of course," she says, "but I don't think it's my place to seek out that kind of information. After all, if anything should go seriously wrong, I'd know about it soon enough! But overall, without too many details, I think they owe me occasional serious reports on the state of their lives."

The expectation that the children should "check in" reasonably often, especially when there are important changes in their lives such as a new job or new friends, was voiced by a large majority of mothers.

Flowing from the discussion on expectations, there gradually came a clearer view that mothers separate help into two kinds —financial assistance and emotional support. It was the latter they were tentative about seeking, while asking for financial help (if it was badly needed) seemed easier, if not ever a truly relaxed or casual step.

Money problems, many women felt, could be solved with less tension because there were clearer objective measurements in the mother's own mind as to whether the adult son or daughter could afford it or not. If the grown children were seen as having moderate or affluent incomes, then mothers agonized less over the idea of accepting monetary help.

One mother, speaking of a brilliant daughter cutting a swath through law school, put it this way: "She'll most likely have a very good income in her thirties and forties, and needing that kind of help—financial—wouldn't bother me near as much as it would if, for some reason, I was forced to move into her home or to require daily care and attention. I'd sure hate to be that needy, and I hope I'm spared from doing that to my child, no matter how much money is around."

Reluctant as most women were to specify what kind of expectations they have or to pin their children to concrete helping measures, most admitted, when pressed, that they *would* turn to their children if the disaster were dire enough and if they had no alternative. Most saw help from their children as a last resort, to be utilized only when all other resources failed.

These feelings, expressed with a lot of prayers and knocking on wood, were, however, right in line with the truth of how most elderly people actually live in the United States. Despite all the talk of abandonment and "warehousing" of old people, the facts are different. They include these realities:

• The family is still the major assistance network for most older folks, although no one knows how long that can continue if health care costs continue to skyrocket.[2]

• Only 5 percent of older people are living in institutions; most are in their own or their children's or some other relative's home.[3] In addition, three-quarters of America's elderly either live with a son or daughter or within an hour's distance of an adult child or other care-giving relative.[4]

• Economic need, while pressing for widows who outlive their husbands by many years, is still slightly ameliorated for people reaching the seventh and eight decades in the years ahead because of the pervasiveness of private pension plans, in addition to Social Security provisions. Too many elderly are below the poverty line, but statisticians believe that the middle-aged, middle-class women in our sample will, on the whole, have somewhat more financial security than their mothers and grandmothers did. (At the same time, the "feminization of poverty" continues apace among younger single-parent female-headed households, and the older-age outlook for such women is disastrous, indeed.)

Given these marginally more hopeful facts about the probable ways in which some older people are going to live in coming decades, and given that most of the women expressed confidence that their children would help in a real crisis, it then became possible to examine together the question of what they would desire, as opposed to what obligations they think their children have toward them.

I asked mothers how, if they had their "druthers," they would most prefer to interact with their children and what they think they themselves will still owe the children as the second half of their own lives unfolds.

On these topics, women were clearer and more cheerful, perhaps because the questions cast them in the more familiar "giving" role.

In response to the first query, "When you are older, and assuming you are able to live independently and do not require money or care from your children, what will you then want from them at that point in your life?", the answer came loud and clear: *consistent contact*

Although mothers were specific about what this meant—a telephone call once a week, a visit once a month if possible, occasional inclusion in important family events—it was also clear that what they were after were signs and symbols from their children.

Although they talked a great deal about the mechanics of staying in touch—the phone call, the visiting back and forth—what emerged was that they wanted signs that their children cared about them, were concerned for their welfare, and would be on tap if needed.

Most of the mothers saw *consistency* of contact as more important than *frequency* of contact. Six phone calls during an illness or two visits in a few weeks if business or vacation brought them near would not be very satisfactory to most mothers if such contact was followed by long periods of silence or absence.

"What would count most to me would be simply staying in touch in some way—I don't really much care how they would do it. Young people are not much in the way of letter-writers; they're used to the telephone and that's okay, as long as it's regular. About once a week would be fine" is the way Louisa Ann W., mother of two sons, phrased her wishes and hopes.

The prevalence of the once-a-week phone call as a deep desire of mothers was most striking; whatever else they may have thought to be a wish or a preference, they kept coming back to the weekly phone call as a sort of "bottom line" of the future relationship.

This rather minimal requirement—it doesn't seem a lot to ask after a lifetime of involvement, for good or ill, with their children's lives—probably should be looked at with some reservations. It represents what women are speculating about now concerning a delicate relationship some time off in an unknowable future. In addition, it assumes that the oft-mentioned independent life so dearly wished for, but not always granted, will be theirs.

In addition to the weekly phone call, there were two other desires that led the "wish list." They were: opportunities to be with the grandchildren (this was also on the list of things they felt their children "owed" them), and being included in significant family gatherings.

However, the tone of voice and emotional coloration of discussing these latter two wishes were quite different from the way in which mothers specified the weekly phone call. When they talked of that call, their voices were firm, making the demand clear and straightforward. But when they spoke of their wish to see the grandchildren or to attend weddings and college graduations, they were more wistful and tremulous, much more uncertain of whether this was a reasonable request or not.

For example, they tended to hedge these latter hopes with qualifications, such as "if it's not too inconvenient for the children" or "if they lived close enough to make the visits easy." Most shrank from any suggestion that the adult children should make extreme efforts to let them see the grandchildren, even though modern young people have made it clear in many cases that they are revaluing family ties and actually *want* their parents to be actively playing the grandparent role for the benefit of their own children.

The mothers interviewed were especially tentative about the hope they could be included in future family gatherings, even when they are very old (see Chapter 5). It was obvious that such gatherings meant life-affirming validation of their existence, offered warmth and love and a supportive network, and gave them a chance to strengthen continuity in the family's life. But they were sadly and deeply uncertain of the appeal of these values to their children. They were also quite concerned, they said, that they themselves, due to frailty or illness, might eventually come to ignore such symbolic contacts with their kin.

Why are these women so tentative and uncertain about some of the things they so dearly want from their children later?

Two answers emerged from their lengthy discussions. One strong causal factor was that, as daughters of now-aged mothers, they felt they were being asked for too much—too much of everything, they said. Most cited endless needs for emotional support and involvement that they experienced as heavy burdens, and again repeated how they wished to avoid burdening their children as they are being burdened.

The second reason is based on the mothers' view of their seventh and eighth decades as a time when the accounts will be balanced and a final tally written in the family ledger. In other words, Judgment Day!

Will the implied bargain they struck when the children were born—to give love and care forever and to receive it in return when they are needy—be honored and observed?

It turned out that for many women, any discussion about what their children may or may not do for them when they are old is seen as a final verdict on their mothering job.

To have to ask for help (most wished their children would offer without being asked) and then possibly to be rejected is the last nightmare before death itself for many women. They would, quite simply, rather not ask, no matter how dire the consequences, than risk being refused.

The fear that their children will, in effect, render a negative judgment on their lives as mothers springs partly from their own massive, lifelong guilt about their mothering performance (see

Chapter 2) and partly from a practical, realistic view that such a negative verdict has been rendered in many families for reasons outsiders can seldom fathom, for causes that may never be identified openly.

"Children at any age are basically selfish, relative to their parents, and the less you expect, the better off you'll be," warned Leslie R., mother of two, grandmother of five. Interestingly, Leslie enjoyed good relations with her offspring; she was often a sought-after guest now, in mid-life, at her children's backyard cookouts, and on their vacation trips.

But Leslie herself, looking toward the next life stage, said she wasn't at all sure she should continue to expect that kind of attention in the future, as her children's own lives became more complex and demanding, and she stoutly maintained that she got along so well because she expected little. Leslie illustrated her point by calling on a piece of folk wisdom from her own grandmother: "One mother can take care of six children, but six children cannot take care of one mother," she told the other women.

Lila Z., mother of four, said, "I know all too well the mistakes I've made as a mother—nobody needs to kick me when I'm down to prove it—and old age is when your kids really let you know how they feel about it. It's pay-up time and I'm as scared as anybody!"

Lila seemed to reflect the consensus, though, when she added: "I hope for the best—my three sons and daughter are all basically good kids. They vary in how much they can sympathize with another person, but on the whole, they're decent human beings and I think things will probably work out okay. I just hope," knocking on wood, "they don't have to be tested too much. But if that should happen—well, we're the kind of people who do what is right."

On the other side of the coin, what does an aged mother still owe her children and perhaps go on owing to the end of her days?

When mothers tried to answer this question, they were much calmer and showed much less apprehension, possibly because they felt on firmer ground examining their own obligations than in trying to guess how their children will handle theirs.

However, it also became apparent that, in trying to find answers to these questions, many women again became entangled in trying to define aging and how it will affect their total behavior, not alone the relationship with their children.

Their struggle to project a model of successful aging and not quite finding the outlines is shared, though many of them did not know it, by professionals in many disciplines, who are still trying to formulate the set of patterns that would be workable for most people.

For some men and women, gradual disengagement from past phases of their lives seems normal and good; for others, deep and active involvement in life on every level seems imperative, even if it becomes unrealistic in their eighties and nineties.

And for still others, some compromise between withdrawal on too dramatic a scale and overinvolvement beyond diminishing strength and resources offers a comfortable path.

The 208 women in our core group took up each of these possible strategies in turn and examined them in the context of what they still would want to offer to their children in their "real" old age, meaning past 75 or 80.

A majority agreed on one primary offering: they want to be attentive grandmas, "needed from a distance" said one eloquent and devoted but still young grandma of forty-eight, for as long as health and strength permit. Being involved with their grandchildren did *not* mean living with them, women were quick to point out. "God forbid I should have to raise another family; I can't think of anything I'd dislike more!" exclaimed Greta L., mother of five adult children and three grandchildren.

But a large majority of mothers felt the tie with grandchildren was precious, and they suffer a conscious sense of deprivation when the grandchildren live so far away that an ordinary visiting relationship cannot be built.

A second emotional offering women feel they owe their own adult sons and daughters is to remain concerned and caring about troubles, and sharing with joys—to show the children they will always be important, even though some women were aware of the tendency of many aged persons to turn more inward.

It was on this latter point—how long can mothers continue a deep emotional involvement with the trials and triumphs of their children's lives?—that the first signs of change in the indissoluble bond began to show.

Speaking slowly as she groped for the right words, Alma B., the mother of three children whose lives had featured a fair amount of "normal" turbulence arising from broken romances and routine job problems, said, "I think I *can* imagine a time when I might say to my children, 'Spare me the bad news and be quick to tell me the good news,' because I'm not sure how old one has to be before emotional fatigue sets in and you just don't want any more grief, nohow!"

Alma's admission that there might come a time when a mother's ability to cope with troubles in her children's lives might wane elicited a good deal of agreement from other mothers, together with a positive determination to try to hold off that time as long as possible.

"It's hard for me now to think I might ever be so worn out and weary that I wouldn't want to actively help. I know I would always care but maybe couldn't do much—if my children were in some kind of trouble—but I suppose it could happen later on," said Bridget M., mother of a grown son and daughter.

In addition to being an attentive and affectionate grandmother, and in addition to staying closely in touch with the unfolding of their adult children's lives, most of the women who answered questions also felt another strong lifelong debt to their children, and that was to symbolize continuity and to hand on family traditions, belongings, and religious and ethnic heritages.

Lizbet T., at 54 the grandmother of five youngsters, was fortunate enough to be included in a grandparents' project one of her grandsons was assigned at school. This required Lizbet to spend a number of hours with her 9-year-old grandson, taping reminiscences of the "old days" before television and space travel, and sharing more family history with him than she ever had before. In addition, she was one of the honored guests when all the grandparents were invited to the school to hear the tapes and exchange family histories.

The event affected this modern, active grandmother, who had just come back from a vacation trip to the Far East, to resume her work as a music teacher when the project developed, in a way she described as "profound."

"Before this happened," says Lizbet, "I never realized that I had so much to give, so much to share, of the past with my children and grandchildren. I love my life now that they're all grown and I'm always looking toward the future—the next holiday get-together, the next bit of travel, the next concert for my students. I'm too young, I guess, to be looking back very much. But after this experience, I can see how, when one is older and perhaps somewhat less active, all these good things you've stored up in your life can be like treasures you take out and shine up for the kids. It was a wonderful experience and has made me much more careful about saving old things from scrapbooks and family albums and such. They're a lot more important and interesting to the family than I ever understood before."

It was clear from Lizbet's description that a possible later role as the link between the past and future for her family was a delightful and warming idea, and several mothers in the group listened intently and vowed they, too, would be ready for occasions when the children and grandchildren showed an interest in the past.

However future reality matches up with the hopes, wistful aspirations, dreams, and expectations of these mid-life women, one central fact was thrown into sharp relief by the thoughts and feelings they shared on the subject of time's passage: The quality of their relationship with their grown children and grandchildren will always be a matter of deep concern and attention, no matter what great age they may attain.

Although there are few things in life sadder than an aged mother weeping over a child's disappointing life or coming to harvest time to find there is no ripeness between them, still women cling to the hope of very great happiness and affectional support in the later years of their lives if they could only be strong and wise enough to keep working away at love and understanding—and if their children would meet them halfway in the effort.

That the generations continue to be immensely vital to each other's lives, no matter how old the mother or advanced into middle age the child, is being reaffirmed and reflected in some new research now underway at Pace University in Westchester, New York.[5]

At Pace's Lienhard School of Nursing, two faculty members, both R.N.s with doctorates in education, are working on a tool for measuring stress in older people, ranging in age from sixty-five to eighty and up. The two professors, Dr. Shirlee Ann Stokes and Dr. Susan E. Gordon, were attempting to track down the stress factors that might lead to illness in those age groups.

But on their way to that goal, they discovered concrete evidence of what the middle-aged mothers in our sample have been discussing here: For the entire lives of women, their children remain crucial to their well-being, and age does not much diminish concern and connection.[6]

Dr. Stokes and Dr. Gordon worked with a group of twenty-five older persons (mostly women, though a few men were included) who helped to identify more than a hundred stress factors, some major, some minor, that cause discomfort to older people. A second group of forty-three older persons ranked these stressors from most to least stressful.

Their findings were surprising. The lead stress factors were not what are commonly imagined—money and health—but rather this discovery: Of the twelve leading causes of stress in older folks, no less than six dealt with relations with their children and grandchildren.

The research team was itself surprised that family relations so strongly led all the other possible stresses and that the more conventional issues of housing, safety, and social activities were well behind all the worries and concerns that women described involving their offspring. Even the anticipated or unanticipated loss of a spouse ranked lower down on the scale than the stress factors involving grown children and grandchildren, the findings revealed.

What most older folks in the study said they thought were the most stressful possible events they could endure would be the death of one of their own children, the death of another close relative (but not spouse), and the death of a grandchild.

These three losses were grouped together at the very top of the stress scale, separated only by one or two points and virtually combining to produce a moving reflection of how people over 65 feel themselves most strongly tied to life: through their children, grandchildren, and other "close relatives," presumably someone standing in a sibling or aunt, uncle, or cousin relationship.

Dr. Gordon, in commenting on this finding, advanced three possible causes for these family-related stresses leading all others: The loss of her children or grandchildren cuts the older woman's tie to the future, her hope of either biological or spiritual immortality and of continuity. She would be bereft of the common parent or grandparent comfort that even after one's death, something of one's self goes on.

In addition, Dr. Gordon proposed that the loss of the younger generation outrages nature, and turns one's orientation to the life cycle topsy-turvy, for the usual hope is that the younger generation will outlive the older. The death of an adult child or grandchildren, therefore, is in the class of catastrophes that shakes the older person's sense of how life is supposed to unfold, of its naturalness and "rightness," as well as eliminating expected sources of comfort and help in old age, leaving a poignant vulnerability.

Although the Stokes-Gordon research, which is still underway, reveals the over-65 woman's concern with reaching into eternity through her family, there were also many important stresses caused not by death but by the way adult children's lives were going.

After the fear of loss, the subsequent stress factors listed by the older people revealed where our sample group of mothers are likely to be finding themselves in another ten or fifteen years: still worrying over unmarried offspring, still concerned— though not judgmental—about the economic hardships of their children. "How will they manage?" was a constant refrain the researchers heard when the children's job or money woes were contemplated with much anxiety by parents, and they were still anxious over deviations from the life course.

Given the fears about getting older that our sample mothers confided, it was also interesting to learn that the women in the Pace group—who already were in the "young old" and "middle old" stages—were finding life satisfying and enjoyable if health and family life were functional. There were few women in their eighties and none in their nineties in the Pace group.

From this and other geriatric studies, however, I'm coming to believe that while no one can forecast any one person's specific later life, Americans don't even seem to know what lies ahead for them in a general way. They know they may live longer than their parents did and, because of medical and public health advances, probably arrive at old age in better shape, but they

oscillate between numb fear and blank ignorance of the possibilities and realistic challenges of later life stages.

Viewed from where the mothers in this book are right now,
I believe we actually need to embark on formal learning, to "go
to school" in some sense, to learn more accurate, updated facts
about modern aging and more constructive ideas about the way
later life-styles might evolve. ("Old age is not a disease, it's
another stage of life," said one commentator.)

It seems to me that the greatest task confronting most women
as they try to imagine moving through time together with their
adult children is to embrace the possible in those relationships,
rather than yearn for immortality or for some unreal attempt at
perpetuating the past days of their young motherhood.

A recent book about older women suggests that the task of the
second half of life is to find and develop those capacities that
have not yet been realized.[7] If women can set about doing that
at any age, I believe it will have a strengthening and rejuvenating
effect on their relationships with their adult children.

Some new investigations into the mother-child bond now underway in the United States and Britain have shown that in the
very first chapter of the mother-child story—birth and infancy—
mothers come to love and care for their babies *gradually* and as
the result of learning and interacting together over weeks and
months.[8]

A folk adage puts it: "A few hours in the hospital don't make
you a mother; loving and caring and raising a child is what makes
you a mother." The gradual development of maternal attachment when babies and mothers grow together is a sweet and
sturdy model, I believe, for similar possibilities in the later
stages of mothering.

As women change and grow, it's possible that their children
keep pace and move into new stages, too—stages that can bring
fresh understanding of mothers as women and human beings.

"Freedom," said novelist Doris Lessing, "is knowing what
your responsibilities are."

Such a freedom beckons over the next horizon of years for
both women and their grown children.

Epilogue

A Note to My Comrades

For several years now, I have been privileged to listen to and talk with hundreds of women about their lives as mothers.

For this book, the focus of our talks was their relationship with their adult children. But as one might expect, we also drifted into talk about the past; indeed, we talked often about their whole lives as women, wives, mothers, workers, and citizens. Much of that discussion does not appear in this book because it does not bear directly on the central theme, although these other roles influence mothering styles and techniques indirectly, as does virtually every life experience.

What I saw and learned affected me on four levels of my own life. As a reporter, I learned information about the actual daily ways that women and their grown children get on together—information I had not known before.

As a mother, I found that my own relationship with my adult children was enriched and illuminated; talks with my comrades on our maternal long marches through our children's lives were like a hundred mirrors in which I saw many facets of my own mothering. Some of these reflections were comforting, some inexpressibly beautiful and dear, others unattractive, and a few reflections made me feel downright miserable.

As a woman, I learned all over again the depth of women's fight to be all that they can be, while trying to do their best for their families and for the web of friendships and familyships in which they feel so embedded.

As a human being who is also a citizen, a worker, a social and political person with a particular class, religion and socioeconomic background, I learned at first hand where the points of breakdown are between the larger society and individual families these women represented.

I saw brief but close-up glimpses of how the world outside the four walls of home continues to put the most Herculean burden on the shoulders of women. Men struggle with racism, of course, but they do not struggle with racism and sexism together—the lot of many women. In addition, women deal in ways that men do not with the gritty, spirit-destroying details of every social problem known in our society.

These include the virulent epidemic of teenage pregnancies (one of the women in my sample was a grandmother at 32); the shocking poverty of minority, women-headed households; the loneliness and isolation of young women who fight the career-family conflict with no national day-care policy and little help at all from the society that has such a big stake in their futures. And above all, women deal in a special daily way with the fact that even stable households with two parental incomes and normal, healthy children must bring up their youngsters under the nuclear shadow.

One could not talk with women on these four levels—as a journalist, a mother, a woman, and a citizen-human being—without coming away from our conversations, our group discussions, and our voluminous exchanges of correspondence full of thoughts, feelings, and impressions that might prove useful for other women if I found a way to share them.

Accordingly, I've put down a few notes for my colleagues in the mother enterprise.

Many mothers and some fathers, too, hearing that I have spoken with so many women, have asked what kind of direction or guidance I might offer on the basis of what I've learned. I hope I have clearly disqualified myself as any kind of credentialed expert in any of the professional helping services, but I can simply tell what I feel as a reporter/mother who has talked to many other mothers. On the basis of this experience, my advice would be:

• *Be more open and less hesitant with your adult children.*   Tact is always in order, but don't hang back, don't claim to feel okay when you don't, and get things out on the table more, in a less fearful way. I have overwhelming evidence that a fake "cool," pretending you're disinterested and distant, just doesn't work. The kids have had your number forever and know beyond any hiding how vital the bond is to both of you. Don't be around their necks, but never hesitate to hug, and to say—affectionately —what's on your mind.

• *Do something about the guilt burden.*   If you think your relation- ship is in a dreadful state, a really nonfunctioning one, and you feel guilty about that, then some outside help seems indicated. If things are really going along okay and you still feel guilty in general, you have to do some work on yourself. If the guilt is irrational and undeserved, you have to work at getting around it, over it, under it, or away from it. It also helps to make a list of all the other influences in your child's life that may have had something to do with what he or she is like, too, including that second-grade playmate who gave your child nightmares for a year. Some women have ameliorated the ever-present guilt by familiarizing themselves with some new research that shows how adaptable the human infant is and how good the chances that whatever Mom thinks she did for two days that was bad, it probably really didn't doom the relationship or the child's psy- che forever.

• *Claim more for yourself.*   On the whole, you did the best you could for your children, and ought to have more recognition for that, even when they are trotting off to the divorce court or changing jobs three times in two months. You also deserve more open pleasure, satisfaction, and reward from their doings, so request some reports now and again. Since you will undoubtedly get 99 percent of the blame when things go wrong, why not a few bouquets when the children stay out of jail or the madhouse or the drug detoxification center, and actually manage to operate like sensible humans in a crazy world?

• *Check into the underground mother network.* It will do you worlds of good to find that nobody produced a child all that much more perfect than yours, that mothers of the so-called successful children are quaking in their boots about problems you never dreamed of, and that when you share the joys and successes with other mothers, it's doubly sweet and the sorrows are halved. You'll also find it a delight to talk with other mothers for hours *without* mentioning the children, and that might be a good exercise for everyone.

• *Connect up with the world in some way.* You and your family do not exist in a vacuum. Social trends, entertainment, style, politics, economics, neighborhood development—all have an impact on that center that is so important to you and it's fun and helpful if you're part of making that impact a good one. It would be wonderful, for example, if older women spearheaded a movement that would so much benefit their children—the movement to get expectant mothers a four-month paid maternity leave whatever part of the work world they are in; to make it, in other words, national labor policy. If young adult pregnant daughters and their middle-aged mothers together stormed Congress, the private sector, and the professions on this issue, it could make so much difference to the next generation of grandchildren.

In addition to these suggested guidelines, many men and women asked me for an overall view or set of impressions that I took away with me from my many contacts with mothers of adult children. Here then, are a few quick sketches:

The first and one of the strongest impressions I gained was that the amount of giving, doing, loving, and caring that women perform routinely in the ordinary course of family life is simply enormous. It cannot help but stagger the minds, eyes, and hearts of anyone who sees it, especially in the aggregate.

But one of the most amazing things about this is that *no one notices!* Here is a looming Mt. Everest of human behavior so different, so radically different, from the human interaction we see all around us outside the home, and it is hardly ever commented upon, except sentimentally.

Everyone takes completely for granted what the average woman does in a day to care for her family; its dimensions are not weighed and balanced in human affairs from one generation to the next. If anything, it is seen as a totally dependable known quantity that is a given, and never varies. (In point of fact, there have been a number of periods in human history when, for a variety of reasons, women were much less involved with their children than are modern mothers.)

Historical figures like kings, queens, and generals may vary from one period to the next in integrity, corruptibility, wisdom, or aggressiveness; artists vary from one generation to the next in creativity and productivity—not every century brings a Renaissance.

But what women do in our own times as they go quietly and almost invisibly about the task of helping their partners through life and raising their children seemed to me, if this is multiplied by millions, to be a model of human relations unique in our species.

As I observed this reality in a hundred different humdrum events where women described their activities as "ordinary," it was hard to imagine any other setting in which so much altruism is processed into human affairs, hour after hour, for days, weeks, months, years, decades.

Of course many mothers are negligent or overprotective, smothering or indifferent; many are blankly inattentive and insensitive and some tragic few are cruel and abusive to their children. *Of course* many women fail utterly to create a warm and effective family life. *Of course* there are thousands, maybe millions, of women who should never have been mothers of all, so poor are they at the job, for whatever reasons. I met several examples of these inadequate or destructive mothers in my research; usually they were the women who withdrew from participation in the investigation as soon as they learned what it was about. For them, relations with their children were either too painful, too irrelevant to and distant from their lives, or too confusing to be open for discussion.

But for the ordinary woman who has successfuly come to mid-life still in reasonable touch with her kids, it's been a long and caring road. As she bends over homework with her third-grader, drives her junior high student to soccer practice, goes back to work to help her college student pay tuition, she performs feats of patience, love, and support over twenty years of active mothering, and possibly another half-century of second-stage mothering, that are mind-boggling in their constancy and effectiveness.

Quite naturally, mothers get tired, not to mention hostile, resentful, burned out, and overwhelmed, many times along that path. But over decades, their performance is incredible—as well as maligned, misrepresented, underrated, and ignored.

The women I talked to describe themselves as unremarkable and average, yet they are people who have lived through illness, death, accident, crime, suicide, breakdown, rape, abortion, drug addiction, depression, and divorce (only murder was missing from my sample) with their grown children and yet remain in the closest touch with the children who survived these disasters and near disasters.

They have faced the blackest midnights family life can produce—often with the fathers of their children, but also very often alone or with companions who were not their children's fathers—and very few have ever cut and run.

Moreover, this particular group of middle-aged women has lived through assaults mounted by the watershed social change of the 1960s on their own values, beliefs, and life-styles, and have remained true to their children, if not to their children's values. They bent in a wild social wind; they did not break. In fact, they are closer than ever to the young adults who, in the 1960s, visited contempt and derision on their patterns of religion, morality, and ethics, and defied every significant aspect of these women's culture.

Today, these mothers have grown, too. They now largely accept unmarried live-togethers in spite of all the silent tears they wept. They pay the bills for abortions that outrage their traditional mores, and they have cradled stoned-out drug-using sons and daughters in their arms and rocked them like babies. Their resiliency in coming back to their heart's center—their children—is something governments and kingdoms well could ponder, and poets and artists well could sing.

The French philosopher Montaigne said that "to storm a

breach, conduct an embassy, govern a people, these are brilliant actions; to scold, laugh, and deal gently and justly with one's family and one's self, that is something rarer, more difficult, and less noticed in the world."

I came away from the life stories of many American mothers feeling that their work in raising families was scandalously less noticed in the world.

Another strong feeling I got from observing many mothers from varied backgrounds was how oppressed by guilt they still are. If they are not actively guilty at a given moment, it is astonishing how quickly that maternal guilt can be reactivated by events in their children's lives. We've already examined, in Chapter 2, some of the methods by which this guilt was so firmly planted, but it was eye-opening to see how persistent and pervasive it is.

I was surprised at how little middle-aged women seemed to know about the other forces in their children's lives that influence their development, how unready they were to shed any guilt in the light of new knowledge about the adaptability and resiliency of children, and how quick to assume an absolutely central role in every bad (never good) turn in their children's personalities and life events.

To me, women didn't seem to be making many efforts to get rid of this load of often irrational guilt, either. It was as though decades of "mother blaming" had fixed a permanent hump on their souls that could never be smoothed out.

Time after time, in face-to-face interviews and in group discussions, I longed to shout, "But that wasn't your fault!" as women recounted incident after incident in which fathers, teachers, coaches, peers, all clearly contributed to the children's problems and then mothers would resolutely go on and assume total blame for the difficulty! They seemed to be saying that if teachers were traumatic, coaches sadistic, and fathers negligent, it was their fault for not making all those people serve the child better or their fault for not creating an atmosphere at home that would arm the child against absolutely everything he or she would encounter in the world. I came to feel that if all caring adults want kids to feel secure and self-confident, only mothers pursue the creation of this armor against reality to the point of near-lunacy.

Knowing that I was talking with many mothers, women would repeatedly ask, in tones varying from wistful to pathetic to defeated, "Tell me, does everyone else feel as guilty as I do?" If I accomplished nothing else in my investigation, I felt satisfied that I could—accurately and truthfully—report that it seemed to go with the territory for just about everyone.

This pervasive guilt may somehow be linked to another problem I found—the terror of aging that is described in Chapter 10.

It might be helpful for mental health professionals, gerontologists, and philosophers to look into whether this desperation about facing old age has anything to do with the feeling mothers might have that perhaps their lives with their children were not yet in acceptable or comfortable shape. Maybe they can never be ready to leave the scene, no matter how old, if they feel there is unresolved, unfinished business with these critically important younger people.

I have taken no steps to test this hypothesis, but it presented itself to me when I began to recall the ways in which mothers described the underlying concern they *always* feel about their children. They used phrases like "I can't put my head down on the pillow" or "I just don't rest easily if something is wrong with one of them," which could be metaphors for not being able to round out their lives comfortably if there are still important things to be worked out in the relationship.

Despite this huge mountain of guilt, women get deep pleasure, reward, and joy from their mothering.

I saw so many marvelous expressions of this, as varied as the personalities of the women. Some are bouncily joyful at the fun and stimulation they get from their young people, some are quietly proud (and others not so quietly!) of their children's achievements, others show a sweet, beaming serenity when they see the well-kept house, the healthy grandchild, the interesting work that their children and in-law children show them.

Here, too, I felt myself enormously privileged to watch that special smile, the special warmth in the eyes, when I was shown pictures of wonderful young adults and beautiful grandchildren. This was the very stuff of life and I was lucky, indeed, to be allowed to share so much of it.

This feeling of a hugely successful harvest was not necessarily a minority experience; it existed in many women, right along with the worry and the guilt.

In fact, despite all the "down" feelings, more than two-thirds of the 208 women in the core group said that their satisfaction with their children was immense and that *their adult kids had either equaled or surpassed* their expectations for them.

Asked whether, if they had it to do over again, they would do it all the same way, the answers can be summed up this way: More than 90 percent said they would definitely have children, about 83 percent were satisfied with the number of children they had, but a sizable minority said they would change some (but not all) of their child-rearing practices.

I found this wish to go back and do things differently as far as the day-to-day handling of childhood growth was concerned especially interesting because my own viewpoint, after listening to women describe their styles and techniques of mothering, was that a refreshing range of differences appeared and yet so many were successful. Mothers who were strict and stern had good results; women who were more permissive and indulgent had good results; and women who just sailed on, unable to give a label to their methods, also had good results. The wide variety of mothering styles that yet resulted in reasonably well-functioning households must give some comfort, I felt, to those simultaneously guilt-ridden women who were sure there was only one "right way" to raise kids. The experiences of the women I contacted suggest that lots of different mothering styles could be effective, given a number of other important elements, such as health and energy, adequate income and housing, and support of various kinds from husbands and kin.

Among the positives, I found one that could almost be termed sublime. That was the effect on themselves of being mothers that women reported. They felt that there was no other experience that produced as much personal growth, enrichment, maturation, a touching of the deepest wellsprings of life.

They said those prizes compensated them well for the endless round of caring and doing that is motherhood.

One of the less sublime impressions I gained from the many women I talked to is that, as a group, they are not as much clued in to the world outside the home as their skills and competencies might suggest they could be.

I got the distinct impression that many mid-life women have left the competitiveness, the speed of movement, the vast and complicated connections of the larger world to their husbands and adult children and have been timid or uncertain about jumping into the fray.

Even when women are working outside the home, they aim low. Many are in the "pink collar ghetto" of low-paying, low-status jobs, but even though these provide many satisfactions—an independent paycheck, a marked contribution to family income, adult socializing beyond the domestic limits—they often do not use the hugely impressive skills which so many women possess, skills of organization and management, of coordination and administration, of good human relations.

It is a commonplace in the United States when public policy and affirmative action programs in the workplace are discussed to say that the 51 percent of the population who are women are underutilized.

But for the largely middle-class women I talked with, their perspective, sadly, is that they feel themselves not ready or able to be better utilized. Many of them talked of "office politics" or "silly kinds of work" as the reasons they did not seek challenges in the work place, but underneath that, I felt a fear of the competitiveness and pressures of the work world for which they had not been trained and that, probably rightly, they did not see how they could accommodate to the draining tasks they already have at home.

Since mid-life women have been programmed largely to put family first and the big outside world second, and since they have a long history of being shut out of all attempts to get into that big world of work, it's going to take uncommon skill and nerve for them to break such old patterns; I had to accept that many very likely will not. The fact that there is blatantly overt discrimination in the outside institutions of business, government, the professions, and the arts doesn't help women battling inner resistances, either.

But I could not be helpful or honest if I did not admit to considerable distress at seeing so many fantastically competent women, who can do such an incredible array of jobs, usually concurrently, remain so uncertain about the realities of how things work, so tentative about putting even a toe in the water.

It seems to me that the larger society desperately needs the coping abilities, the common sense, the incredible stamina, and the sheer day-to-day dependability and maturity of women who have spent a lifetime coordinating details that baffle most men, soothing human beings in various states of rage, frustration, and fear, and consistently keeping a menagerie of humans and animals fed, clothed, sheltered, and functioning reasonably well.

Having been privileged to see so many displays of enviable intelligence, skill, and strength, I will continue to hope that middle-aged women will, before it's too late, begin using their formidable capacities to benefit themselves and others beyond their own families.

. . . And a Note to Our Sons and Daughters

There's no use kidding ourselves—the family as a significant social unit has some massive problems.

It isn't going to die, but it sure is going to change, and you will be part of that change.

One of the reasons I think the death of the family, as announced for the past twenty years and in other times of social crisis, is premature is that, so far, there is no really viable alternative or substitute, though some interesting experiments are always being tried and should be looked into. Communal housing for older folks, for instance, seems to be working well, and certainly co-op nurseries have been with us for a long time, but these are supports and extensions, not substitutes, for the family.

Professor Jerome Kagan of Harvard has made an especially thoughtful statement that pertains specifically to the high technology era you will increasingly inhabit and to the reasons why families will still be a part of your brave new world.

"Without other groups to rely on, modern youth has greater freedom and minimal constraints on autonomy of action," wrote Kagan, "but the price is loneliness and the unavailability of any person or group in which to invest strong emotion. It is for this reason that marriage and the creation of a new family are likely to experience a recrudescence in the West."

The world-famous psychologist continues, "We take it as an axiom that the self resists depersonalization. As modern environments make a sense of potency and individual effectiveness more difficult to attain, freedom from all affective involvements becomes more and more intolerable. Involvement with a family is the only viable mechanism available to satisfy that hunger."

The dilemma, of course, is sharper for our daughters, but if things go as they are presently tending, our sons, too, will share in ever greater expectations for ever more demanding roles. Both will be wage-earners, parents, partners. We cannot offer an easy road.

But we can tell you that parenthood's demands, while heavy, offer rewards that ought not to be too easily turned aside. Our greatest hope is that if you decide against having children, you will do so in an informed way, truly understanding what you have chosen to exclude from your life.

We cannot rid ourselves of history, dear daughters. There is no question that much of family life was purchased at the cost of women's other possible lives—and you may choose to refuse to make such a sacrifice and pay such a cost. If you do, knowing that thousands of women have struggled for your opportunities, we could never make harsh judgments and we promise to try to handle our grandparent anxieties in a noninterfering way.

For our sons, struggling to deal with the new woman (who, in another context, is merely our daughter, your sister) and to be the new father, while remaining the old breadwinner, we understand thoroughly your anxiety when faced with these burdens. And should you, too, decide that the cost of family life is too great for the other things you want to do with your life, we'll try to handle that gracefully, too.

We can't persuade, we can't coax, we shouldn't really have much input at all into any decisions about having children that our sons and daughters may make. In fact, in a recent novel, the son of a close-knit family was moved to tell some of the things that are bad about growing up in a loving family: The intensity is exhausting, sometimes the timing of expressions of love is unwelcome, the magic circle excludes others (just ask a few in-law spouses), and the loving family cannot defeat death.[1]

All true, dear ones. But should you decide to become parents, it will also be one very great way of knowing life.

WOMAN TO CHILD

You who were darkness warmed my flesh
where out of darkness rose the seed.
Then all a world I made in me;
all the world you hear and see
hung upon my dreaming blood.

There moved the multitudinous stars,
and coloured birds and fishes moved.
There swam the sliding continents.
All time lay rolled in me, and sense,
and love that knew not its beloved.

O node and focus of the world;
I hold you deep within that well
you shall escape and not escape—
that mirrors still your sleeping shape;
that nurtures still your crescent cell.

I wither and you break from me;
yet though you dance in living light
I am the earth, I am the root,
I am the stem that fed the fruit,
the link that joins you to the night.

                        —*JUDITH WRIGHT*

Appendix

QUESTIONNAIRE

Vital Statistics

Name
Address
Phone
Age

List your children's first names, ages, and sexes.

Are you _____ divorced or _____ widowed? If so, how old were your children when this happened? _____

What was each child's reason for leaving home?

	College	A Job	Marriage	Other	At What Age?
Child #1	___	___	___	___	___
Child #2	___	___	___	___	___
Child #3	___	___	___	___	___

Do you live with

    ____ your children's father
    ____ a husband who is not their father
    ____ a male companion who is not their father
    ____ none of the above

Where does each child live now?

    Child #1 _____
    Child #2 _____
    Child #3 _____

When the Children Were Growing Up

How much did you enjoy having young children?

    ____ very much
    ____ a fair amount
    ____ not very much
    ____ not at all

Which years of their childhood were the most work for you?

    ____ Infant-4
    ____ 4-8
    ____ 8-12
    ____ 12-16
    ____ 16-20

Which years were the most fun for you as a mother?

    ____ Infant-4
    ____ 4-8
    ____ 8-12
    ____ 12-16
    ____ 16-20

Which years were the most rewarding in terms of emotional payoff and satisfaction to you as a mother?

    ____ Infant-4
    ____ 4-8

_____ 8-12
_____ 12-16
_____ 16-20

When your children were small, was your family financial situation

_____ problematic
_____ satisfactory
_____ comfortable
_____ very comfortable

How important a part did religion play in your family life?

_____ very important
_____ fairly important
_____ not important

When your children were small, how much did you look forward to the time when they would be grown up?

_____ very much
_____ a fair amount
_____ very little
_____ not at all
_____ didn't give it any thought

How would you characterize your affection for your young children?

_____ Very physical (lots of hugging, kissing, and touching)
_____ Moderately physical (occasional hugging, etc.)
_____ Fairly reserved (not much physical exchange)
_____ Very reserved (almost no physical exchange)

Was your approach to child-rearing markedly different from the way your mother raised you? If so, briefly tell how.

Which of the following caused the most intense sibling rivalry among your youngsters? (You may check more than one.)

_____ battles over space or privacy
_____ competition for material possessions
_____ competition for parental attention and approval

_____ competition in school
_____ competition in sports or physical skills
_____ jealousy of one sibling's talent

Do you remember sibling rivalry in general as being

_____ intense and constant
_____ intense but erratic
_____ somewhat intense but rare
_____ rare and never very intense
_____ never a problem

At what ages in your children's lives were they most hostile to you as a parent?

	Infant-4-years	_4-8_	_8-12_	_12-16_	_16-20_
Child #1	_____	_____	_____	_____	_____
Child #2	_____	_____	_____	_____	_____
Child #3	_____	_____	_____	_____	_____

Briefly, what things did you enjoy most about mothering?

Briefly, what things did you dislike most about mothering?

What do you remember as being the most work for you? (You may check more than one.)

_____ cleaning up after the children
_____ childhood healthcare and illnesses
_____ giving the children enough personal attention
_____ getting the children to obey
_____ settling disputes among the children
_____ planning and executing activities for the children

Did you have special problems with any of your children that made raising them specially difficult?

_____ yes
_____ no

Were your children's adolescent years basically happy or unhappy for them?

	Happy	*Unhappy*
Child #1	——	——
Child #2	——	——
Child #3	——	——

Were their adolescent years basically happy or unhappy years for you?

—— happy
—— unhappy

Do you remember being aware that your children were "pulling away" or "seeking independence" during adolescence?

—— yes
—— no

If so, what were your feelings about it? Check those you felt most strongly.

—— happiness
—— worry
—— pride
—— resentment
—— confusion
—— sadness
—— anger

At what ages were your children the happiest?

	Infant to 4	*4-8*	*8-12*	*12-16*	*16-20*	*Older*
Child #1	——	——	——	——	——	——
Child #2	——	——	——	——	——	——
Child #3	——	——	——	——	——	——

At what age did your children most actively seek your approval?

Child #1	——	——	——	——	——	——
Child #2	——	——	——	——	——	——
Child #3	——	——	——	——	——	——

How much did your children's father help in caring for and tending to them while they were growing up (not counting finances)?

_____ more than 50 percent
_____ about 50 percent
_____ about 40 percent
_____ about 30 percent
_____ about 20 percent
_____ about 10 percent
_____ less than 10 percent

Briefly, what were your children's father's important contributions to them while they were growing up?

Mothering the Adult Child

On the average, how often do you talk with each of your adult children?

	Once a day	Once a week	Once a month	Less
Child #1	_____	_____	_____	_____
Child #2	_____	_____	_____	_____
Child #3	_____	_____	_____	_____

Who does most of the calling or visiting, you or the children?

_____ I do almost all
_____ I do more, but not all
_____ I do half, the children do half
_____ the children do more
_____ the children do almost all

Regardless of who does most of the calling or visiting in your family, who do you think is _more_ responsible for keeping in touch?

_____ mother
_____ children
_____ neither

Which of the following have caused serious disagreement between you and any of your children? (Check all that apply.)

____ child's career
____ child's marriage or divorce
____ child's children and/or his parenting techniques
____ children's relationships with each other
____ child's neglect of you and/or their father
____ child's life-style
____ child's moral values
____ child's religion
____ child's failure to achieve
____ child's lack of motivation
____ child's spending habits or attitude toward money
____ your career
____ your marriage or divorce
____ your life-style
____ your spending habits or attitude toward money
____ other (explain briefly)

Which of the following things do your children talk to you about

a) in great detail
b) casually, but not thoroughly
c) only superficially
d) only when a serious problem arises
e) rarely or not at all

their health	a	b	c	d	e
their travel and vacations	a	b	c	d	e
their job	a	b	c	d	e
their social life	a	b	c	d	e
marital disputes or problems	a	b	c	d	e
their sex life	a	b	c	d	e
their children	a	b	c	d	e
their finances	a	b	c	d	e
childhood memories	a	b	c	d	e
their plans for the future	a	b	c	d	e
their fears and anxiety	a	b	c	d	e

Which of the following do your children ask you about

a) often
b) sometimes

c) rarely
d) never

your health	a	b	c	d
your work, hobbies, or projects	a	b	c	d
other family members	a	b	c	d
what you think of something				
they've done	a	b	c	d
how much you love them	a	b	c	d
your opinions about current				
events	a	b	c	d
your advice about a choice they				
must make	a	b	c	d
your advice about finances	a	b	c	d
your advice about child-rearing	a	b	c	d
other (explain briefly)				

Have you and your adult children talked about the things that caused parent-child hostility and arguments during their adolescence or other stages of their childhood?

_____ yes
_____ no

If so, would you say these talks

_____ helped you understand things better
_____ sparked old angers and lead to new arguments
_____ made no real difference

What subjects, if there are any, do you avoid discussing with your adult children because they inevitably lead to arguments or bad feelings?

What are three or four specific things you really enjoy talking about with your grown children?

Which of the following do you talk to them about

- a) in great detail
- b) casually, but not thoroughly
- c) only superficially
- d) only when a serious problem arises
- e) rarely or not at all

your health	a	b	c	d	e
your travel or vacation plans	a	b	c	d	e
your work	a	b	c	d	e
your social activities	a	b	c	d	e
marital disputes or problems	a	b	c	d	e
your sex life	a	b	c	d	e
your finances (income, investments, etc.)	a	b	c	d	e
your future plans	a	b	c	d	e

Have your children told you anything about themselves since they've grown up that you didn't know about them when they were younger? If so, what?

Do you see your children

_____ just about as often as you want
_____ less often than you would like
_____ more often than you would like
_____ far less often than you would like
_____ much more often than you would like

If you knew that your children were happy and well, could you ever *enjoy* not seeing them for extended periods of time—say, several months to a year?

_____ yes
_____ no

Ideally, would you like to see your children

_____ daily
_____ weekly

_____ monthly
_____ every three or four months
_____ once or twice a year
_____ less than once a year

Which holidays, if any, do you usually celebrate together as a family?

Are these holiday gatherings usually at

_____ your house
_____ one of your children's homes
_____ alternately at your house and theirs
_____ somewhere else

Who generally does the planning, organizing, and preparation?

_____ you
_____ your children
_____ both

Can you imagine a circumstance that would cause you to "disown" one of your children—for example, if he or she married outside your religion, cheated you out of a large sum of money, committed a murder, etc.?

_____ yes
_____ no

Which of the following do you think are a parent's *responsibility?*

_____ supervising a grown child's early career decision
_____ paying college tuition, undergraduate
_____ paying graduate school tuition
_____ financing a child's wedding
_____ helping a child purchase a house or business
_____ loaning or giving a child money to make large purchases (baby furniture, appliances, etc.)
_____ baby-sitting regularly for grandchildren
_____ hosting family gatherings at holidays

Now, circle those items in the above list that you have done, whether you believe they are a parent's responsibility or not.

Which of the following do you believe is an adult child's *responsibility?*

_____ visiting or calling you regularly

_____ making sure you get to see the grandchildren regularly

_____ supplementing your income as their own increases and yours becomes fixed

_____ keeping you up to date on the major changes in their career, finances, families

_____ helping more and more with your major purchases, vacations, etc., as you retire and have less income

When your family has a gathering, which of the following emotions would you say operate most strongly? (Check as many as apply.)

_____ excitement

_____ warmth

_____ awkwardness

_____ competition

_____ love

_____ hostility

_____ tension

Briefly, what do you enjoy most about family gatherings?

Briefly, what do you dislike most about them?

Do you enjoy seeing your children individually more than you enjoy seeing them all together?

_____ yes

_____ no

_____ no preference

Which of the following best characterizes your relationship with your son-in-law or daughter-in-law? (Check once for each in-law.)

_____ close and loving
_____ warm and friendly
_____ formal and friendly
_____ cool
_____ hostile

Does sibling rivalry still operate noticeably among your children or between any particular two?

_____ yes
_____ no

If so, is the competition over

_____ your attention
_____ career achievements
_____ social status
_____ financial status
_____ material possessions
_____ children's accomplishments
_____ other (briefly, tell what)
(check all that apply)

How often do you play the role of mediator between the children to keep the peace?

_____ often
_____ occasionally
_____ rarely
_____ never

How would you characterize your affection for your adult children?

_____ very physical (lots of hugging, kissing, and touching)
_____ moderately physical (occasional hugging, etc.)
_____ fairly reserved (not much physical exchange)
_____ very reserved (almost no physical exchange)

Was there a noticeable turning point when the child/parent tensions of adolescence began to dissolve?

    ____ yes
    ____ no

If so, how old was the child when this happened?

	18-20	20-23	23-25	25-30	30 or older
Child #1	____	____	____	____	____
Child #2	____	____	____	____	____
Child #3	____	____	____	____	____

Do you babysit regularly your grandchildren or provide any other service to help save your children money?

    ____ yes
    ____ no

Have you lent any of your children large sums of money?

    ____ yes
    ____ no

If you answered yes to either of the two above questions, do you believe that providing money-saving services or lending money gives you a right to speak up about how your children handle their finances?

    ____ yes
    ____ no

Do you do this?

    ____ yes
    ____ no

Do your children respect your wishes?

    ____ yes
    ____ no
    ____ usually
    ____ rarely

How much do your children know about your finances (income, investments, insurance policies, real estate holdings, etc.)?

    ____ virtually everything
    ____ a good amount
    ____ some
    ____ very little

When it comes to your finances, do they know

    ____ as much as you want them to know
    ____ less than you think they should know
    ____ more than you would like them to know

Do your children always know where you are and where you can be reached?

    ____ yes
    ____ no

Have any of your adult children ever moved back home for an extended period of time?

    ____ yes
    ____ no

If so, for how long?

If any of your children are divorced, how closely were you consulted during the separation and divorce proceedings?

    ____ very closely
    ____ fairly closely
    ____ very little
    ____ not at all

How do you feel toward your ex–son-in-law or daughter-in-law now? (Check once for each ex–in-law)

    ____ close and loving
    ____ warm and friendly
    ____ indifferent
    ____ hostile

How different is your relationship with your adult children from that of your mother's relationship with you?

_____ very different
_____ somewhat different
_____ only slightly different

Are there things your adult children expect from you that you never thought they would expect? Briefly, tell what.

Are there things your adult children do not want or expect from you that you thought they would? Briefly, tell what.

How different is your life now that your children have grown and moved out?

_____ radically different
_____ fairly different
_____ slightly different

Which of the following best describe how your life has changed since your children have grown up? (Check as many as apply.)

_____ more tranquil
_____ less complex
_____ more boring
_____ lonelier
_____ less inhibited
_____ less restricted

If you had it all to do over again, would you

_____ probably not have as many children
_____ probably not have any children
_____ radically change many of your child-rearing techniques
_____ change some child-rearing techniques
_____ do basically the same thing
(Check as many as apply.)

Have your grown children's achievements

_____ surpassed your expectations
_____ equaled your expectations
_____ fallen short of your expectations

A Look at the Future

Answer the following statements true or false

I would never go to my children for financial aid in my old age.	T	F
If I were old and ill, I would rather be in a nursing home than disrupt my children's lives by moving in with one of them.	T	F
If I am ever a widow, I expect to carry on alone and would not expect to move in with one of my children.	I	F
I have given my children a great deal, and I believe that entitles me to their care and financial aid when I am old.	T	F
I believe I could be an asset as a live-in grandmother if I moved in with one of my children's families.	T	F
My children would refuse to let me stay in a nursing home and would want me to move in with one of them.	T	F
Whether or not I am infirm, I would like the chance to live with one of my children and his or her family to play the grandma role.	T	F
If I am ever a widow, I would want to move in with one of my children rather than live alone or with a companion.	T	F
Ideally, I will spend my old age independent of my children.	T	F
Ideally, I will spend my old age living with my children and grandchildren.	T	F
If I have financial difficulty in my old age, I will expect and gladly accept the aid of my children.	T	F

If I accepted financial help from my children I would
always feel a little guilty.   T   F

I'm sure I could not be happy living with one of my
children even if I knew they wanted me and enjoyed
having me.   T   F

References

PREFACE

1. Rhona Rapoport, Robert N. Rapoport, and Ziona Strelitz, with Stephen Kew, *Fathers, Mothers and Society: Perspectives on Parenting* (New York: Basic Books, 1977), p. 347.
2. Kenneth A. Briggs, "Religious Feeling Seen Strong in U.S.," *New York Times,* 9 December 1984, p. A30.
3. J. Weakland, R. Fisch, P. Watzlawick, and A. M. Bodin, "Brief Therapy: Focused Problem Resolution," *Family Process,* 13 (1974): 141–168.

CHAPTER ONE

1. Lillian B. Rubin, *Women of a Certain Age: The Mid-Life Search for Self* (New York: Harper and Row, 1979), p. 15.
2. Elizabeth A. Carter and Monica McGoldrick, eds., *The Family Life Cycle: A Framework for Family Therapy* (New York: Gardner Press, 1980), pp. 171–195.
3. Donald Spence, M.D., and Thomas Lonner, "The Empty Nest: A Transition Within Motherhood," *Family Coordinator,* vol. 20, no. 4 (October 1971): 369–375.
4. John G. Howells, M.D., ed., *Modern Perspectives in the Psychiatry of Middle Age* (New York: Brunner/Mazel, 1981), pp. 329–332.

5. Irwin Deutscher, "The Quality of Post-Parental Life," *Journal of Marriage and the Family,* vol. 26, no. 1 (February 1964): 52–59.
6. Philip Wylie, *Generation of Vipers* (1943; reprint ed., Marietta, Ga.: Larlin Corp., 1979), p. 199.

CHAPTER TWO

1. Ann Dally, M.D., *Inventing Motherhood: The Consequences of an Ideal* (New York: Schocken Books, 1983), p. 13.
2. Ibid., pp. 87, 88.
3. Ibid., p. 89; and Michael Rutter, M.D., *The Qualities of Mothering: Maternal Deprivation Reassessed* (New York Jason Associates, 1974), p. 128.
4. K. Alison Clarke-Stewart, "Popular Primers for Parents," *American Psychologist,* vol. 33, no. 4 (April 1978): 359–369; and Michael J. Geboy, " 'Who Is Listening to the Experts?' ": The Use of Child Care Materials by Parents," *Family Relations,* vol. 30, no. 2 (April 1981): 205–210.
5. Daniel Goleman, review of *The Nature of the Child* by Jerome Kagan, Ph.D., *New York Times Book Review,* 18 November 1984, p. 15.
6. E. E. Werner and R. S. Smith, *Vulnerable But Invincible* (New York: McGraw-Hill, 1982), p. 159.
7. Daniel Goleman, "Traumatic Beginnings: Most Children Seem Able to Recover," *New York Times,* 13 March 1984, p. C1.
8. Ibid.
9. "Analyst Focuses on Life's Early Years: Margaret Mahler Speaks on Child Development," *New York Times,* 13 March 1984, p. C2.
10. Wladyslaw Sluckin (professor of psychology, University of Leicester, England), Martin Herbert (professor of clinical psychology, University of Leicester), and Alice Sluckin (social worker, Leicestershire Child and Family Guidance Service), *Maternal Bonding* (Oxford: Basil Blackwell, 1983), p. 97.
11. Ibid., p. 91.

CHAPTER THREE

1. Lillian E. Troll, "Family Life in Middle and Old Age: The Generation Gap," *Annals of the American Academy of Political and Social Science,* vol. 464 (November 1982): 44.
2. "When Was the Last Time You Called Your Mother?" *New York,* 7 May 1979: 47–54.
3. Troll, p. 46.

4. "Movie Notes," *New York Times,* 10 September 1982, p. C6.

5. René DuBos, Ph.D., "Avoiding Future Shock," *Christian Science Monitor,* 14 May 1974, p. F8.

CHAPTER FOUR

1. Edmund Bergler, M.D., *Money and Emotional Conflicts* (New York: International Universities Press, 1951), pp. 4–19.

2. U.S. Bureau of the Census, *Statistical Abstract of the United States,* Employment and Earnings, D-29-41, Table 656, p. 392; and U.S. Bureau of Labor Statistics, Women's Bureau, *Current Population Reports,* series P-50.

3. "Six Million Women Are Paid More Than Their Husbands, U.S. Says," *New York Times,* 16 January 1984, p. B10.

4. Georg Simmel, *The Philosophy of Money* (1900; reprint ed., London: Routledge and Kegan Paul, 1978), pp. 283–354.

CHAPTER FIVE

1. Jerome Kagan, Ph.D., *Daedalus* (special issue on "The Family"), vol. 106, no. 2 (Spring 1977): 53.

2. Werner and Smith, p. 78.

3. S. P. Bank and M. D. Kahn, *The Sibling Bond* (New York: Basic Books, 1982), p. 60.

4. Ibid., pp. 11, 12.

5. Annie Gottlieb, "The Sister Knot," *Mademoiselle,* November 1980: 249.

6. Bank and Kahn, p. 11.

7. Ibid., p. 201.

8. Virginia Adams, "The Sibling Bond: A Life-long Love/Hate Dialectic," *Psychology Today,* June 1981: 38.

9. Dava Sobel, "Siblings: Studies Find Rivalry, Dependency Revive in Adulthood," *New York Times,* 28 October 1980, pp. C1, C3.

CHAPTER SIX

1. Lorraine D. Siggins, M.D., "Psychoanalysis and Ritual," *Psychiatry: A Journal for the Study of Interpersonal Processes,* vol. 46, no. 1 (February 1983): 3.

2. "Ceremony" and "Ritual," in David E. Hunter and Phillip Whitten, eds., *Encyclopedia of Anthropology* (New York: Harper and Row, 1976), pp. 69, 336–337; and Jessie Bernard, *The Female World* (New York: Free Press, 1981), pp. 27–30.

3. Carol Gilligan, Ph.D., *In a Different Voice: Psychological Theory and Women's Development* (Cambridge, Mass.: Harvard University Press, 1982), pp. 16–17, 21.
4. Carter and McGoldrick, pp. 437–439.
5. Paul Wilkes, *Trying Out the Dream: A Year in the Life of an American Family* (Philadelphia: J. B. Lippincott, 1975), pp. 326–344.
6. Glenn Collins, "Trauma of Holidy Family Gatherings," *New York Times,* 22 December 1980, p. B6.
7. Philip M. Boffey, "The 'Holiday Blues' Are Overstated Ill, Health Experts Find," *New York Times,* 24 December 1983, p. C1.

CHAPTER SEVEN

1. Rapaport et al., pp. 78, 84, 89.
2. Sandra Scarr, quoted in Glenn Collins, "Day Care: Mother's Positive View," *New York Times,* 25 December 1984, p. B78.
3. Andy Merton, "Things Our Fathers Didn't Tell Us," *New Age Journal,* June 1984: 54.

CHAPTER EIGHT

1. Mary Kay Blakely, "Hers," *New York Times,* 2 April 1981, p. C2.
2. Lynn Simross, "When Parents and Children All Grow Up," *Los Angeles Times,* 22 September 1981, p. B7.
3. Judy Klemsrud, "Parents and Grown Children," *New York Times,* 1 November 1982, p. C15.
4. Oscar Handlin, *The Uprooted* (Boston: Atlantic Monthly Press, 1952).
5. Elinor Lenz, *Once My Child, Now My Friend* (New York: Warner Books, 1981), p. 3.
6. Stella Chess, M.D., and Jane Whitbread, *Daughters* (Garden City, N.Y.: Doubleday, 1978), p. 201.
7. Jeanne Hanson, "Vacation Trips Home Good for Parents and Children," press release, University of Minnesota News Service, 30 May 1980, pp. 1–3.
8. Sigrid Linscott, "Medical and Health Notes," *New York Times,* 29 August 1984, p. C4.

CHAPTER NINE

1. Olive Evans, "When Friends Drift Apart," *New York Times,* 16 April 1984, p. B8.
2. K. C. Cole, "The Travails of a Part-time Stepparent," *New York Times,* 14 May 1980, p. C3.

3. Marilyn Machlowitz, "Mothers' Ties to Daughters," *New York Times*, 7 June 1981, p. C52.
4. Klemsrud.

CHAPTER TEN
1. Daniel Goleman, "The Aging Mind Proves Capable of Life-long Growth," *New York Times*, 21 February 1984, p. C1.
2. Staff report, "Growing Old, Feeling Young," *Newsweek*, 1 November 1982, pp. 56–65.
3. Geoffrey K. Leigh, "Kinship Interaction Over the Family Life-span," *Journal of Marriage and the Family*, vol. 44, no. 1 (February 1982): 197–208.
4. Marjorie Kantor, "Inner City Elderly," *New York Daily News*, 4 March 1981, p. 51.
5. Dr. Shirlee Ann Stokes and Dr. Susan E. Gordon, "Development of a Tool to Measure Stress in the Older Individual," unpublished research paper prepared for the 21st Annual Stewart Conference on Nursing Research, 27 April 1984.
6. Ibid.
7. Audrey Borenstein, *Chimes of Change and Hours* (Rutherford, N.J.: Fairleigh Dickinson University Press, 1983), p. 137.
8. Sluckin, Herbert, and Sluckin, p. 92.

EPILOGUE
1. Kagan, *Daedalus*, p. 54.

Index

304

fathers, 150–169
absent at work, 33, 98, 157, 158, 162
aging of, and nurturing ability, 168
in children's growing-up years, 157–164
communicating with, 154–156
failure of, 159–160, 162, 165
as financial providers, 152, 153, 157, 158–159, 160, 161, 162, 163, 164, 166
and friendship with children, 168
image of, contemporary, 164
and launching, 151–152
and money matters, 70, 76, 153, 156
mothers as chief contact between children and, 151, 153, 154, 156, 159, 165, 167
new style, 164–166, 167
rapport with children, newly developing, 154–156
and returnees, 222
stereotype of, 162
strength of, children's fear of waning, 154
telephone conversations of, 46
favoritism, and siblings, 81, 88, 98–102, 103, 105
feelings, owed to elderly, 248
feminization of poverty, 252
filial dependability, 236
financial help. *See also* loans; money
for business failures, 79–80
for careers, 75–76
and control, 6
and economy, 70–71, 83
for education, 5–6
for elderly mothers, 250–251
and fairness among siblings, 80–81, 88
for home ownership, 6–7

mothers' surprise at children's need for, 91–92
as owed to children, 87–89
parents' refusal of, 77
and strengthening family ties, 73–74
and working mothers, 81–83, 84
and "you owe me" syndrome, 87, 88
financial situation
children's, 84, 86–87
parents', 84, 85–86
in parents' youth, 89–90
Flaubert, Gustave, 69
Fleisig, Robin, 231
freeze-frame syndrome, 232–234
Freud, Anna, 27
Freud, Sigmund, 24–25, 27, 30, 32
Friedman, Edwin H., 128
friends
conventional, 172, 173, 182, 184, 187–188, 196–197, 216, 223–224
mothers' mothers not seen as, 171–172, 177
friendship with children, 170–173, 182, 183–188, 195–197, 199, 200, 210, 212, 213, 219
and changing sense of self, 224
and crises, 199, 200, 210, 212, 213, 215
faltering, 223–226
and inherited relationship of the past, 225–226
and postadolescent rapprochement, 189–197
and returnees, 215, 216, 217, 223
of stepparents, 225
strategies for, in unsatisfactory relationships, 226–227
Frost, Robert, 128
future, changing, 228–261
children's fear of, 230–236
expectations for, communicating, 248–249

telephone calls *(continued)*
  collect, 51–52
  content/relational nature of,
    57–59
  costs of, 50–52
  desire for, among elderly, 252,
    253
  and fathers, 46
  initiating party of, 53–54
  and misunderstandings, 48
  and quarrels, 48
  recommendations for, 66–67
  as symbol of love, 57
  voice in, as psychological
    barometer, 55–57
tension, at family gatherings, 132,
  139–141
Thanksgiving, importance of,
  124–125, 129
Thomas, Alexander, 36
traditional mothers, 10, 14–16
  changes in, 229–230
  and family gatherings, 135
  and friendship with children,
    186–187
  and telephone contact, 54
transitional mothers, 9–12, 13–14,
  16
  and family gatherings, 137–138
  and friendship with children,
    184–186
  lack of models for, 10
  and sharing common world of
    work with children, 184–186
  and telephone contact, 54

Troll, Lillian E., 46–47
turning points, children recalling
  mothers' approach to, 196
twins, fraternal, relationship
  between, 101–102

voice, telephone, as psychological
  barometer, 55–57

Wadler, Joyce, 201
Wasserstein, Wendy, 40
Wilkes, Paul, 127
women
  versus men, in child care ability,
    167–168
  underutilization of capabilities
    of, 270–272
women's movement, 11, 15, 229
work
  communicating with fathers
    about, 154–156
  mothers sharing world of,
    184–186
working mothers
  money earned by, 81–83, 84
  sharing of common concerns
    with children by, 184–186
  statistics on, 82
World Health Organization, 25,
  28
Wright, Judith, 275
wrongs, fixing, 32
Wylie, Philip, 13, 54

young old, 240